The
BUSHMAN MYTH

Conflict and Social Change Series

Series Editors
Scott Whiteford and William Derman
Michigan State University

The Bushman Myth: The Making of a Namibian Underclass, Robert J. Gordon

Surviving Drought and Development: The Ariaal of Northern Kenya, Elliot M. Fratkin

Harvest of Want: Hunger and Food Security in Central America and Mexico, edited by Scott Whiteford and Anne Ferguson

Singing with Sai Baba: The Politics of Revitalization in Trinidad, Morton Klass

The Spiral Road: Change in a Chinese Village Through the Eyes of a Communist Party Leader, Huang Shu-min

Struggling for Survival: Workers, Women, and Class on a Nicaraguan State Farm, Gary Ruchwarger

FORTHCOMING

The Myth of the Male Breadwinner: Women, Industrialization, and State Policy in the Caribbean, Helen I. Safa

Literacy and People's Power in a Mozambican Factory, Judith Marshall

Computing Myths, Class Realities: An Ethnography of Sheffield Workers in the Information Age, David Hakken with Barbara Andrews

Sickness, Healing, and Gender in Rural Egypt: A Political-Economy Ethnography, Soheir A. Morsy

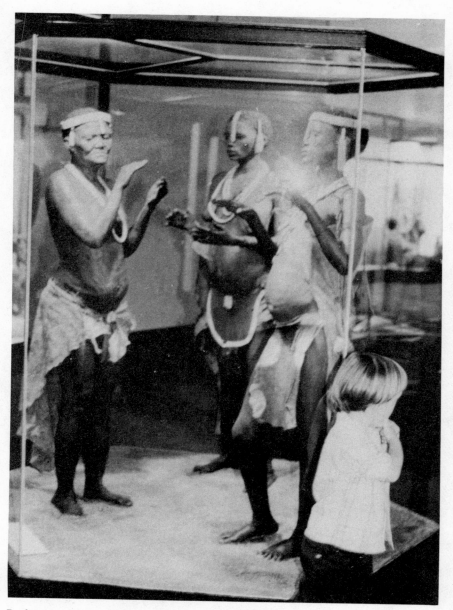

Bushman casts in the South African Museum in Cape Town have always attracted tourists. (Photo courtesy of author)

The
BUSHMAN MYTH

The Making of
a Namibian Underclass

ROBERT J. GORDON

Westview Press
BOULDER • SAN FRANCISCO • OXFORD

Conflict and Social Change Series

The illustrations appearing on the opening pages of parts and chapters are reproduced from Bushman rock paintings of the Tsibab ravine, Southwest Africa. For information about these and other regional paintings, see Geoffrey Williams, *African Designs from Traditional Sources* (Mineola, NY: Dover, 1971).

Published in 1992 in the United States of America by Westview Press, Inc., 5500 Central Avenue, Boulder, Colorado 80301-2847, and in the United Kingdom by Westview Press, 36 Lonsdale Road, Summertown, Oxford OX2 7EW

Library of Congress Cataloging-in-Publication Data
Gordon, Robert J., 1947–
    The Bushman myth : the making of a Namibian underclass / by
Robert J. Gordon.
        p.   cm. — (Conflict and social change series)
    Includes bibliographical references and index.
    ISBN 0-8133-1173-X.—ISBN 0-8133-1381-3 (pbk.)
    1. San (African people).   2. Namibia—Social conditions.
3. Culture conflict.   4. Intercultural communication.   I. Title.
II. Series.
DT1558.S38G67   1992
306.4′089961—dc20
                                                                    91-13486
                                                                    CIP

Printed and bound in the United States of America

(∞)   The paper used in this publication meets the requirements
      of the American National Standard for Permanence of Paper
      for Printed Library Materials Z39.48-1984.

10   9   8   7   6   5   4   3

Contents

Tables and Illustrations

Preface

The origins of this book lie in the alignment of three events: In the early 1980s Greg Finnegan cajoled me into reviewing John Marshall's *N!ai: The Story of a !Kung Woman* during the same period that *The Gods Must Be Crazy* was the talk of the screen. A few months later I was in Namibia when I met documentary filmmakers John Marshall and Claire Ritchie. They invited me up to Tsumkwe, the "capital" of Bushmanland, and the result of that visit, some years later, is this book.

Many scholars and friends have inspired, participated, assisted and aggravated the research on this project. I am grateful to all of them. Rather than risk unintentionally overlooking one or two of these most deserving people, a very real possibility given the large number to whom I am indebted, let me simply give a blanket but heartfelt thanks. Every rule has exceptions, however. The staff of the State Archives in Windhoek and the Inter-Library Loan Staff at the University of Vermont deserve commendation. Without their assistance most of the obscure references in this book would not have been tracked. Most of the photographs were provided by the State Archives in Windhoek and are so identified. The photograph of the delegation of Bushmen with Donald Bain was provided by the Illustrated London News Picture Library. Portions of the material in this book have appeared in volumes edited by Crummey (1985), Schrire (1984) and Wilmsen (1989b).

The prime victims of this book were my family. To them, for their remarkable support, especially in Namibia, I can only be as inarticulate as a Bushman before the Namibian Supreme Court. But they will understand.

And then there are the funding agencies, which, given my genteel poverty-level salary, made this project possible: The Walsh-Price Fellowship of the Maryknoll Missioners, the National Endowment of the Humanities, the Social Science Research Council and the Graduate College of the University of Vermont.

Finally, I would like to dedicate this book to Lorna Marshall, humanist ethnographer extraordinaire, for being such an inspiring role model, not only for how to write, but also for how to age gracefully.

Robert J. Gordon
Roma, Lesotho

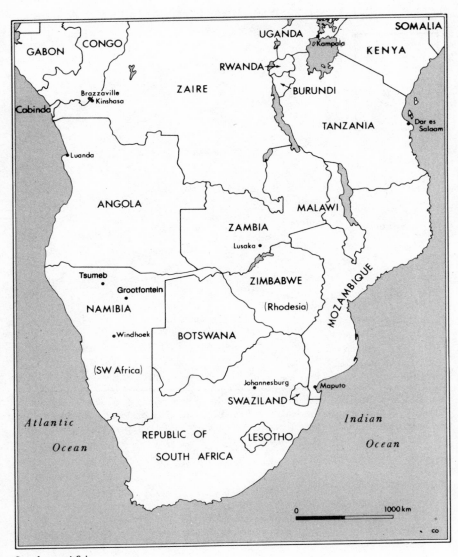

Southern Africa.

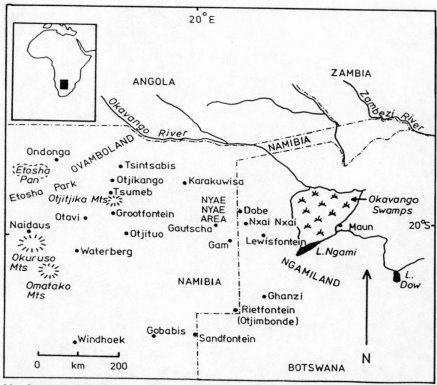

Northeastern Namibia, site of the largest Bushman population. *Source:* Robert J. Gordon, "The !Kung in the Kalahari Exchange," in C. Schrire, ed., *Past and Present in Hunter Gatherer Studies* (New York: Academic Press, 1984). Reprinted by permission.

Chapter 1

The Bushmen: A Merger of Fantasy and Nightmare

Ethnology [is] at once the child of colonialism and the proof of its death throes: a dialogue in which no one has the last word, in which neither voice is reduced to the status of a simple object, and in which we gain advantage from our externality to the other.

—*Todorov*

Some films can kill. One such film was the blockbuster *The Gods Must Be Crazy*,[1] which played to packed houses in the United States, South Africa and elsewhere. This film, with its pseudoscientific narrator describing Bushmen as living in a state of primitive affluence, without the worries of paying taxes, crime, police and other hassles of urban alienation, has had a disastrous impact on those people whom we label "Bushmen."[2]

The film unleashed a veritable vortex of television and film crews on what is officially known as "Bushmanland." In 1982 alone more than nine film crews visited Tsumkwe, including an eleven-member Japanese team and the famous Sir Laurens van der Post, bringing to realization, in an unanticipated form, a prophecy made in 1929 by the traveler Makin: "Perhaps someday, the Bushman will degenerate into that final humiliation—an exhibit by a travelling showman" (Makin 1929:275).

The success of *The Gods Must Be Crazy* gave a major boost to the Namibian Department of Nature Conservation's proposal to develop Bushmanland as a game reserve. In the world envisioned by Nature Conservation, Bushmen would be allowed to remain, provided that they "hunted and gathered traditionally." Of course most tourists would come not to see wild animals but to see "wild Bushmen."

In the same period the South African Defence Force (SADF), which had been fighting a low-intensity guerrilla war with the South West

Africa People's Organization (SWAPO) since the early 1960s, made a concerted effort to recruit Bushmen. Indeed by the early 1980s Bushmen held the unique distinction of being perhaps the most militarized ethnic group in the world.[3] One of the major reasons for military recruitment was the belief that Bushmen were "natural" trackers and thus would be effective counterinsurgency operatives. The SADF also exploited them culturally. The SADF was so proud of what it had done for (and to) these "last representatives of the stone-age" that, as a matter of course, visiting foreign journalists were shown the Bushman base at Omega.[4] These journalists recorded a rich fund of characteristics that the white soldiers attributed to Bushmen. According to one senior officer, "The Bushman's senses in the field are unbelievable. If a patrol has a Bushman with it, then it is unnecessary to post guards at night. The Bushman also goes to sleep, but when the enemy is still far away he wakes up and raises the alarm" (*Die Burger*, 6 January 1982). Another white soldier believed: "They have fantastic eyesight and they can navigate in the bush without a compass or map. . . . With the Bushmen along, our chances of dying are very slight. They have incredible tenacity, patience and endurance. They've taught me to respect another race" (*Time*, 2 March 1981). Even experienced, battle-hardened mercenaries were impressed. A *Soldier of Fortune* article exulted:

> Able to survive long periods on minimal food and water, the Bushman has an instinctive, highly developed sense of danger, and has proved to be an astoundingly good "snap" shot . . . [but his] forte is tracking. . . . If you've never seen a two-legged bloodhound at work, come to South West Africa and watch the Bushman. Actually, the Bushman puts the bloodhound to shame. [In addition, Bushmen are] good at estimating mortar projectile strike distances because of their age-old weapon—the bow and arrow. (Norval 1984:74)[5]

According to that view, the superhuman qualities of Bushmen were grounded not in humanity but in animality. Their inability to herd cattle was attributed to their lack of self-restraint. As they are "extremely emotional," their women cannot be deprived of the men, and this determines the length of patrol (*Pretoria News*, 26 February 1981). *Time* magazine assured us that they are often distracted from a guerrilla track by honey, and when they sight a hyena, they laugh uncontrollably (2 March 1981).[6] The transmogrification of Bushmen is still very much an issue.

The wave on which both the South African Defence Force and *The Gods Must Be Crazy* rode to acclaim both in South Africa and in the United States was clearly part of a larger current in contemporary scholarly discourse. This is the idea that Bushmen have always lived in the splendidly bracing isolation of the Kalahari Desert, where, in uncontaminated purity, they live in a state of "primitive affluence" as one of the last living representatives of how our paleolithic forebears lived. Indeed, the Bushmen, more than any other human grouping in the annals of academic endeavor, have been made a scientific commodity. Their continually rediscovered stature in the eyes of scholars has been exploited not only by academics but also by diverse groups, ranging from the South African Defence Force and the Department of Nature Conservation to ordinary Namibian schoolchildren, who all subscribe to the myth of primitive affluence and its various intellectual contours. Have the Bushmen become prisoners of the reputation we have given them?[7]

Despite the fact that most recent work in the Kalahari has stressed history and the wider context, almost all contemporary anthropology textbooks *still portray* Bushmen as if they live in a state of "primitive affluence." There is no simple answer to that question. In order to begin we must look at the history of research. Nancy Howell, one of the most prominent members of the Harvard Kalahari Project, recalled that the research project of which she was a member ignored the paraphernalia of Western "civilization and poverty"

> because we didn't come all the way around the world to see them. We could have stayed at home and seen people behaving as rural proletariat, while nowhere but the Kalahari and a few other remote locations allow a glimpse of the "hunting and gathering way of life." So we focus upon bush camps, upon hunting, upon old fashioned customs, and although we remind each other once in a while not to be romantic, we consciously and unconsciously neglect and avoid the !Kung who don't conform to our expectations. (Howell 1986)

The Bushman issue raised troubling questions for me, both as a Namibian and as an anthropologist. The dissonance between scholarly textbook rhetoric and actuality was forcefully brought home to me in 1980 when John Marshall, an ethnographic filmmaker, invited me to accompany him to Tsumkwe, the "capital" of the Apartheid-inspired Bushman homeland. What I saw there on my brief three-day visit was profoundly disturbing. I had never been in a place where one could literally smell death and decay, as in Tsumkwe. Indeed the death rate exceeded the birthrate. It was a prime example of what Robert Chambers called integrated rural poverty: The Tsumkwe people were caught within the mutually reinforcing coils of isolation, poverty, physical weakness, vulnerability and powerlessness (Chambers 1984:103).

When I grew up in southern Namibia, stories of the treacherous "wild Bushmen" and how they had to be "tamed" by tying them to

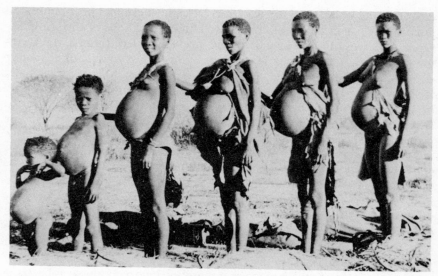

Bushmen: pregnant women and malnourished children. This photograph, taken in the 1930s, has appeared in books and newpapers with misleading captions, such as: "Bushmen after a raw meat feast"; "They have filled themselves with locusts, exactly as did their ancestors, the 'wild Bosjes'"; "Bushmen after a feast." *Source: Windhoek Observer,* July 24, 1982. (Photo courtesy of *Windhoek Observer*)

windmills and force-feeding them mielie-meal were common coin. One of my most vivid childhood memories was looking at a picture in the Luderitzbucht Museum that showed Bushmen being hung from a camel-thorn tree. Was I dreaming? Or are we dreaming now? How to reconcile or indeed evaluate these discordant images of those labeled "Bushmen" is the guiding motif of this book.

The Politics of Labeling Bushmen

The images that I have sketched were not, of course, invented or dropped ready-made from heaven. They are instead the products of discernable sociocultural factors that are firmly located in a history. This book analyzes the interplay among that imagery, policy and history. The indigenous people at the center of this book do not see themselves as a single integrated unit, nor do they call themselves by a single name; it follows thus that the notion and image of the "Bushmen" must be a European or settler concept. The focus is thus not so much on the Bushmen/Kung/Ju-/wasi/San or whatever one might like to call them but on the colonizer's image of them and the consequences of that image for people assumed to be Bushmen.

Social identity becomes meaningful only in relation to others; thus, in order to understand the image of the Bushman, we must consider that image as the product of interactions between those encompassed by the label and their "significant" others. "Only by understanding these names as bundles of relationships and by placing them back in the field from which they are abstracted, can we hope to avoid misleading inference and increase our share of understanding" (Wolf 1982:1). Because the Other cannot exist without the Self, this is a study not only of history but also of the sociology of knowledge.

One of the many issues academics have argued about concerns the label they impose upon these people. Some, like Guenther (1985), prefer the older term *Bushmen*. Others reject this term because they believe it is racist and sexist and prefer to use the term *San* (e.g., Lee 1979:29; Wilmsen 1989a:26–32; Wilmsen 1989b:31) on the grounds that San is derived from the terms like *Sonqua*, which were used by Khoi speakers in the Cape of Good Hope to label these people. More important, they argue that San can be glossed as 'original people', but that explanation must be examined within its (neo)colonial context. Is there any significance in the fact that the fashionable gloss of 'original people' became stylish when scientists were interested in Bushmen as representatives of the Paleolithic? 'Original people' is simply one of many glosses for the meaning of San. Theophilus Hahn (1881) is usually cited as the definitive authority for that gloss. But the matter is much more complex. In his 1881 monograph Hahn wrote:

> The meaning of this term is not quite intelligible, and I frankly confess that, after nine years, of which I have spent seven amongst the Khoikhoi [Nama], I did not succeed in arriving at a quite satisfactory etymology, and I must still adhere to the interpretation which I first gave in the *Globus*, 1870, where I traced the word Sa-[b] to the root *sa*, to inhabit, to be located, to dwell, to be settled, to be quiet. *Sa[n]* consequently would mean Aborigines or Settlers proper. (quoted in Nienaber 1989:831)

However in 1870 Hahn had said of San:

> The meaning is unclear. . . . The nearest explanation is pariahs, outcasts, pursued [*Gehetzte*], an explanation which is grounded in reality. A second explanation is based on the root *sau*, 'to follow' in which case they were the underlings [*Knechte*]. Wallmann, formerly Rhenish Mission Inspector, derives *Sab* from the root *sa*, 'rest' and explains it thus as the original inhabitants [*Sesshaften*]. Also this explanation is not to be ignored. (Nienaber 1989:831)

Nienaber claimed that Hahn's gloss of San as 'original inhabitants' was copied from Wallmann, who used it more as a term denoting teasing in the sense of 'people who enjoy rest'. Nienaber, certainly no radical, noted that this change in gloss was politically expedient to Hahn, as it fitted in well with the emerging theory that the Bushmen were the original inhabitants of the country, who were then dispossessed by the Khoi-khoi and Herero; that theory provided a valuable justification for European conquest of Khoi and Herero in Namibia. Such an interpretation calibrated well with Hahn's political activities in Namaqualand at that time (Nienaber 1989:834).

There are other possible explanations for the origins of the word *Bushman* (authoritatively discussed by Nienaber 1950, 1989). Perhaps the most common explanation and one that has the most credibility is that it is derived from the term *bossiesman,* meaning *struikrower,* glossed as 'bandit' or 'outlaw'. Interestingly enough, the name that the Khoi (Hottentots) gave Bushmen, *Sonqua,* from which the term *San* is derived, also means bandits (Nienaber 1950:37–38). It is significant that early travelers were able to provide a fairly substantial amount of information on the different Khoi groups, their language and customs, but those travelers were unable to provide much information on Bushmen, who were seen as peripheral people. Within the context of southern African history this explanation makes the most sense, whereas the other two folk explanations of origin merely underline the pejorativeness of this social "misbehavior." The term *Bushman* is thus a "lumpen category" into which all those who failed to conform or acquiesce were dumped. It was not an ethnic group but a sociopolitical category derived from the wider setting. The fact that we find it pejorative is testimony to the effective socialization that we as members of that larger sociopolitical entity have undergone.

Contemporary use of the term *San* appears to be restricted to (Khoi) Nama speakers in Namibia, and its continued use by academics serves to further mystify the tragic situation of those labeled "Bushmen." In Namibia, everybody uses the term *Bushmen.* Changing the label does not reduce the racism and invidiousness implicit in the relationship, since words get their emotive content from the social milieu in which they are used. To feel compelled to change the label is to submit to the effectiveness of colonial socialization. In order to confront this restrictive socialization we need to confront the same terms and infuse them with new meaning. Many labels, like "Christian" and "Quaker," were once also highly derisive and derogatory. I use the term *Bushman* because I feel that it is important that we make social banditry respectable again, for of all the southern African people exposed to the colonial onslaught, those labeled "Bushmen" have the longest, most valiant, if costly, record of resistance to colonialism.

Another solution to this issue, and one which Wilmsen (1989a) favored, is to use the term that the people use to refer to themselves. This would, however, fragment the discourse. For example, the following is a partial listing of some of the groups officially recognized with some of the spellings used by academics and bureaucrats:

I. Nama-speaking groups (Nama-San):
   A. Khoe; Kwe; Khwe (Mbarakwengo); Hukwe (River Bushmen) [Kavango and West Caprivi districts]—estimated population: 5,000
   B. Nharon; Aukwe; //Ai-khoe (Naron) [Gobabis district]—estimated population: 1,500
   C. Hai-//omn (Heikom)
      1. Xwaga [Owambo district] (Heikum)
      2. Keren [Owambo and Outjo districts]
      3. Hai-//omn [Grootfontein, Tsumeb and Kavango districts]
         Estimated population: 11,000
II. "Bushmen proper" (!Khu-San):[8]
   D. Angola !Khu (Kung)
      1. !O-!Khu
      2. Kwankala
         Estimated population: 6,000
   E. Ju-/wasi (Zhu-/hoasi) [Grootfontein, Tsumeb and Bushmanland districts]—estimated population: 7,000
   F. //Khau-//esi; =/Auin (Auen; Makaukau) [Hereroland and Gobabis districts]—estimated population: 2,000
   G. Ovambokavango-!Khu (Nogau) [Grootfontein, Tsumeb and Kavango districts]—estimated population: 6,000
III. Cape Bushmen (Cape-San)
   H. !Xo (Magong) [Gobabis, Mariental districts]—estimated population: 300
   I. /Nu-//en (Nusan) [Mariental district]—estimated population: 100
   J. /Auni [Mariental district]—estimated population: 200

(Sources: Malan 1980:13–14; Marais 1984; population estimates derived from Budack 1980)

Contemporary population estimates for Bushmen in southern Africa range from 30,000 to 87,250.[9] In Namibia most Bushmen are to be found in the region known to the white colonizers and some blacks as the Omaheke, a vast, flat, seemingly monotonous, stoneless expanse covering northeastern Namibia. Sometimes this expanse is arbitrarily

Table 1.1   Distribution of Bushmen by District

	1970 Census	1981 Census
Magisterial districts		
Gobabis	5,212	4,837
Grootfontein	3,815	4,461
Tsumeb	3,888	3,506
Outjo	1,347	1,827
Other districts	890	1,288
No. within Police Zone	15,152	17,207
So-called homelands		
Kavango	3,478	2,672
Ovambo	1,814	2,790
Hereroland	911	2,361
Bushmanland	459	2,245
Other homelands	95	357
No. in homelands	6,757	10,425
No. not distributed	—	573
Total	21,909	29,441

Sources: Robert J. Gordon, *What Future for the Ju-/wasi of Nyae Nyae?* (Boston: Cultural Survival. Occasional Paper No. 13, 1984); François Marais et al., *Ondersoek na die Boesmanbevolkingsgroep in Suidwes-Afrika* (Windhoek: Direktoraat, ontwikkelingskoordinering, 1984).

divided into the Kungveld, the Kaukauveld and the Otjimpoloveld. At other times the whole area is referred to as the Kaukauveld[10] (see Table 1.1). The Kaukauveld provides the focus of this work.[11]

Speaking for the Bushmen

My inquiry into how Bushmen made their own history within conditions that were not of their own choosing proved to be a challenge. The Bushmen's role in shaping Namibian history has been denied or ignored by historians as diverse as Vedder (1981), Bley (1971), Drechsler (1966, 1980), Katjavivi (1988) and Mbuende (1986). This underlines the current relative powerlessness of people practicing a peripatetic or foraging mode of existence. History, as we know only too well, is concerned with success stories or with those who wield power or have the loudest voices. As a result Bushmen have been relegated to the shadowy underside of Namibian history.

The search for a Bushman voice proved to be rather frustrating. The Bushmen were remarkably inarticulate, perhaps the most damning evidence of their powerlessness. Not only was there little material in the archives from which one could infer a Bushman voice, but even a close scrutiny of criminal court records and affidavits was disappointing, offering mute testimony to the smothering history of their victimization. Indeed, it is remarkable that they were as articulate as they were in the 1960s and 1970s, but even this testimony is problematic, as I argue in Chapter 22.[12]

In this book, then, rather than treat Bushmen *as if* they are an isolated self-sufficient society, I seek to analyze their role within the wider context of the emergent Namibian social formation. It is not so much an ethnohistory of a particular group as it is a regional history shaped by an ethnographic enquiry.[13]

Most of the information I collected and synthesized belongs to the public domain and is located principally in the Windhoek State Archives. In consulting this material I was struck by the rhetoric and especially the vocabulary used by officials and settlers to describe Bushmen and their relationships to them. This rhetoric is, I believe, an important aspect in understanding the role of Bushmen within settler society. I have thus quoted these texts extensively but have tried, as Todorov put it, to avoid

> the temptation to reproduce the voices of these figures "as they really are"; to try to do away with my own presence "for the other's sake" [and also] to subjugate the other to myself, to make him the marionette of which I pull the strings. Between the two, I have sought not a terrain of compromise but the path of dialogue. I question, I transpose, I interpret these texts; but also I let them speak . . . and defend themselves. (Todorov 1985:250)

The problem is complex on another level as well. Labels or categories like Bushmen tend to be reified by settlers and academics, and as Eric Wolf warned, "by turning names into things we create false models of reality. By endowing nations, societies, or cultures with the qualities of internally homogenous and externally distinctive and bounded objects, we create a model of the world as a global pool hall in which the entities spin off each other like . . . billiard balls" (Wolf 1982:6).

The results of these false models were pervasive in "Bushman Studies," and their political implications in the South African setting ubiquitous. The major intellectual and moral tasks of anthropology flow together in the debunking of dangerous contemporary myths, more so if it has played a role in creating such myths.[14] Working in southern Africa, the social-anthropologist-cum-historian is forced to deal with contradictions on the personal, social and structural levels. This study belongs to that genre of social science literature known as exposé ethnography, the most elementary historical ethnography possible in such situations. As a Namibian I am acutely conscious of both the freedom and the obligation to develop a critique of the so-called national society to which I belong, but by the same token, this study is more than a specific critique of Namibian settler society. If we cannot be proud of the history of settler-Bushman relations, we must also recognize that it is not a simple story and avoid naïve simplifications, whether they be of the "vermin" or "noble savage" variety. The Namibian situation is not unique. Striking parallels can be found with numerous other settler societies, most notably South Africa, Australia, Argentina, Canada, the United States and the English conquest of Ireland. The banality of evil and indeed of genocide is universal. It is my hope that this material might be used to develop a comparative study of genocide and the vulnerability of small-scale sociopolitical formations.

In this book I suggest that the popular image of Bushman, which derives its authority largely from (a selective reading of) the scientific[15] discourse, was used by various parties to reflect their own purposes, including the justification of ethnocide or genocide of those people commonly labeled "Bushmen." Far from being "beautiful people living in primeval paradise," they are in reality the most victimized and brutalized people in the bloody history that is southern Africa. If we anthropologists are concerned about the future of humanity, then it is incumbent upon us to try to understand the processes by which Bushmen were brutalized. More important, we need to try to understand why no scientists seriously addressed the issue of why Bushmen were becoming "extinct."[16]

Storyline

Until recently, ethnographers tended to dismiss the Kalahari Bushman past as timeless and endless; their historic presence begins around the turn of the century. That presence has been depicted as a series of exploitative interactions with whites, unfortunate dealings with blacks and a rather unsatisfactory resolution of matters that leaves the Bushmen straddling an uncomfortable border between Botswana and Namibia, under the effective thumb of the South African government. Bushmen emerged in the major ethnographies as relics of the past, trapped in a fast-moving present frame that supports the notion that they have, until a few years ago, been traditional hunters and gatherers.[17]

The first section of this book explores the historical records relating to Bushmen in the Kaukauveld Kalahari to reveal their complex interrelations with numerous other people through time. It complements the prehistoric findings by Denbow (1984, 1986) and Wilmsen (1989a, 1989b), which suggest several millennia of interaction between Bushman foragers and local pastoralists. In addition, by presenting a record that goes beyond generalizations about economic modes and into the actions and aspirations of individuals, Part 1 describes a situation of complex inter-actions between different groups that is probably analogous to that which pertained centuries earlier in the southern tip of Africa, as recorded in the early colonial Dutch records and analyzed by Szalay (1983) and Parkington (1984).

The picture that emerges is complex and changing. The old notion of these people as passive victims of European invasion and Bantu expansion is challenged. Bushmen emerge as one of many indigenous people operating in a mobile landscape, forming and shifting their political and economic alliances to take advantage of circumstances as they perceived them. Instead of toppling helplessly from foraging to begging, they emerge as hotshot traders in the mercantile world market for ivory and skins. They were brokers between competing forces and hired guns in the game business. Rather than being victims of pastoralists and traders who depleted the game, they appear as one of many willing agents of this commercial depletion. Instead of being ignorant of metals, true men of the Stone Age, who knew nothing of iron (Lee 1979:76), they were fierce defenders of rich copper mines that they worked for export and profit. If this section has a central theme, it is to show how ignorance of archival sources helped create the Bushman image that we, as anthropologists, wanted to have and how knowledge of these sources makes sense of the Bushmen we observe today.

After having discussed life in what early German maps revealingly termed "the masterless area" in Part 1, I move in Part 2 to the onset of the colonial state. It was with the onset of settler capitalism (Denoon 1983) that settlers created the "Bushman problem," which they referred to as the "plague." The plague was not a punishment visited upon the good settlers by the Almighty but was a direct consequence of various state activities, in particular its land policies. The imposition of the state and the resultant land rush had dire ecological consequences. Reigning settler ideology, supported by science, at that time defined Bushmen as "untamable" and believed it was only a matter of time before Bushmen inevitably became extinct. Bushmen did not accept these settler devel-opments passively but audaciously resisted. It was only after World War II that, for a variety of ideological, international, academic and economic reasons, the administration decided to create a Bushman reserve. These factors, including the role of the missionaries and academics in the cultural uses and abuses of those labeled "Bushmen," are charted in Part 3, especially the value these elements of the bourgeoisie attached to constantly reinventing "wild Bushmen."

In exploring the relationship between image and role in society in Part 4, I employ the concept of rural underclass[18] as a framework to examine the nature of the social relationships that led to the particular style of incorporation of foragers into the colonial order. It is in this process that the entity known as the "Bushmen" was created and transformed into an underdeveloped segment of Namibian society. The contemporary social problems in Bushmanland, the Apartheid-generated "homeland," which John Marshall so movingly captured in his film *N!ai: The Story of a !Kung Woman,* are thus not the result of isolation but are rather the product of the texture of the Bushmen's ties with the wider society. Intellectuals, writers and academics played a crucial role in underclass formation by engaging in mystification.[19]

I conclude (Part 5) by extracting some points from this case study that might be pertinent to developing an anthropological understanding of genocide. For an explanation to be satisfactory, it must, as Max Weber long ago insisted, be adequate on the levels of both cause and meaning. Apart from emphasizing the causal processes of land dispossession and techniques of labor coercion, any analysis of these relationships must also include a discussion on the realm of meaning, of culture. I show how, almost universally, writers and academics played an important role in developing the ideology justifying settler expansion, be they mystifications as "vermin" or "beautiful people."

Ironically *The Gods Must Be Crazy* represents a crude but accurate caricature of the Bushman scholarly enterprise, although not surprisingly, most of the academics involved in protesting the film did not examine this issue.[20] Actions, including image making, have consequences. Are academics prepared to accept responsibility? Before they can do that they must be conscious of the effect of their actions. But do they have the requisite self-consciousness? This is no trivial matter. As Robertson pointed out, "The only way in which the vexatious gap between theory and practice may be closed is by restoring to anthropology some overtly moral concerns" (Robertson 1984:301). Such an exercise is necessary if we are to understand the contradictory nature of ethnology. Fortunately it is already a keynote of current research in the Kalahari.

Part 1

What's in a Name?

Chapter 2

Locating the Bushmen

Inspired by David Livingstone's well-publicized "discovery" of Lake Ngami, a youthful Francis Galton determined to be the first European to reach the lake from the west.[1] He did not succeed but instead became the first white traveler to record a visit to Ovamboland from the south. These travels were to win him the Royal Geographical Society's coveted Gold Medal[2] and launch him into London's scientific community, bringing him fame later as the creator of eugenics and election as second president of the Anthropological Institute. His travel reports were to be translated into French and German and cited extensively in the construction of the numerous popular ethnographic surveys that were published in the next few decades.

Galton was the first European to write about travels that skirted both to the south (when he tried to reach Ngami) and the west (when he traveled to Ovamboland), the area that is now defined as the "traditional" stronghold of those people labeled as "Bushmen." Fresh from England, Galton could not help but be aware of the bourgeois interest in Bushmen, as some of the most fashionable shows in England between 1846 and 1850 had consisted of various troupes of South African Bushmen. They had enjoyed a popular, if somewhat controversial, reception (see, e.g., Lindfors 1983). Prichard's treatise *Researches into the Physical History of Mankind* (1st edition 1836–1847; 2nd edition 1851) summarized the scholarly knowledge of the era:

> Writers on the history of mankind seem to be nearly agreed in considering the Bushmen or Bosjesmen of South Africa as the most degraded and miserable of all nations, and the lowest in the scale of humanity . . . these people are so brutish, lazy, and stupid, that the idea of reducing them to slavery has been abandoned. . . . It is no matter of surprise that those writers who search for approximations between mankind and the

inferior orders of the creation, fix upon the Bushmen as their favourite
theme. (Prichard 1851, 1:177–178)[3]

Prichard (and Galton) were, of course, well aware that most of the
Bushmen in South Africa had by this time been annihilated, except for
a few pockets in the Cape Colony and the southern Kalahari.[4]

This then is the historical context in which European scholarly
categorizations of the Namibian or Kalahari Bushmen have to be seen.
Galton's first report of his travels, published in the *St. Helena Gazette* of 31
January 1852, while he was en route back to Britain, is a useful place to
start. Concerning the population of the area traversed, Galton opined:

> South of a line stretching east just north of Walvis Bay is now entirely
> inhabited by tribes of partly civilized Hottentots, called in the aggregate
> the Namaquas. North of this line, live Damaras and dispersed tribes of
> perfectly savage Hottentots; the Namaquas call these "Saen" [or Bush-
> men]—look down on them with the greatest contempt, and catch them,
> as they do the Damaras, for slaves.[5] They are not so diminutive as the
> Bushmen, commonly so called, neither are they quite so low in the scale
> of humanity, though in every other respect they exactly resemble them
> . . . living together with these Bushmen, and hunted down in the same
> way as they by both Damaras and Namaquas, are another and a very
> peculiar race, called the Ghou Damup; they are blacks, speaking no
> other language than Hottentot, and who have retained no tradition
> whatever of their origin; they used to be despised and made slaves of,
> *even by the Bushmen,* but of quite late years community of misfortune has
> much equalized the two races, and they now intermarry. . . . Years ago,
> I presume that the Bushmen entirely conquered them, so that they then
> lost their own language, and about 70 years ago the Damaras came like
> a swarm from their original home [some 10 days east of Cape Cross]
> and overran the whole country, driving both Bushmen and Ghou Da-
> mup together to the hills and other uninhabited places, where they now
> live together. . . . [Referring] once more to the above mentioned line
> (part of which coincides with the Swakop river), after it reaches the
> 19th degree of longitude, both Damara land ceases to the north, and
> Namaqua land to the south of it, and in their place a broad tract of
> Bushman country stretches north and south, beyond which lies the lake
> [Ngami] and its bordering inhabitants. (Galton 1852 [emphasis added])

Galton's traveling companion, Charles John Andersson, who was to
stay on in Namibia, shared his view that Bushmen were simply lower
versions of the Hottentots (Khoi-khoi) but suggested that there was a
different type of Bushmen in the vastness of the Kalahari:

. The Namaqua Hottentot is simply the reclaimed and somewhat civilized
Bushman, just as the Oerlam represents the same raw material under a
slightly higher degree of polish. Not only are they identical in features
and language, but the Hottentot tribes have been, and continue to be,
recruited from the Bushmen. During my travels I never met with a
single specimen of the very smallest tribe of Bushmen, that is North of
the Orange River, but travellers tell me that they are by no means
uncommon towards the East. (Andersson 1855:103–104)

In terms of historical usage, the term *San* thus clearly refers to what
later became known as the Nama-speaking Heikom, and not the Kung
Bushmen. This dichotomy between the Saen/San/Saan, who spoke Nama
and indeed were believed to be impoverished Khoi, and the "genuine"
Bushmen, who were smaller, yellower and spoke a language unintelligible
to Khoi speakers, was accepted by many early European travelers and
long-term missionaries like McKiernan (1954:50), Brincker (1899:126)
and Vedder (1913, 1981). Galton was building on local common knowledge. He was not the first white in the area. On the contrary, at that
time Namibia had at least eighty active white traders as well as numerous
missionaries. Some of them wrote of their experiences. Thus, for example, the Reverend Edward Cook, Wesleyan missionary at Gobabis, noted
in his journal in 1842: "I hear with much pleasure that some of the
people to the East, called Bushmen, are getting a considerable number
of sheep and goats, and are very desirous of obtaining clothing etc. of
European manufacture" (Cook 1849:164). Sometimes Cook identified
Bushmen with the Groot Rooi (Big Red) Namaquas or Hottentots
(1849:167).

His colleague, the Reverend Joseph Tindall, who proselytized in the
Gobabis area from 1839 to 1855, declared that the Bushmen of Damaraland and Ovamboland were originally members of the Grootkarrosses
(Great Mantle) Namaqua "tribe" and had formerly held the Damaras in
submission: "All the other tribes speak of them as the oldest and most
powerful member of the Namaqua." Their Bushman life-style, he suggested, had developed because they had become impoverished Khoi
(Namaqua). He illustrated his argument by referring to a similar process
that was then occurring among the pastoral Herero, creating the so-
called Fieldherero: Herero who had lost their livestock and thus were
left with the choice of either "servitude or the cheerless and miserable
vicissitudes of a bush life" (Tindall 1856:25).[6] And the veteran Reverend
Hugo Hahn in 1858 declared that "the so-called Bushmen from the West
Coast to the Ngami Lake are without exception impoverished Namaqua"
(cited in Nienaber 1989:152).[7]

That Galton found Bushmen to be more than simply a horde of
people incapable of taking decisive action is clear from his description of

how they set up game pits and fences near Otjikango. "The whole breadth of the valley was staked and brushed across. . . . The strength and size of the timber that was used gave me a great idea of Bushman industry . . . and the scale of the undertaking would have excited astonishment in far more civilized nations" (Galton 1889:106; see also Mc-Kiernan 1954:57).

Galton's astonishment arose out of the prevailing metropolitan intellectual orthodoxy concerning Bushmen (as per Prichard). Such was the strength of this orthodoxy that by the time Galton settled down to write his book, he ignored the distinction between impoverished Nama as Bushmen and the diminutive "genuine" Bushmen.[8] Galton was not to be the first to have his observations so clearly fashioned by reigning orthodoxy.[9]

There are obvious ecological reasons why hunting and foraging should have been a viable mode of subsistence in this area for so long. Even today, despite heavy pressure on land resources, and high-technology ranching techniques, parts of this area, like western Bushmanland, are still relatively untouched by either European ranchers or Herero pastoralists. The area's seasonal rainfall was also highly irregular. In addition, the presence of large waterless tracts and the presence of lung sickness and seasonally poisonous forage (*Dichapetalum cymosum*) served to inhibit any but temporary cattle grazing in the area, at least from the western approaches.[10] Most important, although economically within the reaches of the world capitalist system, the area was too removed from the nearest markets. Instead, it offered something more valuable than herding and more easily transportable: ivory and ostrich feathers; it thus attracted numerous mercantile hunters and traders. Indeed Galton's travels represent the proverbial foam of the waves of predatory capitalism that were to engulf the whole area.

Interspersed within this trading network and often extending beyond the ecological zones occupied by pastoralist Nama and Herero and agriculturalist Ovambo and Kavango were people practicing a hunting and gathering/foraging or fugitive type of existence who were usually arbitrarily categorized as "Bushmen" or "Bergdamara." For one to understand the dynamics of their existence, the critical importance of a volatile environment must again be emphasized. The relationship was complex. Drought and epidemics of various sorts would often force proud pastoralists to grub for roots. Similarly, foragers might be forced by drought conditions to enter subservient relations with pastoralists or agriculturalists. There is increasing evidence of the flexibility of foraging systems of people like Bushmen who would adopt pastoralism or rural proletarianization and then later revert back to foraging (see, e.g., Hitchcock 1982). There were also many reports of both Nama and Herero becoming "Bushmen" and later reverting back to their previous mode of subsistence (see, e.g., Lebzelter 1934b:184; Tindall 1856). In sum, hunting and pastoralism (and even agriculture, to a degree) are flexible production strategies: There is no lineal trajectory from the one to the other. Nor for that matter are they mutually incompatible because animals, be they cattle, sheep or game, tend to feed/browse/graze predominantly on different types of plants and grasses.[11] The distinction between foragers and pastoralists is a political one. Fluidity, competition and movement were the dominant characteristics of these communities.

Reading beyond Galton's narrative, it is clear that he found himself in a complex situation. There was an extensive tradition of trade and interaction. Already in 1837 Alexander had found Portuguese trade items in Windhoek. Early traveler accounts present a vivid picture of movement and trade within the area, with, for example, Bechuanas coming to trade for cattle and Herero going up to Angola in search of ironware. Galton's experiences were thus typical. At Jonker Afrikaner's *werft* (place, homestead) in Aigams/Windhoek, Galton reported "blacksmith shops where iron things were forged for the Damaras who brought their cattle in exchange—the place had the appearance of a crowded bustling market the whole year round."[12] On his eastern trip into the Kalahari Desert he encountered a Bushman cooking in a large iron pot at Tounobis (Rietfontein). "The Bushman said that it was given to them by people from a wagon some distance to the east, and who had gone to the lake the previous season," he reported (Galton 1889:16).

On his northern trip, Galton's guides to Ovamboland were Ovambo traders who had come south to Hereroland to purchase cattle in exchange for beads that the traders had obtained from the Portuguese. The traders' leader spoke fluent Herero. The party consisted of twenty-four men whose "necks were laden with necklaces for sale, and every man carried a long narrow smoothed pole over his shoulder, from either end of which hung a quantity of packages. These were chiefly little baskets holding iron articles of exchange, packets of corn for their eating and water bags" (Galton 1889:109). Accompanying the party on its return to Ovamboland were about eighty Herero women. The older ones were looking for food and work while the younger ones, in a display of feminist autonomy, were searching for husbands. Ovambo traders and craftsmen would regularly visit Okahandja (Stals 1968), and in 1857 the Reverend Hugo Hahn on his visit to Ovamboland was surprised to find an Ovambo king speaking Herero and smoking a trader's pipe (Hahn 1985:vol. 4).

There is thus evidence of large-scale commodity movements. Items of trade included beads, food products, pottery, leather, various forms of ironwork, but principally knives, points, bracelets, tobacco, cannabis and

Artist-traveler Thomas Baines's engraving, "Bushmen, a group (Aug. 1861)," based on a pioneering photograph by James Chapman. First appeared in Baines's *Explorations in South West Africa* (1864). *Source:* James Chapman, *Travels in the Interior of Africa,* ed. Edward C. Tabler (Cape Town: Balkema, 1971). Reprinted by permission.

livestock. The ethnological insistence on the social value of cattle unfortunately has hidden the commercial role of cattle. This commodity movement was accompanied by a movement of services, especially iron-working and medicinal work. Ovambo and Damara craftsmen and ritual experts moved around, offering their services on both the short and the long term to Herero and Nama.[13] There were also trade routes extending from the east coast through what is now Zambia and Angola into the present-day Bushman heartland. It was a trade that featured cowrie shells, beads, cattle, ivory and slaves. When the hunter Green was at Lake Ngami in 1856, he encountered Mambari traders. The Mambari trade route went from Benguela, on the Atlantic coast, through northern Namibia to Bulozi, where it linked up with the east coast trade (Tlou 1985:19ff.). Bushmen were very much part of this trading network. In a remarkable testimony to the effectiveness of this precolonial trade and communications network, McKiernan reported that upon receiving word of the Kavango killing of the trader Thomas, Bushmen groups 300 miles away killed their own white employer (McKiernan 1954:170). As in other parts of the world, this vibrant indigenous trade received a massive prod from the capitalist world system but then, within a short period, was stifled by it (Kjekshus 1977).

That even the "genuine" Bushmen, the ethnographically famous Kung-speaking Ju-/wasi of what is now Bushmanland, were involved in this well-developed trade nexus is clear from Hauptmann Mueller's report of a reconnaissance party he led to the Kaukauveld. He found trade items near Geitza, including cowrie shells, glass beads, iron beads, copper rings, Ovambo knives and wooden bowls from the Okavango. There was evidence that Bechuanas often trekked into the area via Lewisfontein for cattle grazing, hunting and trading and that they regularly sold ammunition to Bushmen. They came with horses, wagons and pack oxen and went as far north as Kauara and as far west as Debra. At Tsumkwe, Gautscha, Garu and Nona, Mueller found fresh traces of cattle kraals and dung. The Ju-/wasi kept horns and hides in anticipation of these expeditions. He explained:

> Within a wind screen of the werft Kauara, I saw a bundle which was plaited like a weir basket. I caused it to be opened and found . . . ostrich feathers ready for dispatch! The people of Geitza keep the ostrich feathers still more carefully. They cut a rod of the length of an ostrich feather from a shrub, *grewia spec,* which has a remarkable soft marrow. This marrow they push out and put the ostrich feather in its place. (Mueller 1912:66)

J. H. Wilhelm, who farmed in the Grootfontein district from 1914 to 1919, also presented a vivid description of similar parcels of ostrich feathers, arranged by size and bound in bushels. The choice feathers were protected in reed tubes that were taken by the Kung (Ju-/wasi) to the Okavango River for trading purposes. Such expeditions took place near the end of the winter period, before the onset of the rains, and consisted of several men, led by an experienced elder. To provision such an expedition, Bushmen removed hides from their storage places in the crowns of large trees, placed ostrich-eggshell necklaces in collecting bags, arranged ostrich feathers and gathered snakeskins and antelope horns. Once the expedition reached the Okavango, where they wanted to trade, the leader went forward while the rest of the party waited. While waiting, they ritualistically hid the articles that they thought would be the most valued. The Okavango people awaited these expeditions with eager anticipation, as they needed the animal hides for cloaks and blankets and the ostrich-eggshell necklaces to give to their wives. In preparation for these visits, they built up a large stock of clay pots, assegai points, knife blades, axes, knives and metal rings.

After formal greetings and the smoking of a round of tobacco, Bushmen generally untied their packages and bartering proceeded, with heavy haggling, item by item. The most valuable items, the objects hidden outside the kraal, were kept until last. There was much gaiety after the trading, and Bushmen were given gifts of ground millet, which they cooked while they were entertained by the people of the Okavango until late at night. The following morning they returned home, moving from waterhole to waterhole (Wilhelm 1954:140–144; see also H.J.K. 1921:119).

A different system of trading occurred when the traders (Bechuanas, whites and Herero) moved into the Bushman heartland to trade. Bechuanas came especially for tanned skins, which were renowned throughout the country for their softness. Tobacco was the major commodity traded to Bushmen, and the quantity was measured in three ways: a handful, two handfuls, and the hollow between the chest and the arms when folded (Wilhelm 1954:140–144). In addition to clothing, ironware and cannabis were also regular items (Wilhelm 1954; Bleek 1928); in the southern Kalahari, coffee was also a popular item (SWAA, A50/27, 16 April 1926).[14]

Bushmen (Kung) also traded among themselves. Thus, the Karakuwisa Bushmen were reported to go to Nurugas in order to trade pots obtained from Bushmen at Blockfontein; Bushmen at Otjituo traded with Auen Bushmen. A shirt given by the missionary Vedder to a Bushman at Gaub went to the Auen via Otjituo, and beads emanating from Bechuanaland found their way to Grootfontein (Wilhelm 1954). Bleek, in her study of Naron Bushmen in the Gobabis district, provided an indication of how far-reaching this trade network was. Ovambo knives and metal rings that came from the north via the Auen were found among the Naron, who then traded them to the Koon, who lived south of Gobabis (Bleek 1928).

As befits the winner of the Royal Geographical Society's Gold Medal, Galton, and his compatriots, tended to underplay the fact that many of their "explorations" were secondhand. But every now and then in their texts such references surface. Thus Galton's colleague Andersson reported meeting South African Coloreds[15] who had trekked across the Kalahari with forty-seven wagons to hunt, and both Galton and Andersson found that game had retreated to beyond longitude 20° as a result of large-scale hunting with firearms (Kienetz 1974). One of their near contemporaries, the artist Thomas Baines, found Bushmen at Sandfontein (now Plessisplaas) who could speak Dutch (Baines 1864:94). Galton, then, can be read as representing a complex picture of interethnic distribution and interaction, which was, moreover, contrary to conventional European wisdom. Many early travelers, especially Rhenish missionaries, actively promulgated the image that Bushmen and the (negroid) Bergdamara were the serfs and slaves of Herero and Nama. Such an image made sense in terms of the nineteenth-century unilineal evolutionary models and, moreover, provided a moral justification for the missionary presence in the territory as well as an argument in favor of colonization.

In order to flesh out this complex picture of the role of Bushmen within precolonial northern Namibia, I impose my own categories upon their activities: their copper mining and trading operations and their interethnic relations with pastoralists. I also discuss scholarly attempts to explain Bushmen. Of course, the activities of the Bushmen did not occur within a vacuum but were rather part of a larger process of incorporation into the world capitalist system. Therefore, that wider milieu has to be sketched also, for it provides the key to what was later to happen to Bushmen when their area suffered colonization.

Chapter 3

Bushman Copper and Autonomy

While Bushmen were being entrapped in the vortex of changes brought about by incorporation into the world system, how were they getting on with their fellow indigenes? Two aspects of Bushman life in precolonial Namibia during the eighteenth and early nineteenth century are pivotal. First, Bushmen exercised considerable autonomy. There was no strong centralized authority in the region where most of them lived. It was seen by Europeans as an area that was subject to rival claims by Herero and Ovambo. The botanist-explorer Hans Schinz's remarkable map showed the area as being occupied by (Ovambo) "Ondonga tribute-paying Bushmen" (Schinz 1891). During this time, Herero presence was minimal (Köhler 1959b; see also Schinz 1891). Second, Bushmen were producers of copper; indeed most of these copper deposits were in this locality.

Copper and the Ovambo

Trade, and especially trade and mining in copper, was one of the features that impressed many early travelers in their encounters with Bushmen in this part of Africa. In 1850, Brochado entered Ovamboland from the north. He found:

> On [Chief] Nangolo's periphery about 100 to 125 km away are *Kwankhala* [Kung[1]] who contrary to most other members of this race, are settled and possess large copper mines and have copper in abundance. Only the [o]Ndonga trade with them trading for copper for tobacco, beads and *pungo* [cannabis]. However, the Ondonga do not precisely know where the mine is. Even the powerful Haimbili of Kuanyama is not

allowed direct contact with them. (cited in Heintze 1972:47; see also Schinz 1891:293ff.)

Brochado also reported that Heikom Bushmen traded salt from the Etosha pans, which they made up in sugar-loaf parcels.

The next travelers in the area, Galton (1889:136) and Andersson (1856:182), found that Bushmen brought the ore to Otjikoto, where they traded it with Ovambo. The very notion of Bushmen being engaged in copper mining clashed with the standard stereotype of Bushmen. Thus, the Reverend Hugo Hahn noted his first encounter with mining Bushmen in these terms: "We met two Bushmen today who were taking copper ore from Otjorukaku to Ondonga *on their own account* where they would sell it for corn, tobacco, and calabashes. *This I never expected from Bushmen*" (Hahn 1985:vol. 4, 1034 [18 July 1857], my emphases and translation). Hahn described how parties of Ovambo (and Bushmen) transported the ore in neatly woven baskets made of palm leaves. Filled, each basket weighed 90 pounds, and when food and water were added, each porter carried approximately 115 pounds! These porters performed with impressive military precision, traveling for six to eight hours per day in parties of about thirty men. Apparently one of the reasons why Hahn's party was attacked by the Ovambo king on this expedition was that the king, Nangoro, wanted to appropriate the group's four wagons to transport copper.

The copper was smelted in Ondonga and made into decorative foot rings,[2] which Ondonga then traded further afield with their fellow Ovambo. On his next journey in 1866, Hahn observed that Bushmen were mining the copper near Otavi and trading it to Ovambo, who arrived in large numbers. Bushmen still refused to allow outsiders to visit the actual site of mining. Hahn estimated that between fifty and sixty tons of copper were exported to Ondonga per annum. Other Bushmen[3] collected and traded salt from the Etosha Pan. This trade was just as important to Bushmen as the copper trade (Moritz 1980; Sohnge 1967; see also Palgrave 1877:46).

Obviously, such mining activities were bound to attract the attention of mercantile adventurers, and McKiernan wrote that in 1875 he managed to find the mine after much difficulty. "Old smelting places were plentiful. Calcined stones, charcoal, and fragments of copper ore in heaps" was how he described this very rich ore body. But he felt that the deposit was too far from the nearest port and that lack of water en route made mining impracticable and uneconomical (McKiernan 1954:53–54).

A few years later, Schinz (1891) confirmed the mining activities near what was then the Republic of Upingtonia. He said that these Bushmen owed their allegiance to the Ondonga chief, Kambonde. By that time the

Bushman monopoly on the salt trade had been broken, as the Ukuambi Ovambo and the Ongandjera Ovambo were also engaged in it (Schinz 1891). A Bushman is credited with discovering the immensely profitable mines at Tsumeb (Lebzelter 1934b:42).

These amicable relations extended to Bushmen living within the various Ovambo tribal areas. "I never heard a Damara or a Bushman speak ill of the Ovampo, they always spoke in the warmest terms of their hospitality and honesty," claimed Galton (1852). "The Bushmen appear to be naturalized," he later wrote, "and free to a distance very far north of Caconda" (Galton 1889:142). Apparently, it was not that free a life because they, like all the subjects of Ovambo chiefs and kings, had to pay tribute. This was in ivory. Moller wrote that, like other citizens, Bushmen living in southern Ovamboland paid a yearly tribute in salt, copper ore or game. Game had to be handed over alive because Ovambo feared that Bushmen might poison the Ovambo king (Moller 1974:148, 152).

Ovambo kings appreciated the advantages of using outsiders for sensitive tasks.[4] Bushmen were widely reported to have served as body-guards, executioners, spies, special messengers and professional hunters. They were so effective as spies that Lehmann reported that missionaries complained that Nehale knew about events two weeks before the missionaries did (Lehmann 1956). So trusting were relations between Bushmen and Ovambo that when in the 1860s Andersson went up to Ovamboland after Hahn and Green had been attacked, the Ovambo king fled to a Bushman *werft* for refuge (Vedder 1938). As befitted their mercenary status, the Bushmen were "even more ornamented than the Ovambo themselves, [and were] a kind of standing army" (Galton 1889:142). The Ovambo kings did, on occasion, appoint Bushmen as headmen or fore-men of their bands. These Bushmen chiefs were allegedly powerful, and their followers would, if ordered to, kill men or women. One such Ovambo-appointed headman was Quben Qubu, who had his great place at Andoni, but roamed from Ovamboland to the Sandveld, armed with two muzzle-loaders and accompanied by his several wives. He was widely feared and respected by Bushmen and Ovambo (see *Rex v. Qouigan and Habuson* 1919 SCC and *Rex v. Quben Qubu* 1920 SCC). There is also a case of a chief's wife appointing a Bushman as a foreman over a local Ovambo ward (Wulfhorst 1937).

In times of drought, Bushmen often moved in and lived with Ovambo families, usually those with whom they had previously established trading ties (South Africa 1931; Heintze 1972). When old Bushmen could not fend for themselves, they too would attach themselves to an Ovambo household. After such a move, the men would generally assist the Ovambo in moving their livestock to outlying cattle posts during the winter months (South Africa 1934). Stock theft by Bushmen was unknown, and they would often return strayed cattle (Schoeman n.d.[a]). Indeed, a surprising number settled down in Ovambo-style houses and had fields and cattle.

Perhaps the best social indicator of discrimination involves sex. Intermarriage appears to have been quite common with the Heikom Bushmen, but not so common with the Kung. It was not only a case of Ovambo men marrying Bushman women but also the other way around, and there was no stigma attached to the offspring of such unions. Wulfhorst related the story of a young Kuanyama whose father was a Bushman. The youth went south on a labor contract and later, on his way back to Ovamboland, met some of his father's relatives and decided to stay with them. He eventually married a Bushman woman, who unfortunately died in childbirth, so he returned to Kuanyama (Wulfhorst 1937:37). But it was not just the commoners who intermarried. Prominent Ovambo kings and headmen including Chief Martin of the Ondonga, and the father of the former Ngandjera chief Tshanika were said to be half-blooded Heikom (SWAA, A50/188/5, 1940).[5]

Relationships with Pastoralists

Determining the degree of Bushman autonomy is difficult because claims to the Bushman area were made later by pastoral Herero. These claims are in conflict with evidence by writers of diverse backgrounds showing that speakers of Nama, Oerlam or Herero did not immutably infringe on the traditional areas of Bushmen in the northeast until after the introduction of firearms (see, for example, Wilhelm 1954; Swanepoel n.d.). During the era of booty capital, pastoral Herero "only came to the Bushman country as casual laborers to the Europeans during the hunting season" (Köhler 1959b:16). Similarly, the Kwangari, who were to become most populous "tribe" in the Okavango area, were, at the turn of the century, still largely north of the river because they feared the Bushmen (ZBU 1010[3], Gibson 1981).

Galton reported the northernmost Herero cattle outpost to be at Okamabuti, near the present-day Grootfontein; beyond that was a large tract of land that belonged to Bushmen (Galton 1889:103). Schinz, who was the most reliable and informative early scientific explorer of this area, reported Herero at Okamabuti on sufferance from the Ovambo king, who had taken pity on them as a result of the losses they had suffered at the hands of marauding Oerlams in the south. Shortly thereafter, residential permission was withdrawn and the Herero retreated to the Waterberg (Schinz 1891:351). In 1857, Hugo Hahn passed through the area en route to Ovamboland and referred to the area around Otjituo (now a major center in the government-proclaimed Herero ethnic homeland), Grootfontein and the Otjitjika Mountains as "Bushman-land" (Vedder 1938:308; Moritz 1980). There were no Herero or Khoi in the area.

Ovambo lived to the north of the Etosha Pan but traded with Bushmen who mined copper at what is now Great Otavi. The nearest Herero at that time were south of the Omatako Mountains (Hartmann, cited in Köhler 1959b:15). Under pressure from the incessant raids by Jonker Afrikaner, a well-armed Oerlam bandit leader, some Herero tried to flee northward with their cattle. They intended to join Nangoro in Ovamboland, but on the way to Grootfontein they killed some Bushmen at the Waterberg (another traditional Bushman haunt, now the center of Hereroland). True to his role of "Protector of the Bushmen," Nangoro marched south and routed the Herero at Nuitsas and later again at Grootfontein. Primarily because of Oerlam harassment, a small group of Herero fled to Nangoro in abject poverty and succeeded in gaining asylum (Köhler 1959b; Chapman n.d.).

Who were these Bushmen and where did they come from? One Heikom oral history presents the following reconstruction of their past:

> The first Heikom, Xameb [Tsameb?] came to the Namutoni area from Waterberg. At that time, Namutoni was the drinking place of innumerable elephants. The bushes were very thick and the trees were much higher than now. Thus, Xameb and his people moved further on in the direction of Ovamboland but they did not like the sandy soil of Ovamboland and returned to Namutoni. They were great hunters and were left in peace. Only much later did the Hottentots [Khoi] and Damaras [Herero] arrive. The Xaben [Ovambo] were our first friends and we traded with them. The Herero were the first people with whom we made war. (Schoeman n.d.[a])

The southern advance of Herero pastoralists was checked by some singular resistance by a Heikom Bushman leader named Tsameb. With the first appearance of Herero cattle on Bushman preserves, Tsameb organized raids. This led to Herero indiscriminately killing any Bushman they encountered, whether male or female. Tsameb then set about organizing the various Bushman clans to resist the Herero invasion. Because of the success of these strategies, he became known as chief. Later, he obtained Khoi assistance and forced the Herero to retreat. Tsameb's group became known as the *Kai-ei-kwan* (or *Gaikokoin*, in ZBU 2043, Annual Report, Grootfontein Bezirk, 1913) and had "great places," ranging from Karuchas in the Outjo district to what are now the farms Brandenburg and Wittenburg in the present Grootfontein district (SWAA, A50/67, Hahn to CNC, 5 September 1940).

Tsameb was succeeded by his son Aribib, who continued his father's proud and effective tradition of resistance to Herero and later German encroachment (Hartmann, cited by Köhler 1959b; SWAA, A50/67, Hahn to CNC, 5 September 1940). The fragile unity of the Heikom clans were shattered on Aribib's death in 1905, and those clans were subsequently hunted down by both Herero and Germans, who had by this time settled in the area. As a result, Bushmen were driven from their "great places" like Naidaus and Okarusu to the fringes of the Etosha Game Park (proclaimed in 1907), where they found temporary refuge.

Vedder,[6] testifying before the South West Africa Constitutional Commission in 1936, pointed out that Herero had in precolonial and German colonial times occupied the Okahandja, Omaruru, Otjimbingue and part of the Waterberg area. A few families had "travelled up to the north but they knew very well it was Bushmanland" (SWA Constitutional Commission). Old maps confirm this. A map illustrating the German-Herero war of 1904 showed the northernmost point of Herero settlement to be the southern point of the Waterberg, whereas the Herero settlement nearest to what later became the Epukiro Reserve was at least 150 kilometers distant (Moritz 1980). Other sources confirm the maps. The annual reports from the Grootfontein district point out that before World War I, Otjituo was a major Bushman settlement, and Bleek (1922, 1928) in her pioneering research at Sandfontein, east of Gobabis, found that all her old informants claimed that Herero and Tswana had been middle-aged when they came into their area. Perhaps the most interesting evidence for the recency of Herero contact with Bushmen is to be found in the diary that the Reverend Hahn kept on his journey of exploration from Otjimbingue to Ovamboland in the north. He found that one of the ways his Herero servants referred to the Bushmen was as *ozombushmana*, derived clearly, as he recognized, from Dutch. But he went on to say that the proper Herero name is *ovakuruha* (which can be glossed as 'first' or 'primeval' 'people') (Moritz 1980:21; Katjavivi 1988).[7]

The pioneering anthropologist Gustav Fritsch reported "reliable" Herero as stating that Bushmen had originally occupied the whole land from Ovamboland to the Gariep (Orange River) before they were driven out by the Namaqua and Herero (Fritsch 1872). And Ratzel (1897) pointed out that many names in what was later Hereroland were derived from Nama.

Of course, there were Herero claims to land occupied by Bushmen, but changing the name of the place does not establish title to it. Many of these claims were quite specious. Maherero, for example, claimed the Otavi area with its copper mines on the grounds that the Herero had mined the copper first and that Grootfontein had previously been occupied by Herero. However, as Schinz pointed out, the Herero word for copper was *otjikoporo*, a word clearly of English origin, and, moreover, Bushmen in the area recognized the hegemony of Kambonde, the Ondonga king, not that of Maherero (Schinz 1891).

But what of Bushman relationships where they lived in areas conjointly occupied by pastoralists? Herero pastoral values made for a difficult situation. As Vedder wrote: "One who possesses a herd of cattle which he calls his own, is called a master. One who has not acquired or inherited cattle is of no importance. It is compulsory for such a person to throw in his lot with an owner of property. . . . The poor led a wretched life" (Vedder 1928:175, 207).[8]

Most historical sources concur that Bushmen-Herero relations were bitter. Even Andersson, no admirer of Bushmen and an ardent Herero-phile, noted in 1856: "Some Bushmen surprised and killed eight Damara [Herero] women. This was not to be wondered at, for the Damaras themselves are always waging an exterminating war on the Bushmen. Indeed, they hunt them down, wherever met with, like wild beasts" (Andersson 1856:210–211).

A few years later the artist Baines wrote in his journal:

Another even less welcome piece of intelligence is the confirmation of a report that Chapman's Damaras during his absence had borrowed guns of his servant John, an old soldier of the 74th Highlanders, and instead of hunting as they had promised, had attacked the Bushmen in the hills, killing some, and returning loaded with their almost worthless plunder. This outrage, the result of some ancient feud, is likely to set the Bushmen at enmity with us. (Baines 1864:91)

In 1877, the wife of the hunter Green reported that she had witnessed a Herero and twenty of his men first stun a captive Bushman with knobkerries (wooden clubs), then beat him raw with sjamboks (leather whips), before they finally burned him alive (Tabler 1973:48; see also Jordan 1881:174). Even during the German colonial era, the traveler Moller observed that, in contrast to Ovamboland, Bushmen in Hottentot and Herero areas "live as oppressed pariahs who are unscrupulously exterminated wherever they are found" (Moller 1974:147).

The Reverend H. Beiderbecke, who pioneered the Rhenish Mission Station at the Waterberg in 1873, recalled his frustration in trying to stop Herero raids on Bushman and Bergdamara encampments, where the Herero either killed off the residents or captured the young and strong to serve as slaves (Beiderbecke 1922).[9] Vedder stated that the Bergdamaras and Bushmen "were regarded by the Hereros as having no right there at all and they were looked upon as pests. They were killed wherever they were encountered. Women and children were carried off and put to work at domestic tasks and as herd-boys" (Vedder 1938:143). In view of all the evidence his conclusion seems to be plausible.[10]

Chapter 4

The Incorporation
of Bushmen
into the World System

Galton's visit to Ovamboland in the early 1850s was symptomatic of a new era in which white hunters and traders trekked north in large numbers in search of ivory. This era was the result not of Galton's opening up the area so much as of changes in the industrial countries, especially in the United States. As that country industrialized, the nouveau riche sought new status symbols, and the symbol par excellence was the upright piano. "Every American woman feels bound to play the piano, just as she feels bound to wear clothes," wrote a French visitor in 1860. Post–Civil War affluence meant, according to the *Atlantic Monthly* of 1867, that a piano was "only less indispensable than a kitchen range" (cited in Conniff 1987:85). It is estimated that to meet this demand, between 1860 and 1930, 25,000 to 100,000 elephants were killed per year (Conniff 1987:83–89). Between 1852 and 1860 the production of pianos in the United States increased from 9,000 to 22,000 per annum[1] and eventually peaked at 350,000 pianos in 1910, more than twice as many as the Germans produced, the U.S. industry's nearest competitors. By the turn of the century annually 1 in 260 Americans was buying a piano, compared with a modest 1 in 360 for their British peers.

Although it is generally accepted that most of this ivory came from East Africa, a strong case can be made that Namibia supplied a large proportion of the earlier ivory before its herds were depleted. This assertion is based on the fact that the Namibian coast had long been a favorite haunt of Yankee sealers, whalers and guano collectors[2] and that as the profits from the coast dwindled, adventurers and fortune seekers simply extended their operations inland and switched to ivory. Many of the early hunter-traders were from North America. The risks in the

ivory and cattle trade were high, but so were the profits: Estimates range
as high as between 1,500 percent (Lau 1987) and 2,000 percent (Helbig
1983:38).

Figures and records of this era outline a grim march of environmental denudation toward the northeast, the Bushman heartland. By 1860
game was reportedly "shot out" in southern Namibia (Namaland). In
1865 Chapman estimated the value of the Namibian trade with the Cape
to be between 10,000 and 12,000 head of cattle and 20,000 pounds of
ivory. By 1876 the ratio had changed to 3,000 head of cattle, 5,800
pounds of ostrich feathers and 34,500 pounds of ivory (Davies 1943:130–
131).[3] After 1878 the decline of game was rapid. In 1880 game was
described as "shot out" in central Namibia (Hereroland), and in 1882
the official value of the Namibian trade to the Cape Colony was placed
at a measly 26,016 English pounds (de Kock 1948).

Most of these estimates of the value of trade are based on goods
channeled through Cape Town and Walvis Bay and are thus gross under-
estimates. Not only do we have reports that practically all trek oxen on
Cape roads were Herero oxen, but there were numerous other trade
routes that had different destinations. For example, many traders followed the Nossob and Auob rivers and were based in places like Carnar-
von, Upington, Vryburg and Kimberley. The Nossob and Auob routes
led to Gobabis and Blydeverwachting, both important trading centers,
even rivaling Windhoek. The discovery of diamonds in Kimberley in
1867 served to further enhance this route. During this period there
were major routes coming into use leading to the newly discovered gold
mines (1882) on the Witwatersrand. These traversed the Kalahari either
via Lehututu and Aminuis or via Ngami and Rietfontein (Stals 1962).[4]
As the hunter-traders' sphere of exploitation moved north, the major
northern route of travelers, hunters and traders was via either Karakuwisa or Tsintsabis. Cattle from Angola were often exported to the Rand
mining area, not by ship, as then duties had to be paid, but directly
overland, down to Erikssen's Putz, about forty kilometers from Otjituo.
There they were massed and driven through the Kalahari to Lewisfontein (Ngama), a route that took them through Bushman territory to
Ngami and then to the Transvaal.

This cattle route was apparently pioneered by Axel Erikssen and
probably went through Nyae Nyae. "As it avoided the waterless desert
and the unruly Namaquas to the south, it became the customary route
between the interior and the west coast. Erikssen himself sent thousands
of head of cattle to the interior by this route" (Watts 1926:93; see also
SWAA, A198/6/15). Lorna Marshall (1976:54–59) said that at Gautscha
and Garu, in the Nyae Nyae area, there are three baobab trees with
names and dates ranging from 1876. The implications of this mute

Artist-traveler Thomas Baines noted on this sketch: "Wednesday June 4 1852. The Bushman's Camp and remains of their Rhinoceros. Every particle of flesh or skin b _____ to asc _____ even to the outscrapings of the hoofs. Vangyous June 4." Notice muzzle-loader propped against a tree in the left foreground—indicative of incorporation into the world economy. The long strips hung on poles are *biltong*, or jerky. (Courtesy Royal Geographical Society)

Hauptmann Mueller and Bushman at Gautscha, in the heart of contemporary Bushmanland, during Mueller's patrol of 1911. Photographer emphasized differences in stature by having Bushman hold rifle. (Photo courtesy State Archives, Windhoek)

testimony seems to have escaped many Bushman scholars. They point to the fact that the Ju-/wasi of Nyae Nyae have not lived as isolated an existence as the textbooks would like us to believe. Evidence to support this is readily available. For example, Siegfried Passarge's map of his visit to the Nyae Nyae area in 1898 documented routes traversed by Curt von François in 1891 and Powrie in 1898, and there is also an anonymous listing of "Kaffernwagen" (native traders) from the previous year (Passarge 1907).[5]

These hunter-traders did not rush blindly over the landscape. Instead they followed preexisting trade routes and utilized traditional hunting grounds. Hunts involved a large number of people. Expeditions of up to twenty wagons would leave accompanied by a large number of camp servants and stay away for a few months, usually in the winter, pursuing ivory, ostrich feathers or game horns.[6]

Contemporary Views of Bushmen

Bushmen made ideal camp followers. Schinz found them to be the most trustworthy and reliable of the various "natives." Their loyalty was such that they would allegedly work without pay. This conclusion was also reached by other whites with whom he spoke (Schinz 1891:392). Most hunters reported that Bushmen were very helpful (e.g., Chapman 1868) and would do anything for a small gift of tobacco (Nolte 1886). Indeed the Bushmen's almost-legendary weakness for tobacco was well established. Chapman noted that they obtained tobacco by trading jackal skins in Chapa, a distance of 240 kilometers. On occasion, however, it seems that other hunters had to resort to taking Bushmen hostage in order to force them to be guides (Galton 1889), but they apparently treated Bushmen well during these expeditions. Tales of Bushmen rescuing whites, including Boers, and other blacks from thirst were common (see, e.g., van der Walt 1926; Coetzee 1942; Richard Lee [personal communication]). McKiernan found that Bushmen were always willing to perform even the most dull and menial services and were satisfied with a ration of tobacco, beads or a handkerchief as a reward (McKiernan 1954:77). Generally Bushmen who served as guides were allowed to carry guns and doubled as messengers. Indeed, it is clear that they played a pivotal role in the communications network of the early white hunters and traders (Green 1860; Galton 1889).

The prevailing advice to whites at that time was that Bushmen were usually fine people unless they had been wronged in some way (Tabler 1973:49; McKiernan 1954). Many whites and blacks were apparently killed for raping Bushman women (Andersson 1856:359; Moller 1974:150; Wallis 1936:224). Retributive justice worked both ways. When hunter Hendrik van Zyl heard that a small child of one of the Thirstland Trekkers had wandered off and been killed by Bushmen, he let it be known that there was a limitless supply of tobacco and brandy available at his settlement. He invited Bushmen to participate in this largesse at a specially constructed kraal, and when they were suitably inebriated, ordered them tied up and taken to where the child had been killed. He then invited the Thirstland Trekkers to shoot them. The trekkers declined, so he gave some rifles to the Bushmen attached to the Boers, and after he had read the biblical passage concerning an eye for an eye, ordered them to shoot. Thirty-three Bushmen were murdered in this episode (de Klerk 1977:67).

There were contradictions in the stereotype of Bushmen, which were amplified by the fact that the people so labeled did not constitute a homogeneous group but displayed considerable local autonomy. Familiarity easily bred and easily begot contempt. By the end of his life, for instance, Andersson wrote, "I have come to the conclusion that Bushmen, as a race, deserve no pity" (Andersson 1875:274). However, his disillusionment with them had started prior to this, and on occasion he referred to them as "perfect devils" (1856:140). It appears that generally many hunters and traders appreciated the qualities of Bushmen as hunters and trackers and, above all, as faithful servants; thus they armed them and encouraged them to hunt for ivory and later for ostrich feathers. Travelers encountered Bushmen armed with rifles hunting in the Okavango region, who, on a good day, could net 145 pounds of ivory (von Moltke n.d.[a]). Indeed, some "great white hunters" were so afraid of elephants that they left all the hunting to Bushmen (Chapman n.d.). It was also common for traders to trade ivory from Bushmen (Chapman 1868:157).

By 1860, when the renowned hunter Frederick Green and trader Axel Erikssen established their hunting headquarters at Grootfontein (Vedder 1938:423), it was clear that even Bushmen of the most isolated parts of the Kalahari were involved in this ecologically destructive booty capitalism. On Green's death, the Yankee trader Gerald McKiernan eulogized him: "Frederick Green was one of the most famous of African hunters, Gordon Cumming or no other could compete with him."[7] It was estimated that in his lifetime he killed between 750 and 1,000 elephants (McKiernan 1954:93). The upper reaches of the Omuramba Omatako, a dry river bed with lush vegetation, was a popular and much-frequented area for hunters: There was a large hunting camp at Kara-kuwisa, maintained largely by the "Griqua Bastard," Johannes (Jaq) Kruger.[8] So intense was the hunting in this area that by 1865 Green was forced to move his hunting headquarters to Ondongua (Stals 1968).

Another famous hunter, the Boer Hendrik van Zyl of Ghanzi, visited the Gautscha area in 1874 (Tabler 1973). Van Zyl quickly discovered that the area north of Gobabis to the Okavango River was a "true hunter's paradise" (Burger 1978:42). He employed well over 100 Bushmen (Trumpelmann 1948:16), many of them "shootboys." Indeed, when van Zyl established the world record for killing over 103 elephants in one day (and over 400 elephants in 1877 alone), most of them were accounted for by his Bushman shots. This slaughter took place largely in the area immediately north of the present-day Bushmanland, one traditionally held by Bushmen. These kills yielded over 8,000 pounds of ivory (Tabler 1973:116).

The Demise of the Trade Boom

As more and more traders made their way up to the northeast, trade changed radically and a vicious circle developed that led to the decimation of more and more game as firepower became more accessible. Andersson, for example, reported that in the 1850s a Ngamiland chief accepted three ordinary copper mugs for a large tusk, and that 1,200 pounds of ivory, valued at that time at 240 English pounds, was traded for one musket (Vedder 1938:304). Approximately twenty years later in Ovamboland, 40 pounds of ivory could be exchanged for an English rifle, and 300 pounds of ivory could buy an excellent rifle or a small cannon (Stals 1968:248, 250). The problem was, Andersson complained, that Portuguese traders were coming down as far as 20° south latitude and giving 50 pounds of gunpowder and 100 pounds of lead for a single tusk and the Boers were disposing of their ammunition in a liberal manner to their "colored neighbors" (Andersson 1858:158).

Given such a situation, it was not long before Ovamboland was denuded of game too. The last elephants were killed in the Etosha Pan area in 1881 (de la Bat 1981, 1982), and by 1886, elephants were declared "hunted out" in Ngami (Tabler 1973:65). Some contemporaries raised their voices against this environmental pillage. Brincker, a missionary, wrote strongly about the "stupid, or rather inhuman, way in which ostriches have been hunted during the last few years, so that they have been almost exterminated," forcing traders and hunters to move further into Ovamboland and the Okavango where "they still get . . . a fair quantity of ivory and feathers through trading and hunting themselves in a way which many people would not care to undertake" (cited in Vedder 1938:447).

The death knell to this once-flourishing trade came in 1892 when the Germans prohibited trade with blacks in arms and ammunition in their newly acquired colony (Stals 1968:290–291). This led, naturally enough, to large-scale smuggling between Angola and Namibia, in which Bushmen played a key role. In 1893 there was a minor revival in trade because of the ostrich feather boom, and Bushmen were, at least in the southern Kalahari, major suppliers of the feathers and not above weighting the loads of feathers with some iron or rocks to obtain a better price (Jackson 1958).

Bushmen were aware of what was happening. In 1920, the oldest Bushman at Tsintsabis police station complained to a visitor, "Elephants, lions, and game of all kinds abounded and have only disappeared since the white man came and shot them in large numbers" (H.J.K. 1920). They could hardly not have been aware: So sickening did the governor's brother, Paul Leutwein, find the situation in the German colonial heyday that he complained that "almost all white hunters are 'Aasjaeger' [carrion hunters]" and that the "Boers sit on their ox-wagons, the bible in the one hand, the rifle in the other and shoot all the game that there is to see" (cited in Tabel 1975:89).

Bushmen played an active role in this ecological devastation. Many professional hunters and traders armed Bushmen and encouraged them to hunt for ivory and ostrich feathers. In 1878 the South African resident, stationed at Walvis Bay, reported that the Damaras (Herero) had dropped out of the hunting trade, preferring to develop their considerable herds of livestock than move further afield in search of game: "Today the Bushman is using the heavy elephant gun with deadly effect as ever did Damara, Griqua, or Namaqua, and the Damara ponders over the thought of what the Bushman will do with his gun when the game is gone. He sees the trader pass by with the goods he once bought, to enrich tribes beyond over whom he feels he can lord it no longer" (Cape Colony 1879:136). Such a situation of booty capital attracted various types of people, many of them deviants from their own society. One significant group were the "Thirstland Trekkers."

Upingtonia and the First Namibian War of Liberation

A major incursion by whites occurred with the Thirstland Trek when a motley collection of Boer fundamentalists decided to leave the South African Republic (Transvaal) in 1877 and seek a new domicile. They crossed the Kalahari in a number of treks. The first trek, consisting of fifteen families, totaling sixty-two adults, arrived in what is now Rietfontein (in Hereroland), an area traditionally acknowledged as belonging to Bushmen. There they spent two years recuperating before moving north through present-day Bushmanland to the Okavango River. They spent the winter of 1877 grazing their cattle in the Tebraveld. After many tribulations, they eventually made their way to southern Angola, where they managed to eke out a precarious existence. In 1885 an educated Cape Colored, Will Worthington Jordan, persuaded a group of them to return to the Grootfontein area to settle on farms, which he allocated to them on most reasonable terms. Jordan had, as a result of negotiations with the Ondonga king, Kambonde, obtained a concession for 25,000 square kilometers of territory between Grootfontein, Otavi, Etosha Pan and the Waterberg, on payment of 300 English pounds, twenty-five muzzle-loaders, one salted horse and a barrel of brandy (Radel 1947). Although he subdivided his concession into white farms, he retained all the mineral and trading rights in the area.

In October 1885, the *trekboers* announced the formation of the Republic of Upingtonia, named, on Jordan's insistence, after the prime minister of the Cape in an effort to ensure its support for the precarious republic.[9] Forty-six Boers signed the agreement establishing the republic, and within sixteen months, forty-three farms were allocated. Schinz estimated the Boer population at Grootfontein to be about 500 (1891). However, because of the general uncertainty in the area, arising from Bushman raids and robbery, the Boers did not occupy their farms but concentrated together at a few places where they lived in *hartebeesthuises* (adobe-style dwellings), around which they planted small fields of wheat and corn (mielies). The republic collapsed after the murder of Jordan in June 1886 and was placed under German protection in May 1887. By this time most of the erstwhile settlers had already moved away, either to Angola or the Transvaal (Burger 1978).

The role of Bushmen in this cardinal episode of contemporary right-wing Afrikaner mythology is central. Bushmen were not only directly responsible for the collapse of Upingtonia, but, indeed, Jordan wanted to establish his pocket republic there because of the rich copper diggings that they controlled and admirably exploited. Other traders and adventurers like McKiernan had visited the Bushman mining operations and were suitably impressed by the richness of the lode but were inhibited by the lack of infrastructure. However, this seemed a small problem to a visionary like Jordan, who dreamed of building a railway line from Walvis Bay to Zimbabwe (Wannenburgh n.d.:170).[10] In order to wrest the copper mines from Bushman control, he needed a large number of whites in the vicinity to protect his investment. In one of his first letters to the German imperial official, Nels, President J. G. Prinsloo of the republic complained that "the Bushmen made up a commando and have shot Mr. James Todd and taken everything which he possessed. The Bushmen still wander amongst us. We do not know what they will do to us" (cited in Burger 1978:374).

The small Boer community had to cope almost daily with Bushman reprisals, in which Bushmen invariably had the upper hand because they were often well armed with rifles, which were a legacy of ivory hunting, and were more mobile than the trekkers (Burger 1978; Prinsloo and Gauche 1933:157ff.). Indeed, the trekkers experienced considerable problems in mounting attacks, as they lacked horses and were forced to borrow them from the trader Erikssen on one occasion. Bushman counterinsurgency operations, judging by the few descriptions available, were well planned and successful, involving, in one instance, the confiscation of 500 cattle belonging to the Boer Prinsloo in one day (Prinsloo and Gauche 1933). A longtime Grootfontein resident, the surveyor Volkmann, recalled in the 1930s: "As far as I can remember, the first Boers who came into this district in about 1880 had to leave very soon again, as there were too many Bushmen living here so that they were unable to protect themselves against the continuous stealing of the Bushmen" (SWAA, A50/67, Volkmann Letter). As Upingtonian President Prinsloo explained in his last letter to Reichskommisar Goring in June 1887: "Due to our inability, we are obliged to move from here. It is due to our weakness and the rebelliousness of [local] nations which endanger the safety of our families that we are leaving, but should this land be taken into possession by some other possibility, we would like to retain our rights" (cited in Burger 1978:380). Thus ended the first successful Namibian war of liberation.

Chapter 5

Classifying Bushmen: Itinerant Scientists

In the northeastern Kalahari lived what were later to be distinguished as two distinct Bushman "types." The physically larger Nama-speaking Heikom, or San (Vedder 1981 [1934]) and the smaller "genuine" Bushmen, consisting mostly of the Kung who spoke their own language(s). The latter lived to the northeast and southeast of Grootfontein, whereas the Heikom lived predominantly to the northwest and east of Grootfontein. The Heikom, and their Gobabis district relatives, the Naron, were said to be easily distinguishable from the Kung on physiological as well as linguistic grounds (Fourie 1928).

Between Galton's pseudoscientific visit and the next one by a scientist, the botanist Schinz in 1884, a revolution had occurred in southern African anthropological studies and the ways in which scientists conceptualized Bushmen. This revolution occurred on two new fronts, the disciplines of physical anthropology and philology.

The physical anthropology discourse was to dominate "Bushman studies" in terms of numbers of scientific papers produced. In 1872 Gustav Fritsch published the first anthropological study of southern Africa. His *Eingeborenen Südafrikas: Ethnographisch und anatomisch beschreibt* was based on three years of mobile fieldwork. Fritsch claimed to be able to distinguish physiologically between Bushman and Hottentot (Khoi) and argued that they were indeed separate races. Bushmen constituted the Ur-race of Africa (see also Fritsch 1880) and were incapable of learning a European language. Consistent with this stance he also provided a new interpretation of the origin of the word *Bushman*. It was derived, he said, from the Dutch word meaning "bush person" rather than "bush inhabitant," that is, it referred to a mythical race that was, zoologically speaking, between humans and apes. In the evolutionary scheme of things, thus, Bushmen came *prior* to humans. Proof of this he found in the diary of the first Dutch commander at the Cape, Jan van Riebeeck, where reference was made to *Bosmanneken,* which in Batavia referred to orangutans (cited in van Reenen 1920:14).

Using Farini's research and Chapman's photographs for the northern Kalahari as well as German research among the Bakuba (where there were dwarfs known as Batua), he later argued that Bushmen had originally occupied the whole of Africa. They represented the "zerstreuten Überbleibsel einer ursprunglichen Bevölkerung . . . das immer mehr ausstirbt" (the scattered remains of the original population who are increasingly dying out). It was he who coined the much-quoted term *unfortunate child of the moment.* Ratzel attributed this to their paedomorphic features and their mental "fatal thoughtlessness":

> The inclination of the moment is decisive with him, and this explains all the contradiction and bad qualities which has made him, of all South Africans, the most detested by white and coloured men . . . what makes him an outlaw and puts him outside the pale of humanity is the cruelty with which he carries out his raids. The Bushman is the anarchist of South Africa. On the other hand, wherever he comes, as a servant, into permanent relations with white men, he has always the reputation of trustworthiness . . . [but] it seldom happens that he ever comes over into the "tamed" state, and still more seldom that he perseveres in it. The fear of the Bushmen has indeed produced an effect in the disforesting of South Africa; since the colonists in order to guard against stealthy attacks, removed the bush near their dwellings. (Ratzel 1897:267–8)

In philology, the pioneering work of Wilhelm Bleek, conducted in the 1860s on Bushman prisoners captured in the northern Cape and sent to work on the Table Bay Breakwater, had begun to have an impact. Bleek argued that linguistically Bushmen were distinct from Khoi. Bushmen were not, as most had suggested, simply impoverished Hottentots.[1] Writing for a popular audience, he explained the difference as being the same as that of English and Latin. The ideological impact of his theories linking Bushmen and Khoi to the "ancient Coptic tongue of Egypt" (Wilmot 1895:47) was immediate and long-lasting,[2] although they underwent continuous tinkering to keep abreast of metropolitan theoretical fashions. Thus by 1875 he classified the Hottentots as kindred to the Bantu and distinct from Bushmen (Bleek 1875). Bushmen were not the lowest stage of humanity but in many ways closer to European culture (Bleek 1875), and this tied in well with archaeological arguments of the day that saw European rock art as being created by a Bushman-like race.

Later commentators, like Ratzel, felt that Bleek had overemphasized the linguistic similarities and ignored the ethnographic differences.

Bushman and Hottentot languages were peculiar because of their isolation and "the inherited enmity between Bushman and Hottentot served to keep the old racial characteristics distinct" (Ratzel 1897:259). Instead Ratzel wished to "draw attention to the far-extending points of resemblance, both in mode of life and in bodily build between the Bushmen and the so-called dwarf races of the interior" (Ratzel 1897:260).

As Cape government philologist, Bleek was succeeded by Theophilus Hahn. Born of missionary parents in southern Namibia, he was the first South African to earn a doctorate in philology (on Nama, which he spoke fluently). Hahn was also one of the first people to publish material under the rubric of ethnography (Hahn 1867) and ethnology [*volkekunde* in Afrikaans (Hahn 1870)]. To Hahn, neither the connections to the ancient Egyptians nor the distinction between Bushman and Hottentot was quite so clear-cut.

> Firstly . . . that the ancestors of the "Red men" had begun to climb the first steps of the ladder of culture and civilization, we have no reason to doubt, even if we had no proofs to that effect. But there is such a proof, which allows us an insight into the state of culture the Aborigines had reached—namely, the language which is still spoken by the last Mohicans of the Hottentot race, especially by the nomadic tribes of Great Namaqualand and the present Griqualand West.
>
> We are entirely at a loss to understand the arguments which have induced some philologists to trace a relationship between the Hottentots and old Egyptians, and we are equally perplexed to understand how the same authorities could doubt for a single moment the kinship of the Hottentot proper [Khoi-Khoi] and Bushmen [San]. In fact every colonist from the border will look with amazement at the man who would try to convince him of the non-relationship between Bushman and Hottentot.
> . . . For the present we have to state that, linguistically speaking, we never can and we never will consent, to acknowledge a connection between the Hottentot and the old Egyptian languages, unless such indisputable proofs and arguments are produced as shall fully agree with the system of out present Comparative Philology. (Hahn 1878:258–259)

Despite the good reception that Hahn's book, *Tsumi-//goam: The Supreme Being of the Khoi-Khoi* (1881), enjoyed from Max Muller, the foremost philologist of the time, Hahn never received the attention that he warranted. Perhaps he was a bit of a colonial rough diamond. Certainly the intellectual savaging that he gave Hyde Clarke's paper on the (putative) relationship between South African and Australian languages, read at the South African Philosophical Society, did not help. Clarke was, inter alia, president of the Royal Statistical Society and vice president of the Royal Anthropological Institute. Hahn's tenure as government philologist was rather short.[3]

This then was the state of knowledge when that remarkable Swiss botanist-explorer Hans Schinz (1858–1941) set out in 1884 to undertake a survey of the northwest that had been commissioned by Adolf Luderitz. The latter had purchased land concessions around Angra Pequena, from which he was to launch the German colonial state on the sands of Namibia. He traveled extensively until February 1887 and then published his major work *Deutsch-Südwest-Afrika* in 1891. It was Schinz who first separated Kaukauveld Bushmen in different groups. On the basis of his travels in 1884–1887, he classified them into two main groups: the Heikom, whom he called Nama-Bushmen because of the language they spoke (Galton's Saen); and the I Kun San, who were subdivided again into those near the Aha mountains, the I Gu (Ju-/wasi). Near Lake Ngami were to be found the Gani. Between Ghanzi and Rietfontein, Schinz placed the //Ai San, who spoke a language closely related to Hottentot (Nama, Khoi). The //Ai San were unable to understand their neighbors the Au San, who spoke a language closely related to the I Kun San (Schinz, 1891:388–393). Schinz's division of Bushmen matches the current distribution of Bushmen surprisingly well. He estimated the Kalahari Bushmen at 5,000, of whom 3,000 to 3,500 were of "unmixed blood" (Ratzel 1897:266). Distinguishing racially pure from "bastard" Bushmen was to be a major concern of the next generation of Bushman researchers.

Part 2

The Colonial Presence

Chapter 6

The Imposition of the Colonial State

Shortly after the collapse of the Republic of Upingtonia, the official presence of the German colonial powers started to be felt in the northeast. At the onset, policy was dictated by the elementary fact that the first colonial governor, Theodor Leutwein, had limited military power to enforce his decisions. To compensate for this shortcoming he developed pompous, elaborate ceremonies around the ritual of treaty making.[1] So enthusiastically did Leutwein encourage such treaty-making rituals among his officers that some bewildered indigenes found themselves signing the same basic treaty with several different German officials! Bushmen, too, were subject to such rituals.

On August 31, 1895, Leutwein concluded a treaty with the "baster"[2] Johannes (Jaq) Kruger, which recognized Kruger as captain of all the Bushmen and Damaras living at Gaub. In return, Kruger promised to carry out all instructions given to him by "higher authorities in every detail." The representative of the South West Africa Company, the conglomerate that had taken over Jordan's extensive land concessions, was made his immediate superior and given sole rights to dispose of land in the vicinity (Voeltz 1988).

Johannes Kruger was the son of a Griqua[3] hunter who was informally acknowledged as the headman of the Waterberg Bushmen and Damaras. Kruger *père* and *fils*, with their numerous armed supporters, contributed substantially to the depletion of game, especially elephant, in this area (Vedder 1981 [1934]:501). Later Kruger *fils* described what the treaty entailed:

> I knew the Bushmen had no real Chiefs . . . and I told Leutwein that
> Bushmen would not readily submit to a Chief, especially as I was not a
> Bushman. The reply was that as I know the language and the people, I

might have influence over them. . . . After the agreement was signed, Hartmann [the SWA Co. representative] gave me 5 Marks a month. I had to provide labourers for the Company. I then tried to collect people to live in Ghaub which, under the agreement was given to us. I collected in time 212 Heikom Bushmen . . . also 110 Berg-Damaras, and these with the 35 Hottentots, all lived on my werft. . . . But the Bushmen only remained a short time, as there was not enough "veld kost" [wild fruits, roots, herbs, etc.] for them to live on. . . . So they returned to the bush. Later on, the Bushmen began to offer their services as labourers on the farms of the German settlers. The majority of the Heikom . . . left the bush and came on to the farms. Then the trouble started. The German farmers refused to pay them their wages, they said food and tobacco were enough for them. They did not want money. The food was poor and the Bushmen complained to me. I spoke to Lt. Volkmann, the German magistrate, . . . he made promises, but nothing came of them. [Then the settlers started using Bushmen wives as concubines.] They deeply resented it. . . . I made representations . . . but the trouble continued. (South Africa 1918:144–145)

Leutwein also concluded a treaty with Bushman "Kapitän" Fritz Aribib at Naidaus, recognizing him as chief of all the Western Bushmen, in the hope that these "fugitive and shy" people would be controlled (Leutwein 1906:88). A few years later, in 1898, Hauptmann von Estorff concluded yet another "protection treaty" with Bushman "Kapitän" Aribib.[4] In it Aribib ceded to the Germans a large parcel of land stretching from Grootfontein to Outjo for a small subvention of 500 marks, protection and the permanent right to forage in that area.[5]

Aribib received his annual subvention regularly until his death. But after his death and the declaration of the northern portion of this area as the Etosha Game Park, Bushmen were expelled from the park and forced to work for white ranchers. Aribib was a "captain" of some influence. He had managed to check the northward expansion of the cattle-herding Herero to Ombaongomba (Gaikop), Otjenga (Agob), Otji-warongo (Kaknobio) and Okomsu (Kileib). He was a loyal ally of the Germans because he had been shot on the instructions of the Ovambo King Nehale in 1904 for killing a number of Herero who had fled from the Germans to Namutoni.

Some commentators have suggested that by drawing up treaties of this nature, Leutwein was simply displaying his ethnological ignorance, not understanding that Bushmen did not have chiefs. Even if this were true, it is irrelevant, because in his system of control, Leutwein concentrated on the personalities of men of influence.[6] Already in the early twentieth century there was considerable discussion in legal circles as to the validity of these treaties. An international lawyer, A. H. Snow, sum-

Bushman Captain Aribib with wives and bodyguards, photographed by Governor Leutwein in the early 1890s. Aribib was so powerful that the Germans were forced to sign treaties with him. (Photo courtesy of State Archives, Windhoek)

marized the dominant opinion: "The term 'treaty' as applied to an agreement between civilized State and an aboriginal tribe, is misleading, and such an agreement is, according to the law of nations, a legislative act on the part of the civilized State, made upon conditions which it is bound to fulfill since it insists that the aboriginal tribes shall be bound by their part" (Snow 1921:127). Leutwein, by fulfilling the "civilized State"'s side of the agreement, thus recognized the legitimacy of the agreement.[7]

That Bushmen were rapidly incorporated into the colonial political economy is clear from Table 6.1, showing reported criminal convictions in the Grootfontein district in 1898–1899. The cases listed, in which men defined as Bushmen dominate, constitute the tip of the proverbial iceberg. Farmers were legally entitled to administer personally up to twenty-five strokes and frequently did so (Prozess Wiehager, *Südwest Zeitung*, 1907:40). Indeed, often in cases that called for state intervention, the state had to abdicate in favor of action by settlers because it did not have the resources to exert itself. The well-known "Paasch affair" is a case in point. Settler Paasch and his family had trekked by ox-wagon up to the Kavango, where, except for a daughter who was captured, the

Table 6.1   Convictions, Grootfontein District, 1898–1899

Name	Offense	Punishment
Bushman Keiseb	Let horses stray	10 cane strokes
Bushman Pomokeib	Let horses stray	10 cane strokes
Herero Hans	Stole poultry/eggs	25 cane strokes
Bushman Hans	Let flock stray	15 cane strokes
Herero Katjiteivi	Sent child to steal	20 cane strokes
Bushman Kambonde	Let horses stray	20 sjambok strokes
Bushman Landmann	Stayed from work	15 sjambok strokes
Herero Katjekeibe	Continued laziness with troops	9 days in chains and 25 sjambok strokes
Hottentot Richter	Escaped prisoner of war	5 years in chains and 25 sjambok strokes
? Herman	Stole from master	4 weeks jail and 25 sjambok strokes

Source: Fritz Muller, *Kolonien unter der Peitsche* (Berlin: Rutten & Loening, 1962), p. 95.

entire family was killed by the local populace. Settlers demanded retribution. When this was not forthcoming, a party of nine settlers, with the compliance of the district commander, who blessed them with fifty cartridges each, set off on a rescue mission. The rescue was successful, but the effort resulted in a number of Kavango and Bushman fatalities (Mattenklodt 1931:217; Spies 1948).

By 1905, in the state's view, Bushman life was considered to be of even less worth than that of other blacks; the state started making an ominous distinction between *Eingeborenen* and *Buschleute*. The Wiehager case is illustrative: Wiehager, a twenty-two-year-old Outjo district farmer and reserve army officer, was tried and sentenced to three years' imprisonment for killing two Herero women and a child who had deserted his service. While out on appeal, he captured and murdered three Bushmen, and even though he had previously admitted to killing them in a private letter to the local district commander, he was found not guilty and discharged. So outrageous was this verdict that the government was compelled to appeal it, and at a rehearing in Windhoek, he was sentenced to five years' imprisonment (to run concurrently with his previous sentence). Wiehager, an affluent settler, had defending him a Berlin lawyer who brought in numerous witnesses, including the chief army surgeon, who testified that Bushmen had a "treacherous" nature and that the military had orders to shoot every Bushman that did not stand still when ordered to do so (*Südwest Zeitung*, 1907:15, 40).

Bushmen did not accept these measures passively. On the contrary, bandit gangs, which were formed as a reaction to these measures, received notoriety in the colonial press. In this period two gangs were prominently featured. Living alongside Fritz Aribib (of treaty fame) at Naidaus was another chief, named Korob, who during the German-Herero war of 1904, joined forces with the Herero and even fought alongside Herero at the decisive Battle of Waterberg, where the Herero were routed. After this battle, Korob and his followers continued raiding white farms in the vicinity of the Okarusu Mountains. On occasion, they also ambushed Ovambo laborers returning to Ovamboland. Members of his gang included not only Bushmen but also Herero. According to newspaper accounts, they were "cruel, cowardly, and cunning, and fighting them was extraordinarily difficult," as they would vanish without a trace while they "still have numerous rifles which we have not been able to remove" (see Prozess Wiehager, *Südwest Zeitung,* 1907:17).

Another bandit leader who came to prominence during this time was the Kung-speaking (Seiner 1913a; Lebzelter 1934b:20) Namagurub, of the Kum'gau. He lived north of Grootfontein on the Tsintsabis-Kavango route. Namagurub and his band were also well armed with rifles and had extensive trade links with the people to the north of the Kavango River. He is said to have killed a white farmer in 1907 and toward the end of 1911 was believed to have masterminded the theft of some 150 head of Herr von Spiegel's cattle. It took the Germans more than four years to apprehend him. He even planned to launch an audacious full-scale attack on the German police station at Blockfontein, which was on the Nurugas route to the Kavango and quite a distance from his "traditional territory." The Germans conceded that had they not been tipped off by the Nog'au Bushmen, Namagurub would probably have been successful. In 1911 the Germans finally managed to raid his very large *werft,* and when they set it alight, the *werft* exploded because of all the hidden gunpowder and bullets (Seiner 1913a, 1913b; von Zastrow 1914:3–4).

The Nama-Herero War of 1904–1907 marked a watershed in Namibian history in more ways than one, and its impact on Bushmen was devastating. The agricultural potential of the Grootfontein district, with its abundant rainfall and plentiful "open fountains," was highly touted by the earliest colonial entrepreneurs (see, for example, Burger 1978), but development was hindered by the large concession companies.[8] However, during the war of 1904–1907, the colonial authorities intervened and forced large land companies to start selling off farmland. Part of the motivation for this was the realization that an increased settler presence would make for better control of these rural areas. Prospective settlers were given the most favorable terms if they had the high initial capital outlay, or were *Schutztruppe* who had taken their discharge in South West Africa (Bley 1971; Goldblatt 1971).

In addition, the urgency occasioned by the war resulted in the rapid extension of the railway line to the mines at Tsumeb. This meant that Otavi was linked to the coast by 1906, Tsumeb a year later and Grootfontein by 1908.

The significance of the railway line for Bushman pacification should not be underestimated: It provided an invaluable mechanism and motive for farm settlement in the district. Rohrbach calculated that for a farm to be economically viable, it had to lie within a radius of 150–200 kilometers of the railway line (Rohrbach 1907). The completion of the railway resulted in a massive influx of white settlers. Indeed, the district had its most rapid growth of settlers ever during the five-year period 1909–1914 (Oelhafen von Schoellenbach 1926), and by 1911, there was nearly twice as much settled land in Grootfontein as in the second-most-settled district (Gad 1914). By 1913 Grootfontein district had the second-largest number of farms in the territory, 173 (2 less than Omaruru, which had a large smallholder scheme), 35 more than the next-most-farmed district, Windhoek (Wellington 1967:218).

This influx of settlers and "development" led to a labor shortage and a renewed appreciation of the value of Bushmen as laborers. In 1908 for example, the *Südwest Zeitung* (25 November 1908) reported that a patrol from the Waterberg had rounded up fifty Bushmen in the Tsumeb vicinity and transferred them to the Tsumeb Copper Mine as laborers. To the west, the Outjo District Council expressed concern in 1910 at all the grass fires and ordered all Bushmen, who were believed to be the arsonists, to report for work. A police patrol succeeded in rounding up more than a hundred of these supposed vandals, but all escaped shortly after the patrol reached Outjo (Kruger n.d.).

An additional catalyst for Bushmen entering the labor market, and certainly a factor leading to the "Bushman Plague" of 1911, was the establishment of game reserves and the strict enforcement of game laws. Game reserves were first proclaimed in 1907 and accompanied by a ban on the hunting of giraffe, buffalo, eland and kudu cows.[9] All three game reserves encompassed land belonging to Bushmen. The inhabitants of Game Reserve No. 3, what is now the Namib-Naukluft Park, were hunted into extinction before World War I. The treaty Aribib signed with the Germans, which guaranteed protection and habitational rights to an area including Game Reserve No. 2, or what is now known as the Etosha Game Park, although never nullified, was simply overlooked. Bushmen resident in the park were rounded up whenever possible and sent out to work on white settler farms.

The political implications of game park proclamation were transparent: All the proclaimed royal game, by coincidence, happened to be those that were relatively easily hunted by the local indigenes without firearms. This act was part of a wider policy to create a rural proletariat. Moreover, two of the three proclaimed game reserves, namely Game Reserve No. 1, which was centered on Karakuwisa, and Game Reserve No. 2, centered on the Etosha Pan, straddled the main routes to the labor reservoirs of Ovamboland and the Kavango River, and their reputed population of "wild Bushmen" was later to form a convenient deterrent to prevent desertion of migrant contract workers.

There is a lack of primary data on how Bushmen were treated in these reserves, but at Namutoni in Game Reserve No. 2 there was a policy of sending out patrols to collect Bushmen, feeding them corn for which they had to work, and then forcing them to seek a "permanent" home elsewhere (ZBU 2043, 10 March 1910). The situation in northern Namibia mirrors that of the southern Kalahari, where Major J. Herbst observed: "The strict enforcement of the game laws has made the country unsafe for [Bushmen]. They profess to be unable to understand by what right Government protects the game, and invariably ask to be shown the Government brand on the animals" (cited in South Africa 1918:146).

Chapter 7

The "Bushman Plague" of 1911

In 1911 events came to a head. Headlines in the settler press referred to the "Bushman Plague," the "Bushman Danger" and the "Yellow Peril." There were two main sources for this moral outrage: First, a rash of stock thefts and, eventually, murder of whites in the prime settler-farming area of Grootfontein. Second, numerous migrant workers returning to Ovamboland and the Kavango River region after a spell in the newly opened mines were robbed by Bushmen, and this had a devastating impact on sorely needed labor recruits.[1]

The attacks on the migrant labor supply lines started in 1909 and increased in tempo, so that by 1912 the Luderitzbucht Chamber of Mines was forced to lodge a strong protest. Gangs of three to five Bushmen, armed with bows and arrows and the occasional muzzle-loader, would hold up parties of up to sixty unarmed Ovambos and relieve them of their tin trunks crammed with precious articles assiduously acquired during their labor contracts. The chamber urgently requested the government to "please be so kind as to immediately start with the sanitization of the Bushman hordes in that area" (gütigst unverzüglich die Sauberung der dortigen Gegend von Buschmann-Gesindel in die Wege leiten zu wollen) (cited in Budack, 10 October 1980). The government response was to strengthen the local police and to dispatch a company of the *Schutztruppe* (*Südwest Zeitung*, 19 November 1912). Their efforts at apprehending these Bushmen were singularly unsuccessful: "So desperate had the Ovambo become by then that they were paying an enterprising Outjo wagon-owner between 3 and 4 marks per bundle to transport their possessions between Outjo and Okakeujo. The wagon could take an estimated 50 to 70 such bundles. Other Ovambo had started to mail some of their possessions to the post office at Okakeujo" (*Südwest Zeitung*, 19 November 1912).

The frustrated military commander attributed the success of the brigands to ecological and social factors: Bushmen constantly moved around, lived away from water holes, obtained supplies of rice and millet through trade with Ovambos and, indeed, were often sponsored by Ovambo chiefs and headmen like Tshanika of Ongandjera, Ipumbu of Uukwambi and the subchief of Olekunde in the Ondonga area (see also Köhler 1957:61–62; ZBU 2013, Letter, Outjo District Commandant, 20 January 1913, ref. 02842). A year later, the Outjo district commandant complained that the only solution was for police to accompany the Ovambo workers, since it was impossible for the police to "clean up" the areas owing to the thick bush and hidden fountains. Ultimately, he felt, the only solution was the construction of the planned railway line to Ovambo (ZBU 2013, Outjo, Letter 21 May 1914, ref. 1147/14).

In the Grootfontein district, similar raids were taking place, but because fewer migrants were involved, those raids attracted less publicity. There, in 1910, within the space of two months, Bushmen had launched three successful attacks "creating a feeling of great uncertainty amongst the 'Ovambo' who now are reluctant to go to Tsumeb for labor" (ZBU 1010, 14 September 1910).[2]

Contrary to press reports, the "Bushman Plague" was not visited upon the good settlers or innocent migrant workers by supernatural forces. Settlers followed the familiar pattern of blaming outsiders for their woes, asserting that Bushmen were encouraged to rob returning migrant workers by the Ovambo kings and headmen. On the contrary, the raids were a product of a combination of ecological factors like drought, coupled with state-sponsored activities like enclosure. With only 42 percent of the average rainfall, 1910 had been a bad drought year (Wellington 1967:43). The situation was to be aggravated by the fact that four out of the following five rainy seasons were also below average.

The settler outcry reached crescendo pitch with the killing of Sergeant Alefelder. Theodor Seitz, the supposedly liberal governor (Gann and Duignan 1977), saw the "development of the Bushman danger" as similar to events that had occurred in the Cape Colony in the 1700s, thereby supposedly demonstrating the inherently recalcitrant nature of Bushmen.[3] Seitz concluded that "while it is not possible to use such means [punitive commandos] as were used by the settlers 150 years ago against the Bushmen today, the hostility to culture of our Bushmen forces us to adopt stringent measures" (ZBU 2043 W11). He opted for what he knew best: The number and power of police and military units in the troubled area were increased. In Verordnung J. nr 26883/5391, dated 24 October 1911, he proclaimed, inter alia:

Now that the Bushman's attitude toward other natives, white colonizers, officials, and police has become so hostile that it had led to the death of one settler and one police officer, an end must be put to this danger. Therefore with regard to the use of weapons by police in dealing with the Bushmen, I am amending the following:

1. When patrol officers of the state police are searching Bushmen areas, breaking up their settlements or searching for cattle thieves and robber bands, they must have their weapons *ready to fire* at all times, using of course the utmost caution.
2. Firearms are to be used:
   a. in the *slightest* case of insubordination against officials.
   b. when a felon is either caught in the act, or when being hunted down, *does not stop on command* but tries to escape through flight.
3. The native police servant who is accompanying or guiding a patrol may carry a firearm, model 71 [Mauser rifle] with full responsibility in all areas where the Bushmen live. . . .

The way in which State officials are to act towards Bushmen is regulated by the following rules. Even though it may be difficult, one should strive to keep the Bushmen at work. Forced dislocation of a Bushman werft may only take place if they have been stealing stock or robbing or have attacked Europeans or their native workers. . . .

If some of the male Bushmen who have been arrested are strong enough to work, they should be handed over to the district authorities at Luderitzbucht to work in the Diamond Fields. (ZBU 2043 [emphasis added])

Seitz's immediate subordinates felt these draconian measures did not go far enough: The commander of the *Schutztruppe* felt that the *Verordnung* was unsatisfactory because the term *felon* would raise problems and thus urged that the proclamation be amended to read that *any* Bushman who did not stop on command could be shot. Since it was impossible to say from which *werft* the alleged culprit came, "it is nearly futile not to break up and arrest the members of all the settlements in the area where the patrol is operating." The district commandant of Outjo went further: He wanted to include Bushman women in the definition of Bushmen, as they "were just as dangerous" (ZBU 2043). Only one district commandant, Beringar von Zastrow, of Grootfontein, felt that these measures were too draconian; nevertheless, his protests were muted.

Because, even then, it was common knowledge that Bushmen were known to flee at the sight of any patrol (see, for example, Hester 1973), this *Verordnung* constituted, in effect, a warrant for genocide. Seitz's actions were not taken in an intellectual vacuum. On the contrary, they occurred at a moment when academics were engaged in a major controversy as to whether Bushmen reserves should be created.

Academics and the Notion of a Bushman Reserve

The academic who provided the immediate reference point for the debate was the geographer Siegfried Passarge, who in 1907 published a compilation of his contributions to the *Mitteilungen aus des deutsches Schutzgebiets* as a book entitled: *Die Buschmänner der Kalahari*. His research was based on a sojourn of a few months in the Kalahari, where he was accompanied by a Dutch-speaking Bushman. Most of his information is derived from white traders or Bechuanas, as he found it difficult to get information directly from Bushmen: "Nothing is more changeable, undependable, and unpredictable than the character of the Bushman; it combines within itself the greatest imaginable contrasts, virtues, and vices" (Passarge 1907:2). As a race, Bushmen were on a closed development path, he claimed. They were incapable of adopting to agriculture or pastoralism (132). He concluded that the only policy in a settlement situation was to exterminate them: "What can the civilized human being manage to do with people who stand at the level of that sheep stealer? Jail and the correctional house would be a reward, and besides do not even exist in that country. Does any possibility exist other than shooting them?" (124).[4]

Professor Felix von Luschan found such proposals unacceptable and suggested that, on the contrary, a Bushman reserve should be created in the "interest of science" (von Luschan 1908). The *Deutsche Kolonial Zeitung* (1908:91) endorsed this suggestion and the following year carried a strong plea by Lieutenant Gentz, an officer with many years of experience in Namibia: "With the death-knell of these people ringing, one wishes that there was a reserve for them, as there are for the lazy Herero and Hottentots. A reserve where they can live in peace and where they can maintain their lifestyle so important for scholarly research" (*Deutsche Kolonial Zeitung*, 1909:452).

Argument was joined from other quarters. The Grootfontein District Council requested that all "nonworking" Bushmen be placed in a reserve, and Siebert, a government medical doctor, made a strong appeal: "[Bushmen] are unsuitable as settled employees and the relinquishment of their nomadic lifestyle spelled their doom. While they were of little economic value, they were of large scientific value. And even the Cameroons had a law which protected gorillas by placing them in reserves" (ZBU 2043, 24 September 1911).

Copies of the Siebert letter were sent to all the relevant district officers for comment, which were all predictably unfavorable. For example, the Maltahohe commander replied that it was debatable whether there were any full-blooded Bushmen left and a reserve would simply provide a hiding place for runaway servants. Bushmen had excellent potential to serve as herd boys. He concluded that "a wild animal (or gorilla) can be held captive for breeding in which case the race would not become extinct by the process of natural selection. It is not possible to hold a Namib Bushman captive because they are still human beings, but they have no pride in their race, in fact they are without racial consciousness" (ZBU 2043, 2 December 1911).

The Gobabis commandant felt that it would be better to domesticate Bushmen. They could be tamed into becoming useful workers through a gradual process. Reservations would not work because Bushmen would settle at the boundaries and would then escape into the settler farming areas where they would be shot, thus hastening their demise as a "race" (ZBU 2043, 8 December 1911). The Outjo commandant intoned that it would require violence to get Bushmen settled on a reserve and the reserves would simply provide congregation points for bandits and stock thieves. Their scientific value was minor compared to the security threat they posed to white settlers and Ovambo contract workers (ZBU 2043, 12 December 1911).

The following year, the question surfaced in the German Reichstag, where Deputy Mumm pleaded for a reserve for the "poorest of the poor . . . the slaves of the slaves." Bushmen were a product of a tragic history, dispossessed by farmers and railroad companies, and riddled with venereal disease. As a reserve, Mumm suggested the area stretching from the Grootfontein farms to the Kavango river (*Südwest Zeitung*, 16 July 1912). In 1914 he again unsuccessfully renewed his plea for a Bushman reserve. Many felt that the area beyond the Police Zone constituted a de facto reserve (von Zastrow 1914; Mueller 1912), and this served to justify government inaction on the reserve issue.

Probably the strongest argument against the wholesale "eradication" of Bushmen was the so-called economic argument, originated by the Austrian academic Franz Seiner. Seiner had traveled and published extensively on Bushmen during the height of the "plague." As a geographer he wrote about their distribution, dividing them into four groups: first, the Kaukau, who lived in an area that at that time did not border on any settler farms. They were supposedly the most warlike and possessed firearms and were known to attack Herero and Bechuanas. The second and third groups were the Kung au, a northern group, and the Nog'au (Ju-/wasi) who lived north and east of the Omuramba Omatako (river) as far as Tschitschib. The fourth group consisted of the Kung, under the notorious bandit leader Namagurub. Seiner noted the considerable mobility of these groups: They moved east at the onset of the rainy season and returned to the "border" areas in the winter months, when stock thefts were said to occur. Different groups used to live within a few kilometers of each other (Seiner 1913a; 1913b). Seiner estimated the

Kung population in the northeastern portion of Grootfontein at 7,000. The total Bushman population he put at about 12,000 (cited in Lebzelter 1934b:19).

The only way to "tame" Bushmen, Seiner argued, was to have the men deported to the coast and the children and wives placed on farms. The way to make Bushmen into reliable laborers was to start with the children and resocialize them from an early age, divorced from their traditional milieu and their parents. Bushmen were in no danger of extermination by the farmers, he argued, because they had a vast "natural reserve" in the Kalahari. A far greater threat for them was bastardization with various elements in this "no-man's-land." Farmers preferred wild "pure" Bushmen, as the wild "Bastard Bushmen," who constituted the vast majority, were naturally prone to theft and murder. The way to round them up was to strengthen police patrols with more "intelligent" natives who knew the area. At the same time, Seiner felt that by having the women placed on farms they would mate with local blacks, leading to an overall superior laborer (Seiner 1913b). He argued (Seiner 1912) that the semierect penis of the Bushmen was a distinctive racial characteristic and that Bushmen could be identified by the angle of penis. Three out of five Bushmen examined had horizontally projecting penises, but with the admixture of Bantu "blood" it began to droop. According to Seiner, all the northern Bushmen, that is, those north of Grootfontein were "Bastard Bushmen" (hybrids) (Schapera 1930:58) and thus were not an Ur-race worthy of protection.

Seiner had influence. In a letter to the imperial government in Berlin, bypassing the local colonial authorities, he complained about conditions Bushman prisoners were living in at the inhospitable, desert harbor town of Swakopmund. He was, he claimed, not raising the matter for humanitarian reasons, but rather out of concern for the immense waste of potential Bushman labor. To back up his complaints, Seiner included photographs. These made the governor more sensitive because, as a bureaucrat noted in the margin of Seiner's letter, "if Seiner publicizes such photographs, the administration may expect to be attacked most sharply."

Seiner's protest led to minor modifications in policy. The governor explained to the Colonial Office in Berlin that he had not approved of the suggestion of removing all Bushmen to the coast. Only adult male Bushmen who were certified as healthy by a physician and physically capable of work would be deported to the coast because "a more objective view of the situation must take into account the fact that the Bushmen are by no means only harmless children of nature, but constitute a serious danger to more intensive settlement of the fertile northern districts. Weakness cannot therefore be justified by any means in the treatment of the Bushmen" (ZBU 2043, unsigned rough draft, Govt. Whk. to Col. Sec., Berlin, September 1913).

Seiner was not a solitary academic voice. One should also take into consideration the remarks made by Leonard Schultze, a renowned geographer-anthropologist with extensive fieldwork in Namibia and New Guinea. Schultze had made a close study of the Nama, indeed his book *Aus Namaland und Kalahari* (1907) is widely regarded as being the definitive study of the Nama (Vedder 1928:150) and Bushmen:

> If we consider the natives according to their value as cultural factors in the protectorate, then one race is immediately eliminated right off: The Bushmen. The Bushmen lack entirely the precondition of any cultural development: the drive to create something beyond everyday needs, to secure or permanently to improve systematically the conditions of existence, even the most primitive ones like the procurement of food. In the course of centuries he has come into contact with cultures of all levels; in conflict with them he has often enough had the knife put to his throat; tireless missionaries have attempted to save him from such struggle, to protect and to join him as the modest member to a civilized community; but the Bushman has always run away. He feels better out in the Sandveld behind a windscreen of thin leaf thorn-bush than in a solidly built house with a full pot and regular work—as long as he is *free*. Colonists cannot count on such people; they let them live as long as, at least they don't do damage. But when they don't fulfill this requirement, they have been killed off like predatory game. The idea has been considered to preserve the Bushmen in reservations as the last remnants of the primordial past of the human race, just as elsewhere attempts are made to save endangered animal species. But we won't be able to afford the luxury of leaving fallow the required land areas and everything else which man requires for the maintenance of the species without inbreeding. (Schultze 1914:290 [emphasis added])[5]

In the intellectual foment that constitutes any academic discipline, there are always counterarguments and counter-streams, and although it appears that the position taken by Schultze was dominant, there were at least two lesser counter-streams, both of which had some impact on Namibian ethnology: These were the romantics and the slightly more humanitarian mission–oriented ethnologists like Vedder, later the doyen of Namibian ethnography. But even they accepted the belief that extinction was the inevitable destiny of the Bushmen: It was simply a matter of humanely assisting in the transition. Vedder actively advised the administration on how to circumvent Bushman resistance to dispossession of their lands by settlers. He also later argued for the establishment of a

Bushman reserve, not out of pity or concern for the Bushmen as people, but because of their value as a scientific commodity.

The Influence of the Missions

What influence did the missions have on the formation of Bushman policy? After all, in contrast to the vocal newly arrived settlers, the missions could claim to have long experience of dealing with Bushmen. In 1873, the Rhenish Missionary Society established a station at Otjo-zondjupa (now Waterberg), where most of the early members were not Herero but Damara and Bushmen (Baumann 1967:151).[6] Even at this early stage of missionary penetration, the value of Bushmen as potential converts was discerned. In 1879, for example, Missionary Schroeder made a special journey into the Kalahari to contact Bushmen and, on his return, argued for the formation of a special "Bushman" mission, but the general uncertainty prevailing in the country prevented any action being taken on his proposal (Budack pers. comm.).

In 1893, the Reverend Mr. Kremer started a mission station at Gaub, near Grootfontein, and soon acquired 9,000 hectares of surrounding land from the SWA Company. Ostensibly, the intention was to use this area as a reserve for the Damara and Bushmen in order to prevent their proletarianization (Driessler 1932:48). The baster Jaq Kruger was to serve as headman. An official church history reports that at first Bush-men were "unapproachable. Sometimes they came to visit, *wolfing* down the food that was set in front of them and then quickly disappearing. When Kruger tried to get the Bushmen to live on the estates and grow gardens with seeds which he would provide, they laughed at him and said that if they did this, they would die" (Driessler 1932:72).

From the start there was an effort to manipulate the image of the Bushman to the benefit of the church. Kremer had a little Bushman girl named Dissi live in his household for over a year. He described her thus: "Nearly every day she either lied, stole and swore, or else did things with such a degree of falseness and perfidity, that one was forced to question whether such a child could really have been made in God's image and be worthy of salvation. Yet in spite of all this, she had to be led to this salvation" (cited in Driessler 1932:72). The rather self-serving message is obvious: The ignobility of the Bushman is contrasted to and enhances the noble dedication of the missionary.

A major force in Rhenish attempts to gain Bushman converts was the arrival of Vedder at Gaub in 1911 to start a school. He appears to have been an important influence on von Zastrow, the Grootfontein district commandant. Vedder, shortly after his arrival, asked von Zastrow to provide him with some captured Bushmen whom he could train to serve as government interpreters. Von Zastrow gladly obliged (Grimm 1928:299). By treating these Bushmen flexibly, that is, letting them "wander" during the rainy season, but with a government pass, Vedder gradually succeeded in building up his "flock" of Bushmen. By 1913, he had twenty-two and at the outbreak of World War I, the number had risen to some five dozen. At this stage an optimum seems to have been reached. As there was not enough food in the vicinity for all the Bush-men, many of them returned to their own areas (Driessler 1932; Grimm 1928). Bushmen were drawn to Gaub because it offered them a place where they could escape the harassment of the settlers. Understandably the missionaries did not publicize the fact that most of these Bushmen were forced to live on the mission station. Connivance between mission and state was inclusive.[7]

Of the major mission groups, the Catholics had the least immediate influence on Bushman policy. The Oblates of Maria Immaculate came to the country in 1896 and by 1908 had established a church at Groot-fontein. In December 1910, they visited their first Bushmen, a group of Heikom on the farm Chusib, and shortly thereafter baptized their first converts—seven adults and thirty children. Working with a few catech-ists, Father Schulte managed to concentrate on the farms Strehtfontein, Otjihaenena and Auuns, where flourishing colonies of Catholic Bushmen emerged.

Like the Lutherans, the Catholics found it financially rewarding to cooperate with the government in housing captured Bushmen. In 1912, Father Schulte spelled out the Church's policy:

> Some colonialists helped us in that way insofar as they had Bushmen working and living on their farms. It is the government's goal to get the other Bushmen who still lead a nomadic life, to settle them in locations especially built for them. If the mission will support the government in this regard, we can be sure that the government will accept and support our work among the Bushmen. It is in any case the goal of the Catholic Mission to get Bushmen out of nomadism and to have them living in allocated areas [as boarders]. (Schulte 1912:21–22)

Education Through Labor

After wide-ranging discussions in both government circles and the press, the emergent articulated consensus on the "Bushman problem" was that the "gradual education of the Bushmen to labor" was the only answer. In this, the governor felt, settlers were making a contribution that deserved recognition because, of the 2,829 Bushmen enumerated in the 1912 census, 997 were already working for settlers (ZBU 2043

W11). However, there was also intense discussion, involving academics
like Seiner, on whether it was indeed possible to "habituate the Bushmen
to labor." In November 1913, the Landesrat concluded that it was practically impossible to habituate adult Bushmen to labor and that efforts
should thus be directed toward the children. Hauptmann Hollander, in
commenting on the Landesrat decision, agreed: "The youngsters can be
made to work but only if the children are taken away from their parents,
which in these cases can be done without much ado" (ZBU 2043 W11,
undated memorandum).

Bushmen arrested for various offenses, especially stock theft, were
deported to other districts, where they could learn the dignity of labor.
Typically, arrested families were sent to farms in distant districts. For
example, Grootfontein arrestees were sent either to Warmbad, in the
south, or to the coast, whereas Bushmen from Hasuur (Aroab) were sent
to Windhoek. The chief criterion in determining where Bushmen would
be sent appears to have been that the districts should be well developed
and have no unattached Bushmen around who might entice the convict
laborers to desert. Mindful of a potential outcry in Europe, officials
placed Bushmen with specially selected farmers, who were specifically
instructed to employ them only as herdsmen and to provide them with a
plentiful supply of food. It was not necessary to pay these workers wages
for the first six months.

Government discussion centered on strategies for achieving this
transformation of youthful Bushmen from vagabonds to villeinage (to
use an old fashioned word). Much favorable comment was given to the
efforts of Gobabis farmers Lemke and Balzer, who allowed large numbers
of Bushmen to congregate on their farms, so that if one took off for a
few days, he could be replaced by another. Alternatively, as Balzer
organized it, Bushmen would work one day and then have the next day
off in order to forage *veldkos* (field food). The police at Oas, Gobabis
district, also allowed Bushmen to congregate at the station, where they
were gradually habituated to the idea of work by being sent on occasional
errands or given other light tasks. Once these Bushmen became used to
Europeans, they would be given to farmers as per instructions from
Windhoek (ZBU 2043, 1 December 1912). Unfortunately, as a bureaucrat in Windhoek pointed out in a handwritten draft in the same file,
there was a major difference between theory and practice, and the
Bushmen of Gobabis would be driven to self-defense activities if the
police continued the policy of indiscriminately arresting them and placing them with local labor-short farmers.

Moreover, a real concern of colonial officials was the fear of arousing
the ire of the liberal and socialist metropolitan lobby. Thus, the governor
wrote to the Outjo commander (*Bezirksamt*) that he could not approve the

forced removal of all Bushmen from the Outjo district because not only would it cost too much (50,000–60,000 marks per annum) but, more important, it would cause a "very undesirable public discussion if natives who have not broken the law were to be removed as prisoners to an area where the climate would kill many of them" (ZBU 2043, 22 February 1913).

Chapter 8

From Policy to Practice

With characteristic thoroughness the Germans launched more than 400 anti-Bushman patrols, covering 60,000 kilometers in 1911–1912 (Stals 1984:84). Some of the results of all this activity are reflected in Table 8.1, showing the number of convictions, by ethnic group.

In practice, legal niceties were largely ignored when it came to dealing with Bushmen. Despite a clear order that Bushmen living peacefully, especially those outside the Police Zone, were not to be persecuted, police still raided *werfts* outside the Police Zone and brought in all the captured males, who were then distributed to farmers in the hope that they would "habituate" to the dignity of civilization through the sweat of their brows (ZBU 2043, rough draft, Govt. Whk to District Office Gobabis, November 1913).

Assuming that a Bushman was fortunate enough to survive the capture process, what future was there for him? Governor Seitz acknowledged in the Landesrat on 24 April 1912 that there were many difficulties in the Grootfontein, Outjo and Maltahohe districts because of Bushmen and that it was thus necessary to make punishments more severe (*Südwest Zeitung*, 24 July 1912). As if sentencing a fourteen-year-old youth to a year's imprisonment and two times fifteen strokes was not severe enough! There were a number of different categories of punishment, which were often used in different combinations. First, there was corporal punishment, the most basic form. Then there was also imprisonment, with or without chains, or deportation, either to another part of the district or to another more distant district. Finally, of course, there was the death sentence for crimes of murder and armed robbery.

These penalties were believed to have different degrees of effectiveness. The district commander of Outjo (ZBU 2043, 20 January 1913, ref. 02842) complained that seized Bushmen placed with farmers merely deserted. All attempts to educate Bushmen as workers had failed and

Table 8.1   Convictions, by Ethnic Group, Grootfontein, 1913

Charge	Bushmen	Ovambo	Herero	Damara	Other
Laziness	4	2	8	0	0
Stock theft	10	0	0	0	0
Theft	17	7	12	7	5
Disobedience	14	13	21	14	1
Vagrancy	3	0	5	2	0
Desertion	27	22	16	9	0
Insult	1	0	5	1	0
Drink	1	0	3	1	1
Incitement	1	16	0	1	0
Fraud	1	0	4	4	0
Assault	1	0	0	1	1
Escape	2	2	0	0	0
Other	3	0	0	6	1
Robbery and murder	5	0	0	0	0
Total	90	60	76	46	9

Source: ZBU 694, "Gefängniswesen, 1898–1915," State Archives, Windhoek.

would continue to do so until the opportunity to hunt and rob was taken away from them. The only solution, he felt, was for all Bushmen to be removed from the district, placed in a situation where they could not rob and forced to work for a living. There were good opportunities for this at the Luderitz diamond fields.

It is not known how many Bushmen were punished according to these various categories, but a letter from the secretary of Grootfontein (ZBU 2043, 15 September 1913) is indicative: There were twenty-seven Bushman males, twenty-four females and twenty-four children captured and living in the district. Of these, twelve men, two children and two women were being sent to Swakopmund. The women were the wives of men killed in skirmishes with troops, so, it was reasoned, they would undoubtedly hate whites and if set free, would perpetrate further cases of brigandage. Officials had unsuccessfully tried to settle vagrant women and children on surrounding farms, but they had run away. Data on the Bushmen deported to Swakopmund are contained in Table 8.2.

At Swakopmund, a major Bushman holding center, conditions were abominable. In one survey listing thirty-two Bushmen, fifteen had died within a year, one had syphilis and another was said to be suffering from scurvy (BSW 1/1/81 G35).[1] And this after the government had tried to improve the situation after Seiner's protest!

German colonial administration was structured in such a way as to discourage whistle-blowing, and thus in all likelihood Bushman abuses were underreported.[2] An exception was Beringar von Zastrow, the commandant of the vast and potentially rich Grootfontein district, the area

Table 8.2   Data on Bushmen Deported to Swakopmund

Offense	Punishment
Stock theft	6 years in chains
Resistance and provocation	5 years in chains
Stock theft (2 cases)	2 years in chains
Stock theft (2 cases)	1 year in chains
Stock theft	6 months imprisonment
Stock theft	1 year imprisonment and 2 × 15 strokes
8 × vagrancy (8 cases)	Banishment from the district

Source: BSW G35, "Gefängene Buschleute, 1911–1914," States Archives, Windhoek.

where most Bushmen lived. There major disagreements on Bushman policy between the district commandant and his district secretary were common, a situation pregnant with the possibility of bureaucratic sabotage.

Von Zastrow was exceptional, both in his liberal championing of the rights of Bushmen and in his knowledge of them.[3] Concerning the demography of Bushman attacks, von Zastrow observed that most attacks occurred in the Nurugas (presently Maroelaboom) and Choantsas areas, which had the oldest and most heavily settled farms. Areas with heavy concentrations of Bushmen but few farms, such as Otjituo and Namutoni, were remarkably free of brigandage. Most of the trouble was caused, he felt, by the (Heikom) Gaikokoin "tribe" and was directly related to the increase in white farms in the area. Many Gaikokoin employed on these farms had tried "to stir up unrest among their people by inducing them to run away." Soldiers had been brought in but were counterproductive, as they captured only the old and infirm and thus added substantially to the already high prison-mortality rate. Indeed, von Zastrow argued, the extension of "Bushman patrols" had exacerbated the situation. Banditry resulted from ill-treatment on farms (von Zastrow 1914:5–6): Most stock thefts were committed not by "wild" Bushmen but by fugitive Bushmen who had previously worked on farms where they had been ill-treated and were thus driven to commit these crimes out of motives of revenge.[4]

Von Zastrow proposed to deal with Bushmen by issuing identity discs (which were similar to the metal passes issued to blacks) and to reward Bushmen with food and tobacco if they kept these discs for extended periods. This made Bushmen easier to control. He also intended continuing his policy of close cooperation with the missions. Bushmen who settled on mission stations were granted immunity from legal prosecution as long as they remained on the mission land: "I know that the farmers who need workers will be angry with the mission as well as the

German-era postcard, group of farm-laborer Bushmen. Far from being "pristine beautiful people," living in the bracing isolation of the Kalahari, most Bushmen even at that time were forced to work on farms and were being proletarianized. (Author's collection)

administration, but according to my information they, but especially the new farmers, are not yet ready to teach the Bushmen. This is why the Bushman always runs away from the farms. I am rather for winning a lot of workers through a slow process of understanding than having a few farmers happy for a short time" (ZBU 2043 W11).

In classic liberal terms he believed that Bushmen did wrong because they did not "understand"; thus for first offenses like "leaving a job without notice," "letting the farmer's cattle stray" or "gathering veld food," they were only to be cautioned. But in second offenses or in more difficult cases like stock theft, Bushmen were to be transported to the coastal towns of Swakopmund or Luderitzbucht (ZBU 2043 W11, von Zastrow, memo "Über die Buschleute").

Local settlers were irate at such actions. At Farmer Association meetings they demanded that all Bushmen be deported to a large reservation on the eastern side of the Omuramba Omatako, and that those captured outside this reserve should be deported to the recently opened Luderitzbucht Diamond Mines. These demands received much publicity and support in the press (see, e.g., *Deutsche Kolonial Zeitung*, 1911:17, 73; 1912:463–464; 1913:88; *Südwest Zeitung*, 1912:13).[5] Von Zastrow attended many of these meetings to point out the impractical and uneconomical nature of these proposals and remind the farmers that they were contributing to the problem by not employing herders but hiring Bushmen to hunt full-time. He argued that the system of mobile police stations was achieving more satisfactory results. Von Zastrow set out his arguments at length in a memorandum, which was later published in the prestigious *Zeitschrift für Ethnologie*. It is worth citing at length. The economic role of the Bushmen in the development of his district received major emphasis:

> Bearing in mind also the small number of natives now in the whole Protectorate, one cannot afford to pass over these people without consideration. . . . More than half of the farmers would not be able to carry on their business were the available Bushmen labor to vanish.
>
> The opinion so generally expressed that the Bushman cannot be utilized as a laborer because he will not remain on a farm and is too weak is not correct. It must be understood that these people have spent their entire lives wandering about in the open country, never doing complicated work with their hands. They cannot just give up their accustomed way of life to become settled industrious workers. In spite of the good food they get from the farmer, they miss their customary food from the bush and it is a law of necessity to allow them to procure this. They have the need to wander like nearly every other native and it should not be considered odd if they leave their jobs. The present generation cannot change its habits that quickly.
>
> It is remarkable to observe how the Bushmen serve the purpose of farm laborers. They learn to plow, to cultivate tobacco, to control oxen transport, and whatever else a farm laborer must do. Many remain for long years on the farms and become indispensable to the farmer.
>
> [Concerning the feasibility of reserves:] It is impossible to limit the Bushmen to a small area, for they are used to a life of constant wandering. Even if this were possible, the question of how to feed them would prove insurmountable.
>
> The Bushmen live a nomadic existence because their diet changes with the seasons and the area. Thus, one would either be forced to make the reservation very big, or else the government would have to provide them with food. The former would make even a somewhat accurate check on the people impossible, whereas the latter suggestion would be impossible for the state to meet.
>
> The forming of reservations will be carried out as far as possible. Specific water and police stations have been made known to the Bushmen. There they can live and do as they please, as long as they do not break the laws. Thus, there are now over 200 people living at Otjituo and some in Nurugas and Namutoni.
>
> The suggestion has also been made to push them out of the inhabited areas back to the Sandfeld. But the plausibility of this suggestion falls apart in view of the hostilities between the different tribes. The animosity between the old and the new inhabitants would flare into vio-

lence and the newcomers, knowing that they were weaker, would withdraw in flight back to their tribal homelands. The loyalty which Bushmen
have to their land is great: they won't give up their homeland even when
their lives are at stake.

Other proposals, such as extermination or the deportation of whole
tribes, are so absurd as to merit no consideration. (von Zastrow 1914:5–
6)

The only local public support von Zastrow appears to have enjoyed
was from Missionary Vedder at Gaub, who wrote a series of articles on
the Bushmen for a local newspaper (Vedder 1913). He cautiously agreed
that Bushmen could work well as farm laborers and tried to explain the
"problem" as rooted in Bushman territoriality.[6]

Within settler society, von Zastrow's ideas were heretical and he was
roundly abused by farmers (see, e.g., Walbaum n.d.). Even his subordinate officials, such as District Secretary Link, wrote strongly worded
memoranda to Windhoek disagreeing with von Zastrow's policy. Link
pointed out that von Zastrow's policy of "education through work" could
only succeed in those (rare) areas with a low settler density and plentiful
veld food. He felt that the police were too weak to deal with the problem
and that military reinforcements were urgently required because it was
the appropriate time to raid Bushmen, who were congregated at the
water holes prior to the onset of the rainy season when they would
disperse. All Bushmen so "collected" should be transported to the Luderitz diamond fields.[7]

Despite von Zastrow's policy of discouraging the infliction of corporal punishment on Bushmen (von Zastrow and Vedder 1930:433), the
data on Table 8.3 suggest that he was simply ignored.

Ignoring von Zastrow's and Vedder's voices of comparative reason,
farmers preferred to give credence to wild rumors circulating in the
district, namely, that Bushmen were engaging in cannibalism and had
sworn that they would kill every white farmer (e.g., *Deutsche Kolonial
Zeitung*, 6 December 1913). Link was forced to write to the *Deutsche
Südwest-Afrika Zeitung* (24 December 1913) denying these stories. Farmers
engaged in violent self-help (*Südwest Zeitung*, 1913:104), often in the form
of retributive commandos, like the one that attacked Bushmen residing
in the Otjitjika Mountains, when many Bushmen were reported to have
been shot (*Deutsche Kolonial Zeitung*, 1913:672–673). Other farmers found
it more rewarding, at least financially, to hand over Bushmen captured
in the veld to the police for thirty marks per head (ZBU 2043 W11,
rough draft, Govt. Whk to District Office Gobabis, November 1913).

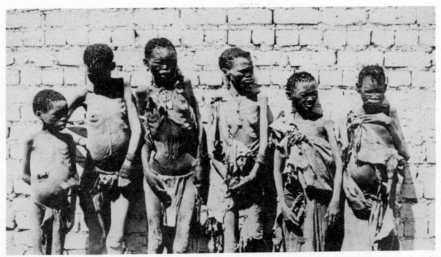

Emaciated "wild" Bushmen from the Kalahari, circa 1912. They were clearly victims of both a severe famine year and repressive colonial policy. (Photo courtesy of State Archives, Windhoek)

Table 8.3   Punishment for Desertion, Grootfontein, 1913

Punishment	Bushmen	Ovambo	Herero	Damara
5 strokes	0	10	0	0
10 strokes	4	0	9	3
15 strokes	19	1	2	5
20 strokes	3	0	0	1
40 strokes	1	0	0	0
3 days	0	20	0	0
1 month	0	0	3	0

Source: ZBU 694, "Gefängniswesen, 1898–1915," State Archives, Windhoek.

Chapter 9

Bushman Hunts and Bushman Gangs

Away from the press and the clubs in Grootfontein, the most common settler strategy was to shoot any Bushmen suspected of stock theft. The case of *Rex v. Becker* 1916 SCC is instructive. Shortly after the occupation of Namibia by South Africa, Farmer Becker of Hedwigslust rode out accompanied by his "boy," Bushman Max, searching for his thirty-two stolen cattle.[1] He surprised a party of Bushmen eating one of his oxen and, without even dismounting, proceeded to shoot two males and four females (including two small children), although they had offered no resistance. The witness Max ran away: "I did not report the matter to the police because I was afraid the Baas would have killed me if I did so. I ran away when we got to the house. I ran to the Sandveld because if I went towards the police station the master might get me in the road and shoot me." The newly arrived South African military police investigated the case because Becker had bragged to them about the Bushmen he had shot.[2]

Similarly, in a sworn statement, farmer Thomas admitted: "In 1911 I had a fight with Bushmen. I shot one and wounded, I believe, 3 or 4. I was never tried by a German court for having shot these Bushmen. I have accompanied the German police and troops when they used to hunt Bushmen, but I do not know how many Bushmen I shot then" (*Rex v. Thomas* 1917 SCC). German records credit Thomas with having shot an additional three Bushmen (including one female). In 1915, farmer Böhme of Kakuse West wrote to the governor, complaining that von Zastrow was not providing him with adequate protection against Bushmen and that he had been forced to shoot a Bushman vagrant—one of his workers who had deserted. He complained that he would no longer be able to hire Bushman labor, as "I am now sure to be made to feel the Bushman's revenge" (ZBU 2043).

On occasion farmers tortured their workers if they suspected that the workers might have information that would lead to the recovery of lost stock or the apprehension of the alleged culprits. In *Rex v. Voswinkel*, Tingaib,[3] Voswinkel's concubine, made a sworn statement that went as follows:

> Xuiseb was a little boy. I was at work in the kitchen and heard Xuiseb crying and accused telling him not to. I heard the sounds of blows. Joseph, Wilhelm, Xuiseb and accused were in the room together. Freda and I afterwards saw Xuiseb in accused's room. He was fastened around his neck, arms and legs with Bushman rope. . . . He had marks on his back where he had been beaten and he was bleeding freely. I had to wash the blood from the floor afterwards. Accused and Wilhelm later took Xuiseb away. Xuiseb was fastened to accused's horse with Bushman rope. He had no clothes on, only a lappie hanging in front. [Xuiseb was not seen again. Tingaib's statement was corroborated by numerous other witnesses.] (*Rex v. Voswinkel* 1918 SCC)[4]

Bushman Patrols

By 1915 it became clear that von Zastrow's policy had collapsed because despite the fact that South African troops were invading Namibia in the south and that the Germans were desperately short of troops, the governor felt constrained to move a company of sixty *Schutztruppe* to the Grootfontein district to deal with troublesome Bushmen. The journal of one of these troopers, Walbaum, provides a vivid doocument of what happened on these "Bushman patrols." He noted matter-of-factly that armed Bushmen were shot on sight (Walbaum n.d.:47), even when Bushmen did not realize that whites were in the vicinity. Captured Bushman women were used to carry supplies (and for other purposes). He described how they came upon a Bushman *werft* where two Bushmen were digging out a wild pig from a burrow. These men denied that they had received a message that Walbaum's guides were supposed to have given them, so they were summarily hanged, and while they were swinging from a nearby tree, Walbaum's group completed the task of killing the wild pig and enjoyed a "superb" meal. On another occasion, they succeeded in surprising and capturing two men and two women. "We sent both women ahead and when they were five yards away, by arrangement Falckenburg and I shot them in the head from behind. Both of them did not feel their deaths" (Walbaum n.d.:47).

The following extracts from Walbaum's journal capture the banality of these hunts better than I can:

After 3 km we reached an open field where Jan (the guide) showed us to go down. One km in front of us some Bushmen were busy digging out uintjies [tubers]. Now Jan did not want to walk in front anymore, because he did not want to have anything to do with the shooting. We discussed our next step for a moment so that we could encircle them. We had to sneak up to them like one does with game. On a sign, we all got up with our guns ready to shoot. We were about 50 to 70 meters away from them. The Bushmen stood in astonishment. When we approached them, 10 or 12 men ran away. Falckenburg and one of our natives shot two. Unfortunately, I missed. (Walbaum n.d.:42)

Indeed, death was often preferable to capture:

(Prisoner) Jonas said he did not know Sus (a farm which had been raided recently by Bushmen), well he did not want to know Sus, but the women said they saw him as he cut the boy's heart out [not verified by court records]. The people were asked how many people were involved and how many guns they had, as well as who had killed the other (white) farmer. They said nothing. I hit them until the blood was running down (in streams). They behaved badly and said their brothers would kill us all. I told them I would get them all. At night I tied each one naked to a tree. It was ice cold and they stood far from the fire; they tried to untie themselves with their feet. The watchman hit them all over with a sjambok. At 4 o'clock in the morning—the coldest time of the night— they started begging: "Mister, if you bring us to the fire we will say everything." I told them that they had to wait because I was sure they were not mistreated enough.

At five o'clock we untied them. Jonas told us everything, but his bad behavior he did not change. The woman stayed near the fire with her child during the night. All the men had bad lacerations on their shoulders from trying to untie themselves by rubbing their shoulders on the bark of the tree.

At 8 o'clock we took the scoundrels to the bush where we found the right trees in no time. A few boxes were piled up, ropes were tied onto branches—the men were put on the boxes with their hands tied and ropes placed around their necks. We kicked the boxes over and they were dead in seconds, because their necks were broken. All four of them had burst veins in the lower leg after they died. In twenty minutes they were dead. The women we took to Wiesental [farm]. (Walbaum n.d.:49)

Even with an officer present, justice was often summary. Take the case of Lieutenant Venuleth, a reserve officer, who during the early days of World War I was in charge of a patrol and came across a band of fifteen indigenes. They scattered, but his patrol succeeded in capturing an elderly man and woman. At his farm he formed a court-martial, with

German justice, circa 1914. A postcard bearing this photograph was available in settler society and appeared in the South African blue book documenting Germany's treatment of indigenes. (Photo courtesy of State Archives, Windhoek)

himself as president, assisted by his two sergeants. Later in a South African court, Venuleth admitted that "the Court was held in order to shoot the natives," whereas Sergeant Schultz, one of his assistants, opined that "being Bushmen they should be shot at sight. I had the right to shoot because they would not stop, because they had arms, and were suspected as spies. . . . It is quite sufficient if they do not stop when called upon." In a sworn statement, Venuleth justified his court:

> The reasons why the court found the accused guilty of stock theft were as follows: 1) the complaint of the population of continued stock theft; 2) the fact that the accused were *Bushmen, not vagrant Hereros;* 3) the further fact that in the north Bushmen are a great nuisance and always stealing cattle; 4) the fact that we found at the camping place of the Bushmen a great number of skins and bones of cattle; 5) and finally, I recognized in the two natives the Bushmen who had stolen and slaughtered a sheep in October 1914 on my own farm. At the time I did not have the Bushmen punished, in the first place because it was only a small loss and further because I had then no authority and I did not want to bring them to the police, as this would have meant the greatest trouble. (*Rex v. Venuleth* 1916 SCC [emphasis added])

"Bushmen captured by protectorate police in the Keetmanshoop district for murder and robbery," according to the caption on this German-era postcard. (Author's collection)

The South African judge hearing the case said in his judgment: "Venuleth was at once President and complainant. According to his own remarks and the statement of Schultz, a member of the court, no charge was made against the native accused. They were not present, no evidence was led. They were convicted and sentenced in their absence and shot. Now it is difficult to mention any principle of justice and law which has not been violated." Yet Venuleth was found not guilty and discharged on the grounds that a South African court had no jurisdiction over an offense that should be tried under German martial law (*Rex v. Venuleth* 1916 SCC).

The "Notorious" Hans Gang

The gang that Corporal Walbaum so enthusiastically pursued was the "Notorious" Hans Gang. Of the various bandit gangs, we have the most information on this gang because of the large number of court cases its members provoked. The gang existed during the early, heady days of World War I when the Germans mobilized and then lost the colony to the South African occupation forces. In its heyday, Hans's gang

Bushman prisoners incarcerated in the coastal town of Swakopmund. The enforced nudity represents an attempt to dehumanize the people. The geographer Franz Seiner took this photograph in 1911 to protest the fact that the two people marked with an X did not have arms and thus could have engaged in stock theft only with great difficulty. (Photo courtesy of State Archives, Windhoek)

had up to seventeen rifles and a large quantity of ammunition. The number of rifles and people who were associated with the gang fluctuated, peaking at between thirty to forty, mostly Bushmen and a few Damaras. But when the final capture came, the gang consisted of nine males plus women and children (Walbaum n.d.).

Hans, a Heikom, was reported to be a good hunter who was employed by a German farmer named Wegener. When Wegener was mobilized for service against the South Africans, Hans collected a small gang of followers, which at Easter 1915 killed a German farmer named Ludwig for stealing the wife of Hans's friend Max. Ludwig's offense was not a sudden irritation. Max had complained to the police at Nurugas about Ludwig's relations with his wife. The police apparently told her to return to her husband, but she had refused (*Rex v. Feuerstein* 1918 SCC). After killing Ludwig, Hans and Max took to the bush and led a life of brigandage. They persuaded other Bushmen employed on white farms to join them. As one of Hans's followers later explained in court, he had worked for farmer Buchheim until 1913 but had not been well treated and so had left and resided in the bush. It was there that Hans had come to him and asked him to join him, as he knew how to shoot. Hans claimed that the Germans would soon be chasing all the Bushmen in the vicinity and that they would have to resist with arms (*Rex v. Johannes Fritz* 1918 SCC). Other members also joined out of fear of the settlers: This was the dominant factor in determining Bushman behavior in those parts: "We ran away because we were frightened of the white man. White people shoot Bushmen so we were frightened of them" (cited in *Rex v. Feuerstein* 1918 SCC). A short while later, Hans shot and killed another farmer, Muller of Knakib, a farmer who used to boast about the large number of his Bushman concubines.

The South African blue book, *Report on the Natives of South West Africa and Their Treatment by Germany,* published in 1918, confirmed the above pattern: Thefts were committed by fugitive Bushmen who had previously been farm laborers when they had been badly fed and flogged, but the chief cause of all the "Bushman" trouble, the blue book said, was when farmers used Bushman wives as concubines (South Africa 1918:148–149). Lieutenant Hull, the South African magistrate who replaced von Zastrow, was more candid: "It seems that the Bushmen have lost all faith in the white man's methods [of justice], more especially as their women were being constantly interfered with by both farmers and police" (ADM 13/26, 6 November 1915).

Bushman fears of settler reprisals were well grounded.[5] Within a short period, as we saw, special army units were delegated to deal specifically with the "Bushman problem," even though the country was on a war footing. However, German patrols were not especially successful because of the "dense bush and shrub," and in January 1917, the "notorious" Hans was reported to still hold "considerable sway" in the Gorobab and Choiganeb (now Otjituo) areas (ADM 13/35, 26 January 1917, 3360). Farm laborers reported that Hans threatened to kill all natives who worked for whites (*Rex v. Feuerstein* 1918 SCC). The gang reportedly killed Fritz, an Ovambo, for displaying marked profarmer sentiments · (*Rex v. Massinab* 1918 SCC).

Walbaum described a virtual state of siege among the farmers. They could not burn lights in their houses at night for fear that Hans and his band would shoot them out. Most of the farm labor in the area, especially Bushmen working for unpopular farmers, had absconded with a goodly number of goats and cattle. The army and farmers responded with brutality.

Given this brutality, it was not surprising that Hans retaliated in May 1915 by attacking the farmhouse at Sus that was serving as a temporary police station in the operations against him. He attacked while the owner and his family were away visiting and the police were out hunting. With three armed men, Hans razed the farmhouse and killed three Herero laborers in their huts but did not touch the women. "The whole house was demolished. Every window was broken. In the house nothing was left: suits, clothing, laundered children's clothes, food, tobacco, schnapps, and 200 marks in money: everything was stolen" (Walbaum n.d.:48). Hans's gang also took ten head of cattle and a model 71 Mauser rifle (*Rex v. Feuerstein* 1918 SCC). In a later court case involving one of the participants in this raid, it emerged that the three black farm workers had caught Max, and that to rescue him, Johannes had been compelled to shoot them (*Rex v. Johannes Fritz* 1918 SCC).

German reprisals were swift and, as we have seen from Walbaum's journal, brutal. Walbaum's patrol captured four males and two rifles in a surprise raid, because the Bushmen were "totally soaked from the schnapps" (Walbaum n.d.). They also managed to capture the wife of Max, who had been Ludwig's concubine. Because of her value as a hostage, Walbaum had a farmer, Reyelien (Regelen), personally deliver her to headquarters in Grootfontein. Despite severe and urgent warnings to be careful, Regelen was surprised by Max at dawn one morning twenty-seven kilometers from Grootfontein. Max killed him and rescued his wife.

Under pressure from the Germans, Hans and his band retreated to Tsebeb water hole, from where, in September 1915, they launched a raid that shocked the local settlers. Max ordered a follower, Johannes, to go to the farm Goroab West and kill the owner, Eckstein, because Eckstein had recently abducted some Bushman women from Tsebeb water hole to his farm, perhaps hoping that they would attract their men to follow them there and work. Max did not go on this mission because he was suffering from bad eyes. Three Bushmen under Johannes, armed with two rifles, set off to exact justice. At the farm they spoke to various farm workers, including Andreas, in the mielie fields; they told Andreas not to accompany white men when they went into the bush and stole Bushman females who were doing no harm. In a carefully laid ambush, two white farmers, Ohlroggen and Korting, were killed. Eckstein was not with them. At his trial, Johannes took the blame for both killings, even though the killings had been committed with two different rifles.

During 1915 and 1916 Hans and his gang continued to harass the embattled white farmers, scaring away their laborers and stealing stock. It was not indiscriminate harassment, however, but was focused on a few farms. Farmer Tributh of Sus reportedly lost nearly all his livestock. Farmers Ackermann and Baumgarten claimed that they had lost nearly a hundred head of cattle, and Voswinkel, Wynack, Thomas and Wilhelm also reported heavy losses. Farmers put a reward on Hans's head and on their own initiative revived the German government reward of 200 marks for every rifle removed from a Bushman. Farmers organized unofficial posses, and Bushmen continued to shoot at army patrols.

In October 1916 Hans was killed. Early one morning, after donating five head of cattle to a *werft*, Hans and a small party of followers, including women and children, were walking along, playing a long, bowlike musical instrument called a *chas*. They had only one rifle, which August, a loyal follower, was carrying. Hans had an infected foot and was hobbling along. Galloping toward them came Feuerstein, an ex–post office clerk who was interned at Sus for the duration of the war. The band scattered, except for the unarmed Hans who, because of his infirmity, stood still. Feuerstein charged up and emptied his pistol at him. He then cut off Hans's head, so that, as he later explained, he could claim the reward. The South African court that tried Feuerstein for this crime could find no extenuating circumstances and sentenced him to death. This sentence shocked the local expatriates, but Feuerstein, together with his friend Voswinkel,[6] managed to make a daring jailbreak and eventually reach Europe via Angola.

After Hans's death, Max appears to have taken over the leadership of the gang. The gang's existence was short-lived, however, as South African troops managed to fatally wound Max and capture the other members. For his services in making this possible, a Bushman informer was rewarded with a princely sum of 1 pound!

Part 3

The Sacred Trust

Chapter 10

South African Rapprochement

German and South African policy toward Bushmen, vacillatory as it was, shared a number of common assumptions and contradictions. Both agreed, in essence, that it was merely a matter of time before Bushmen disappeared off the face of the earth. Such a stance accorded well with the unilinear pseudo-Darwinist doctrines of the period, which saw Bushmen as one of the lowest strata.[1] If this chapter illustrates one point, it is this: "Bushman Policy" was not a monolithic object, unanimously agreed to and consistently implemented. Rather it played to a diverse cast and audience: farmers, police, magistrates, mine owners, missionaries, migrant workers (but never Bushmen themselves), whose voices were often articulating contradictory demands. And when it came to policy execution, the implementers exercised a remarkable degree of autonomy beyond that allowed by the public service regulations. Their actions and interpretations were remarkably inconsistent.

Initially the South African Occupation Forces were concerned to show the world how much better they were than their German predecessors and consequently were more tolerant toward Bushmen. This is well reflected in early reports from the Grootfontein district. As new, but experienced, colonizers, they felt that German settler claims were exaggerated. The first annual report for 1916 issued by the military magistrate reported only one case of a white being fired upon by Bushmen (resulting in the death of the former's black servant). A number of "wild" Bushmen were sentenced to one month's imprisonment on the grounds that they were suspected by local settlers of stock theft but, because of lack of evidence, were charged with vagrancy instead.

Below the level of magisterial rhetoric aimed at superiors, a different world existed. Early in 1916 a number of men, women and children were arrested at Grootfontein on charges of stock theft. The magistrate wanted them removed to Windhoek by train, as they might try to escape. The men were thus transferred to Windhoek "wearing a complete suit of German chains" (ADM 273, 13 January 1916). The Windhoek jailer acknowledged receipt: "The said prisoner was completely chained and roped around neck, wrist and body. He left his teethmarks on the chain" (ADM 273, 19 January 1916).

The military magistrate, Frank Brownlee,[2] realized that proof of having "no visible means of support" or "passes" was problematic (ADM 3360, 12 July 1916; 15 December 1916) and accordingly instructed police not to arrest Bushmen on charges of vagrancy. If Bushmen wished to retain their nomadic life and white farmers continued to lose stock to Bushmen, the latter would not be allowed to squat on farms but should retire beyond the limit of the farming area. "I am convinced that the humane treatment meted out to the Bushmen prisoners in our jails is not without its good effect," he concluded. This approach was endorsed by the secretary of the protectorate, who extended it to other parts of the territory and added that this policy prevented the police from becoming victims of Bushman retaliation.[3] Less than three months later, however, Brownlee was reporting a "serious recrudescence of thefts and shooting of cattle" (ADM 3360, 20 February 1917). In response the crown prosecutor instructed: "No effort should be spared and no possible step disregarded towards the successful prosecution of native stock thieves. As you are aware, such thefts are apt to provoke the sufferer to regrettable[4] reprisals of a far more serious nature" (in *Rex v. Anton and three others* 1917 SCC; LGR 1/2/1–6). Nevertheless, Bushman stock theft continued to such a degree that a number of farmers were forced to abandon their farms later that year.

The typology of "wild," "semitame or wild" and "tame" Bushmen became well established by the early 1920s in the settler discourse on understanding Bushman behavior.[5] The basis of this typology was both spatial and economic. "Wild" Bushmen were those who were not permanently incorporated into the settler economy and generally lived beyond the Police Zone. Then there were the "semitame or wild" Bushmen, who came from beyond the Police Zone to work on settler farms on a temporary or seasonal basis. Finally there were the "tame" Bushmen, who were permanently "habituated" to employment on settler farms. This typology formed the grid on which Bushman behavior was explained.

Generally it was accepted that stock theft was committed by "wild" Bushmen, but beneath this dogmatic assertion was the suspicion, occasionally voiced, that this avowal was sometimes a deliberate ploy fostered by farmers and some academics (for example, Doke 1925:43) to absolve farmers from being held accountable for the situation. Indeed, farmers were known on occasion to exaggerate their stock losses in order to claim various tax breaks and relieve the pressure from the Land Bank to repay loans. Farmers inevitably tended to blame Bushmen, and in this they were sometimes assisted by government officials.

A popular version was to attribute Bushman behavior to biological factors: Bushmen simply *had* to have meat. Echoing this widely held view, Brownlee observed that the "tendency" toward cattle theft could be understood as a consequence of game's becoming more scarce. Provocation was not involved, although he had noticed "that certain thefts are wanton in nature and that more cattle or sheep are stolen at a time than can possibly be consumed by the thieves . . . [this] illustrates . . . a trait of barbarian character which is rather difficult to explain in words, but may be on account of an inherent lust for slaughter" (ADM 3360, 10 April 1917).

Other officials were not so ingenuous. Thus, in his annual report, the director of lands gave his considered opinion that "the Bushman is generally dubbed as dangerous, both to the farmer and his cattle; they are said to steal great numbers for slaughter, and also to attack isolated farmers, but with regard to these depredations, I think that treatment hitherto meted out to these people is, and has been, the cause of most of the trouble. Personally, although I have met hundreds of Bushmen, I have never had any trouble" (SWAA, A521/3, Ill-treatment of Natives, 1919). Indeed some officials became quite sensitive to the ploys used by farmers. In 1925 the Gobabis magistrate complained that "most farmers bordering the hinterlands graze their stock on the crown lands and during the rainy season the stock stray and the cry of stolen stock by Bushmen is made too easily in order to get the Police assistance for its recapture" (SWAA, A50/27, 22 July 1925). These "truths" were to be continually rediscovered.[6]

Given the belief in the inevitable demise of Bushmen, policy was based on "practical" considerations that were well expressed by Lieutenant Hull in 1915: "Every effort should be made to induce them to work on farms even for short periods. . . . On the other hand, stern repressive measures must be taken with sheep stealers and other criminals, or in time the whole Bushman nation will join in the sport of spoiling the farmers and shooting their servants" (ADM 3360). But Bushman policy was never taken seriously. Indeed the secretary of the protectorate plagiarized the above quote from Hull and used it in his circular as official policy (Schoeman 1975:169).[7] The influential Native Reserves Commission of 1921, which laid the cornerstone of segregation as policy, felt that "the 'Bushman problem . . . must be left to solve itself' and that 'any Bushman found within the area occupied by Europeans should be amenable to all laws' " (South West Africa 1922).

Land and Murder

In this coalescence of different agendas, encouragement of white settlement took precedence. For a variety of reasons, such as neutralizing the German settler element, strengthening its own colonial claims and alleviating the "poor White problem" in South Africa, South Africa encouraged white settlement in Namibia.[8] Indeed, the proverbial tail was wagging the dog: White South Africans believed that land was available virtually for the asking in an area they dubbed "Bushman land and Baboon country" (Wellington 1967:272). Indicative of their attitude was an article entitled "The People Eaters of South West" in a popular Afrikaans weekly, which claimed that the "so-called wild Bushmen are complete cannibals."[9] What is interesting about the article though are the accompanying photographs. The first is captioned "Where a Boer drove in his first stakes. Compare this with the picture of a year later." The second photograph is of the same place and is labeled "Beautiful dam and fruit trees." The message is obvious to even the most thick-skulled reader: Bushmen are inhuman and thus whites are justified in taking over and "developing" land which "they" are "wasting" (*Die Brandweg* 1920).

Indeed the administration's Bushman policy conveniently dovetailed and reciprocally bolstered settler interests. As J. Herbst, the secretary of South West Africa, put it in 1919: "The only policy . . . successful in overcoming the [Bushman] trouble is the settling of a European population in the area where these raids occur. When this particular area . . . [is] more thickly populated, the Bushmen will retire and seek new fields" (ADM 112, 25 October 1919, 3360). The van Ryneveld killing provided a major ideological authorization for this policy.

The van Ryneveld Affair

If there is one event that set the course of white-Bushman relationships, it is the white version of the van Ryneveld murder. There are several versions[10] of how the magistrate of Gobabis, F. J. van Ryneveld, went "unarmed" to discuss peace with Bushmen but was treacherously shot with a poisoned arrow and later died in excruciating agony. Given the elaborate myths that have emerged around this killing, it is important to examine what really happened. The van Ryneveld case also provides a valuable case study of the workings of the informal justice system and Bushman resistance.

Heavy cattle losses reported by Gobabis district farmers in 1922 were blamed on Bushmen moving south from the Grootfontein district. One of these farmers, a Mrs. Bullik, wrote a particularly touching letter

A band of Bushmen brought in by the police in the Gobabis district for illegal hunting, the evidence for which is in the foreground. The policeman on the left is Sergeant Zaal/Saal, who was Magistrate van Ryneveld's interpreter. (Photo courtesy of author)

to the administrator. She pointed out that she was a widow with six young children who was attempting to farm by herself and was suffering heavily from Bushman depredations. The administrator immediately ordered an investigation, and a police patrol was dispatched but was attacked by Bushmen and compelled to retreat. Magistrate van Ryneveld was then ordered to investigate by contacting the Bushmen through intermediaries to ascertain the cause of the disturbance. He was specifically instructed to avoid force.[11]

Zameko, whose gang the administration blamed for killing van Ryneveld, was perhaps the best-known bandit in the interwar years. Since 1915 he had been "squatting" and occasionally working on the Bulliks' isolated farm, Alexeck. Relations among Zameko, the other Bushmen who constituted the sole labor force on the farm and the Bulliks were generally amiable. However, after Mr. Bullik died in 1921, relations between Zameko and the Bulliks deteriorated rapidly, with Mrs. Bullik charging that the number of missing livestock had risen dramatically. In a six-month period, she claimed to have lost 28 cattle out of a herd of 450. When she protested one particularly obvious case, Zameko was said to have threatened her and her daughter. Her report of these events brought the police out in force.

According to official reports, Zameko had a strong personality and amassed a considerable following. Estimates range from 150 (SWAA, A396/7, 21 July 1922) to 300 (Sangiro 1954). They attacked and drove away the first police patrol sent out, plundering the police wagon of all its canvas. Van Ryneveld reported that the Bushmen at the Bullik farm were from the Grootfontein district (they were Aukwe) and that they "say they are going to fight and know they have done lots of damage . . . [they would] sell their lives dearly . . . [they] say straight out they are going to make war" (SWAA, A396/7, 12 July 1922). A month later, the priest in charge of the Epukiro Catholic Mission reported that local Bushmen had recently killed cattle and threatened to shoot a Catholic brother. The situation was aggravated by the absence of *veldkos* (wild roots and berries). There were rumors among the local black population that the northern Bushmen were going to make war, kill Mrs. Bullik and take all her tobacco. More significant, the priest reported, the Naron Mission Bushmen, who lived south of the Epukiro River, had decamped and joined their erstwhile northern enemies, the Aukwe (SWAA, A396/ 7, 17 August 1922).

Van Ryneveld reported that 7 "domesticated" Bushmen who had worked for Mr. Bullik until his death the previous year had become a band of stock thieves. Caught red-handed by Mrs. Bullik, they had threatened her and fled into the bush with about 150 of their relatives. Since January, they had allegedly slaughtered over seventy-five head of Mrs. Bullik's cattle. After the "scrap" with the police, several of the band had broken away and 8 had been captured. The rest fled into the waterless area west of the farm, where the police could not follow them. The magistrate felt that "Bushman's attitude all bluff when a number but dangerous when 2 or 3 . . . [and] must be vigorously dealt with" because they would affect other peaceful Bushmen. The cause of the disturbance he attributed to: (1) the absence of police supervision; (2) the widow's being alone and defenseless; (3) and the lack of *veldkos* and game. His successor, Grayson, endorsed these reasons but felt that the most important factor was "Zameko's undoubted contempt for the Administration" (SWAA, A396/7, 21 July 1922).

Four days later, van Ryneveld and a small patrol of three native constables, a tracker and a white sergeant set out to interview Zameko. Despite the warning from Saal, an experienced native corporal, that Bushmen would not know the difference between the magistrate and the police, and that the matter should best be treated as a simple police expedition, van Ryneveld apparently insisted on trying to talk to Zameko. The patrol made contact with the fleeing Bushmen, and the tracker and native police all shouted not to shoot as they were not police but had come in peace. Rhetoric and observation simply did not mesh, for they were in uniform and were carrying cocked firearms. In the ensuing melee, van Ryneveld was wounded by an arrow and four Bushmen perished. Saal immediately rode to the magistrate's aid, but van Ryneveld refused to let Saal wash and treat his wound, so deeply ingrained was his racism. He preferred to wait for the white sergeant to arrive and greeted him with the words, "Viljoen, I am finished." Sergeant Viljoen removed the arrow and the group waited for van Ryneveld to die.

The effect of van Ryneveld's death was immediate and dramatic. A patrol that had set out on 24 July 1922 to assist van Ryneveld was promptly strengthened with special constables recruited from the local settlers. This patrol had verbal "orders to act as circumstances require and as the region was outside of the Police Zone, long reports were not to be expected" (Sangiro 1954:134–135). The patrol, which eventually numbered nineteen whites and sixteen blacks, was initially unsuccessful in tracking down this large party of Bushmen. Telegrams sent to the administrator recorded the progress of the patrol: August 9—"Castle reports Bushmen split into bands of 5 to 20"; August 22—"On 18th, Sgt. Castle came upon Bushman marauders on Eiseb who attacked patrol at once. Six Bushmen killed, 23 captured, including leader. No police casualties. Prisoners and 60 women and children being brought in"; August 29—"Six more Bushmen caught. 1 died"; September 2—"Twenty-six Bushmen escape on night prior to arrival in Gobabis. 19 recaptured. Special constable fined 5 English pounds for negligence" (SWAA, 396/7).

A short while later, Grayson, the acting magistrate, held an inquest into the deaths of the six Bushmen. Sergeant Castle described how, on August 18 at about 9:00 A.M., he and his patrol of twenty-five men had crossed over a recently burned tract of land that stretched for approximately a mile towards a dense thicket of hook-thorn, where some Bushmen had been spotted. The patrol had extended in a prearranged manner and, penetrating a heavy flight of arrows, had managed to reach the *werft*, where they captured twenty men, women and children without a shot being fired. Then Castle heard several shots and found that some of his men had been forced to fire in self-defense; he had also been compelled to fire blindly into some dense bush in order to stop the barrage of arrows. The action lasted for fifteen minutes and resulted in six Bushman deaths, but surprisingly no police or Bushmen were wounded. "It was just great luck that nobody was hit. The Bushman shooting was bad that morning and I attribute it to the cold." Other affidavits from policemen corroborated their sergeant's evidence and elaborated on some of the details. Apparently many women and children were also armed and had fired at the police. The Bushman whom Native

Constable Boomskop killed had been seen with the party that had attacked Magistrate van Ryneveld. Despite several incongruities in the sequence and timing of events, the evidence of the various policemen was surprisingly consistent. The only Bushman to give evidence at the inquest said that they had been surprised by the police attack, as they had not expected it, and claimed that Zameko had told them to kill the police. Grayson, the acting magistrate, ruled that the police had acted entirely in self-defense, and this ruling was accepted by the administration (LGO 1/1/1–16; LGO N 5/1–2; SWAA, A396/7).

This finding is unsatisfactory for several reasons: First, it is clear that Grayson had, in his report of 17 September 1922 (SWAA, A396/7), prejudged the inquest when he observed: "It is hoped that it will be found that the police acted entirely in self-defence in this little matter of history." Second, nobody followed up the small inconsistencies in the police evidence. Third, why was only one Bushman asked to give evidence at the inquest? Fourth, because the Bushmen had been fleeing from the police and had burned the veld as an early warning device, it was obvious that they were expecting an attack, so the element of surprise must be questioned. Fifth, as it is generally believed that Bushmen are accurate with their arrows up to fifty paces and most of the action took place at a range of between thirty and fifty yards, it is indeed "lucky" that no police were hit! Sixth, it is statistically significant that in the indiscriminate firing of the police into the dense bush no Bushman was wounded. Finally, various accounts given a few years after the events differ significantly from the inquest findings. Sangiro, for example, said that in the short and sharp attack, three horses were killed, and that after the Bushmen had used up all their arrows, they had fled, that not a single Bushman had surrendered and that they had to be chased down by horse and manacled. He reported that thirty-seven Bushmen had died and sixty had been captured (Sangiro 1954:134–135).

Morton Seagars, who was one of the police on that eventful action, reminisced: "We captured about a hundred-and-fifty Bushmen . . . when we arrived back at the base camp with them, they made a determined effort to get away, and a running fight took place in which a dozen or so of them were killed" (Morton Seagars 1941:558). Yet no one queried the findings of the inquest.

The van Ryneveld affair had far-reaching implications. Grayson wrote to the resident magistrate in Ghanzi, Bechuanaland, to warn him that some of the Bushmen involved in the affair might try to cross the border. He claimed that they had been raiding cattle on a large scale and warned that they would threaten anyone who tried to pursue them. The Ghanzi magistrate, A. L. Cuzen, reported that a large number of Bushmen had crossed from Rietfontein in Namibia to Okwa, sixty miles south of Ghanzi. These Bushmen informed Cuzen that "they could not live in South West Africa because the laws there punished them for killing game, and they were required to carry passes. They stated quite simply that if they were not allowed to kill game, they would kill cattle" (Hermans 1977:61).

Despite its obvious pro-German propaganda intent, the summary of the impact of the van Ryneveld affair on the Bushmen by B. Voigt rings true:

> After Magistrate van Ryneveld was murdered by an unknown Bushman, an evil time emerged for the entire Bushman population. Everywhere in the Protectorate the British-Boer soldiers and the police were instructed to prepare to flush out the Bushmen and to destroy the hordes. The Bushmen, being used to the mild procedures of the Germans, did not at first take this prosecution seriously not defending themselves since they expected short jail sentences. None of them remained alive: neither man nor woman nor child were spared. How many Bushmen suffered this tragic fate no one can determine precisely. While during the German era every fatal shooting led to interrogations, inquiries, and resulted in thick official files which were later used by their enemy as welcome evidence for German atrocities, the British–South African government is silent about similar measures and prefers not to commit such actions to paper. The Bushman plague in the settled part of the territory has been eradicated completely, and the farmers, even those of German extraction, are not angry about the change. (Voigt 1943:149)

After serving a short sentence, Zameko was reported to be living near Alexeck in June 1924. Mrs. Bullik's troubles, however, were far from over, and she was forced to write to the administrator on more than one occasion to complain about Bushman depredations. These resulted in large special patrols being sent out in 1927, 1930 and 1935. It would be foolish to feel sympathy for Mrs. Bullik. In one of her letters to the administrator, she reported that she had been shocked to find on a recent visit to the Gobabis hospital that "four Bushmen, who had received lashes in gaol, came into the operation room. They pulled down their trousers and a white nurse administered to each one of them a white cloth with ointment thereon. That was enough for me!" Bushmen arrested for killing cattle should, she suggested, "be lashed with a sjambok tipped with the same poisoned arrowhead. If they have wounds, these should be covered with arrow poison ointment, so that the wound can also hiss and foam and so that Mr. Bushman can also feel the pain" (SWAA, A50/67, Letter to Administrator, 5 December 1927).

The Bullik legacy lived on. In 1950, a farmer in the Gobabis district presented some "Jottings on the Epukiro Bushmen" in which he noted that "a certain Polish-Silesian settler family in the most remote corner of the vast Gobabis district used to shoot Bushmen at sight anywhere in the territory which they had claimed as theirs. The mother of this family proudly displays Bushmen skulls acquired in the early days of their settling" (Pyper 1950:51; Green 1952).

The impact of the van Ryneveld killing and the official policy use of "settlement" as instrument of "taming" were clear from a statement made by the administrator a few years later:

> We make no attempt to civilize the Bushmen. They are untameable. They are the savages who shot Magistrate van Ryneveld with poisoned arrows a few years ago. They attack parties of natives from Ovamboland on their way to work on the mines. I have had to send two punitive expeditions against them this year, and more by good luck than good management, we captured some of them and punished them severely. The territory is so large and the Bushman so cunning that an army might seek them in vain. But it is all fine country, splendid for sheep and cattle farming; and it is only because there is so much unoccupied space in the inhabited areas that we are not contemplating any large settlement in the north at present. (cited in Chilvers 1928:276)

The legacy of this policy is obvious from the territorial dispossession of Bushman lands.

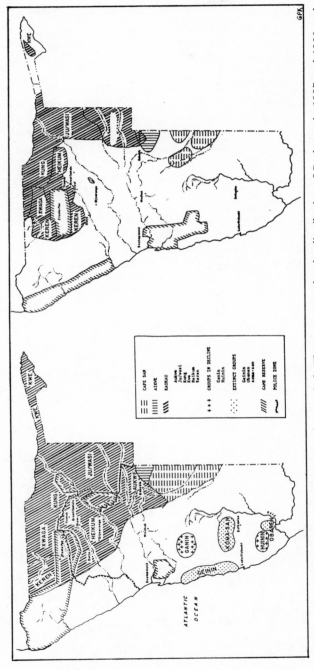

Bushman land dispossession during the Mandate period. The two maps plot the distribution of Bushmen in 1937 and 1980 and, although not completely accurate, provide valuable indices of territorial dispossession. *Sources:* Adapted from Paul Glass, "Die Buschmänner in Deutsch-Südwestafrika," Ph.D. dissertation, Königsberg University, 1939; Kuno Budack, "Die Völker Südwestafrikas," *Die Allgemeine Zeitung* (Windhoek), 6 June 1980.

Chapter 11

Laboring Legitimacy

In addition to land, settlers required labor. The 1916 annual report of the Grootfontein military magistrate had already addressed the question of farm labor. Like its German predecessors, it suggested that Bushman "children should be taken when young and apprenticed to some useful calling but it will need several generations of apprentices to produce a Bushman fit for labor even supposing the apprentice does not take the first opportunity to desert" (ADM 112, Annual Report 1916). Although there is no record that this was official policy, it certainly was informal policy for a number of years.[1]

Bureaucrats in Windhoek, the capital, were quick to follow the lead of their field officers. Thus the (in)famous blue book pointed out: "There is no doubt about it that should South West Africa receive an influx of white settlers after the War, the problem of native labor will become acute. The gradual training and utilization of the Bushman for farm work . . . is therefore a subject which cannot be waived aside without serious consideration" (South Africa 1918:146).

Farm labor was universally disliked. The deputy police commissioner observed that "natives do not like working for farmers; they say the hours are long, and they get very little food and no clothing, and they very much prefer working on the mines or on the railways. This is quite universal, and is something for the farmer to think about" (H.J.K. 1921:59).

Thus while decrying Bushman labor,[2] farmers had little choice but to utilize it. However, given the low image of the Bushman, state officials were ready to overlook the illegal arrangements that some settlers created in order to enhance Bushman productivity. The concord between state and settler is well illustrated by the sympathetic response of the administration to farmer Friederich's request for the remission of a 50-English-pound fine for being an accessory to an assault on Bushmen by his Bushman farm workers:

Mr. Friederich is entitled to protection. The cost, however, of maintaining an adequate police force would be enormous and it is not possible to deal with all the calls. . . . Farmers must therefore necessarily rely on their own efforts to bring the offenders to justice. In such cases, it is not unnatural that owners are inclined to take the law into their hands, more particularly when the expense and time involved in bringing the culprits to the Magistrate's Courts is considered. At the same time, if the jurisdiction of the Courts is disregarded, retaliatory attacks by the natives will ensue and farmers generally will suffer. (ADM 3360, C.-Clarke to Mgte., Gtftn., 6 April 1923)

Inexpensive labor has long been a critical factor in the settler political economy because commercial cattle ranching has always been marginal. In 1923, for example, the manager of the Land Bank wrote a special report on agriculture in the Grootfontein district. Of the 682 surveyed farms in the district, he found that 225 were held by land concession companies, Of the rest, although 220 farms had been occupied a few years earlier, by 1923 only 100 farms were being worked, by around seventy farmers. He attributed the moribund status of farming to an absence of markets, inexperience, periodic droughts, locusts, lack of organization and inadequate capitalization (LGR 3/2/1).

Bushmen, as cheap labor, were brought to work on farms in increasing numbers. In German times, von Zastrow had noted that over half the farms in the Grootfontein district were run on Bushman labor (von Zastrow 1914) and the blue book suggested that there were over 1,500 Bushmen employed on the Grootfontein farms (South Africa 1918).

Legalizing Action Against Bushmen

Although many farmers felt that the leniency displayed in court cases had encouraged Bushman depredations, rapprochement between the government and farmers was soon stimulated by the passing of two pieces of legislation. These were the Stock-theft Proclamation (Proc. 5/1920) and the Vagrancy Proclamation (Proc. 25/1920). The Stock-theft Proclamation allowed magistrate's courts to impose heavier penalties than would normally have been within their jurisdiction.[3] In addition, the magistrate could impose a compensatory fine up to the value of the stock stolen, and failure to pay this could invite additional sentences of up to six months. For the purpose of prosecutions under this proclamation, each animal stolen constituted a separate charge.

The vagrancy law was even more draconian and easier to use to secure convictions and to chain workers to farms.[4] Not only was it intended to stop "depredations," but it also served as a procurement device to meet the farm labor shortage because magistrates could, in lieu of imprisonment, allot the offender to either public or private employment. This law was aimed specifically at containing the "Bushman Danger" rather than regulating black migrant workers. Not only was this alluded to in official correspondence, but contextually the case is very strong. Bley pointed out, for example, that by 1908 over 90 percent of the total black male population was employed by settlers, and of the pastoral Herero and Nama, only an estimated 200 males were not employed by whites (Bley 1971:250). There was little need to control Herero rural workers with laws, as they were controlled by the fact that they were trying to replenish their livestock, which immobilized them, as they were dependent upon white farmers for grazing rights.[5] Commenting on this legislation at the 1923 Permanent Mandates Commission meeting of the League of Nations, Lord Lugard, a famous British colonial administrator, made the obvious point that all Bushmen might be described as vagrants in terms of Proclamation 25/1920 and thus subject to forced labor. The South African delegation did not respond.[6]

Fear as Social Control

Despite Brownlee's ostensibly humane Bushman policy, his successor, R. H. Gage, was so horrified to see incarcerated Bushmen "trembling with fear," their "terror was pitiful to behold" and "nothing short of cruelty" that he wrote a personal letter to the government secretary (for which he was duly reprimanded, ADM 13/26; 13/35, Gage to Gorges, 21 December 1919). Terror and the invocation of fear became the strategy of choice for government officials. Indeed, fear of the police was a common feature, and police consciously manipulated it as a social control device. Dorothea Bleek noted in her report to the administrator that the Bushmen

> are dreadfully afraid of the white man, particularly the policeman, who appears to them merely an arbitrary tyrant, as they don't understand the laws . . . half the convictions of Bushmen under the game laws would not take place, if the accused did not let themselves be frightened into owning to the police. . . . [The police] take care not to warn the natives that anything they say will be used against them. When Bushmen appear in court they have no idea of what would be accepted as a defence or in mitigation of sentence, and the interpreting is mostly done by native constables who are anxious to please the white policemen they serve under and to "make a case." (Bleek 1922:48–49)[7]

Indeed, she even suggested that Gobabis Bushmen often welcomed white settlers as protection against the police (Bleek 1922:40).

Dorothea Bleek, one of the first professional anthropologists to work among Bushmen, here photographed working with a group in Sandfontein in 1921. (Photo courtesy of South African Museum)

At Outjo, the western end of the area occupied by Bushmen, the magistrate observed: "These aboriginals are already so scared of the police that if they see that the area . . . is being regularly patrolled they might leave on their own accord" (ADM 3360, 6 September 1921).[8] State support for maintaining this situation was both direct and indirect. For example, my archival research showed that when police used firearms against Bushmen, the subsequent official enquiry always found that the police were justified in that use. As one investigating officer put it: "A bow and arrow in the hands of a Bushman is just as dangerous as a firearm" (contrary empirical evidence from the van Ryneveld case notwithstanding). Sometimes, the same policeman was featured in a number of enquiries. One such person was Jacob Hybeb, a native constable, and in Brownlee's words, an "invaluable Bushman . . . in rounding up Bushmen." In *Rex v. Orthey* 1917 SCC, Hybeb shot and killed a Bushman who had refused to stop while stealing mielies (ADM 3768/7, 17 February 1917). There is no record of his being punished for this. Shortly afterwards, he was accused of having shot and killed a Bushman witness who had attempted to escape before he could give evidence. In this case, he was represented, most unusually for a black, let alone a Bushman constable, by Dr. Lorenz, one of the top lawyers in the country. Not surprisingly, the court ruled that it was justifiable homicide and he was found not guilty.[9]

In contrast, any Bushman action against the police was viewed very seriously. This is exemplified most strikingly in the case of a Bushman who had shot two arrows at a police patrol; he was captured five years after the event and sentenced to three years because "he had no reason to shoot at the police" (*Rex v. Duma* 1938 SCW).

The Elusive Bushmen as a Police Problem

Frustration was the order of the day for the administration. Additional special patrols were ineffective and uneconomical, as they had to resort to tactics such as night marches and dawn attacks to secure a few arrests, and then these were usually women or the old and infirm. These captives were, however, held hostage in order to arrest the real culprits. Sometimes, the authorities had to resort to deception in order to arrest Bushmen. One officer described an early morning raid:

> At 6:30 a.m. I arrived at the Bushman kraal, on my arrival the Bushmen ran away. I called them back and said they need not be frightened for me as I was looking for Germans. Two of them returned. I gave them tobacco to smoke as I did not intend doing them any harm, then all the Bushmen returned . . . they had a smoke and I gave instructions to have them arrested and charged for murder . . . as I was putting on the handcuffs the Bushmen ran away. I caught three, Corporal van der Merwe caught three, and three ran away. I then gave instructions to fire but not to hit, which was done. Native Constable Fritz killed one Bushman by accident. (ADM 3768/7, Sworn statement, Lt. B. Burger, October 1918)

In summary, the original police strategy was to arrest "all and sundry in the neighborhood of the crime" (ADM 3823/8, Gage to Sec., 9 October 1919).

The difficulties involved in policing Bushmen are reflected in the negative imagery and associated strategies used by policemen in their "Bushman patrols." Consider the following description of the Outjo district: "This district is *infested* with Bushmen, who undoubtedly do a great deal of harm to the stock of farmers and though all cases are energetically investigated, it is most difficult to catch the offenders, who are more like *jackhals* than human beings. . . . I feel quite certain that it will be futile to expect them to leave the Police Zone by gentle means, such as asking them to leave" (SWAA, A396/11, Deputy Police Commissioner, 6 September 1921).

The negative imagery was shared by all policemen, from the deputy commissioner down to the lowest white constable. The deputy commissioner in 1921, after describing a "Bushman custom" of poking a sick child with a burning stick, concluded: "Can you imagine anything more dreadful than this, gentle readers, and mothers of children? Yet this is a custom among a people who live within your boundaries" (H.J.K. 1921:177). Another article, describing police duty in the "real Kalahari" for *Nongqai*, the official police journal, described Bushmen as the "scourge of the Border farmer . . . too lazy to work . . . the lowest type of human being, if not actually the lowest . . . accumulation of filth . . . horribly cruel in their hunting . . . like a pack of wolves. Like wild animals, these Bushmen will run at sight of a European, but when cornered they can be very dangerous" (Billy 1928). The following quote from Bushman patrol veteran, Head Constable Sargent, dispels the myth that it was always the farmers who were "hard," whereas the police were the impartial public servants simply doing their duty:

> In the Kalahari Bushman we have rather a shy, cruel, treacherous, and dangerous native, he has come very little in touch with culture and he roams about doing damage to game and forestry that he is able to do, and when opportunity arises he makes it his business to ambush the Ovambo labourers.
>
> Stock theft is the root of all the trouble. . . . Farmers have informed me that the Kalahari Bushmen when permitted to live on their farms as they like, have often returned stray stock and are at least worth their food when doing odd jobs on the farm. This may or may not be, but still stock thefts are on the increase and in many instances farmers are afraid that if they take steps against the Bushmen and have them punished, they will be the sufferers in the long run, so they think it best not to report the matter [since this encourages the Bushmen]. (SWAA, A82/27, Post Commander, Grootfontein, 11 December 1924)

Sometimes Bushmen engaged in stock theft, according to the police, because they enjoyed being hunted down.[10] These attitudes underline an important structural feature: Policemen, because they did not have to live with the consequences of their actions in the local community, had a greater potential to abuse Bushmen. They could conveniently forget the magistrate's instructions.[11] Thus, although they often dehumanized Bushmen, they were not averse to elevating them to human status in order to commit the occasional rape (*Rex v. Smith* 1917, Outjo; also ADM 148).

In trying to obtain information, police often engaged in crude torture. Two cases provide illustrative material. In *Rex v. Smith, Odendaal and Abraham* (Grootfontein, May 1940; LGR 1/2/1–6), the accused, a police constable, a farmer and a native constable, were charged with the culpable homicide of a Bushman who had apparently admitted his guilt in committing a theft but was of no assistance in locating the stolen goods. The deceased was tied to a tree after being assaulted, and the accused ordered all the local Ovambo laborers to dowse him with water. The Bushman died. The court dismissed the farmer and found the two policemen guilty, not of culpable homicide, but of assault, because the death might have been caused by tetanus! In imposing sentence, the court considered the following factors: (1) the youth of the nineteen-year-old constable; (2) the manner of handcuffing; (3) the long duration of the water throwing and (4) "possible negative influence of the stupid Ovambos." The white constable was fined 50 English pounds or six months imprisonment, and the native constable was given the choice of 25 English pounds or six months imprisonment. Cases such as these emerged only by accident because Bushmen were too intimidated to complain.

Such fear of the police was (and is) widespread and has deep historical roots. In 1940, for example, "Cocky" Hahn, the Ovamboland commissioner, sent an angry telegram to Windhoek reporting that his native constable had arrested some Bushmen who were being pursued by white police and farmers for alleged stock theft. During this fracas the Otavi police had opened fire on them as soon as they had been spotted. Hahn's native constable concluded by "asserting prisoners will be too frightened to mention foregoing in court" (NAO 33/1, 8/1940). A police investigation officially absolved the police from any misdeeds. The Bushmen were sentenced to three years for shooting the constable's horse. Such tactics were often required, as Sergeant Brooks, a veteran "Bushman expert," once explained, because "Bushmen are terrible liars and when cornered appear dumb and ignorant" (SWAA, A50/101, 20 April 1936).

It was believed that the best way to "corner" Bushmen was to wait for the winter months when they were too cold to move rapidly and congregated at water holes. The police could then demonstrate their power by, for example, shooting a dog or two, at which "the Bushmen showed anxiety and allowed themselves to be captured" (Wendt 1981:45). Bushmen captured in such a way were then charged with a battery of offenses like trespass, vagrancy, hunting, unlicensed bows and arrows, failure to pay dog tax, and so on. And while the parents awaited trial and served their sentences, their children were placed in the "protective care" of white farmers.

It is, of course, also necessary to describe what happened to Bushmen once they had been apprehended by the police. Bushmen were chained and sent off to prison, frequently in Windhoek. But even if they were caged, sometimes special precautions were taken. As late as 1946, A. Courtney-Clarke, the brother of the erstwhile secretary for South West Africa, wrote an outraged letter of protest:

In the instance of these 12 boys, it appears they have been chained together on one chain and taken from one farm to another, the journey to Grootfontein occupying at least seven days. They were all beaten up by the native policeman in charge, one seriously and another, an old man who could not keep pace with the others, has his legs and soles of his feet badly lacerated and is unable to stand. Both these cases are now in the Native Hospital. (SWAA, A50/67/1, Courtney-Clarke to CNC, 23 May 1946)[12]

There was a general acceptance of the fact that Bushmen died in jail if given too long a sentence. Indeed, it seems that most Bushmen have had a relative who has died in jail (*Rex v. Zh. Boesman* 1934 SCW). In order to counteract this, the jailers would on occasion allow the Bushmen out of the central prison in order to "graze" in the veld and the administration contemplated constructing an open-air place of confinement, but a lack of funds prevented this scheme from eventuating (Ahrens 1948:119). The Grootfontein magistrate tried a new tack: "The Court has, instead of long terms of imprisonment, shortened the sentences and imposed lashes in every instance. This unfortunately, did not have the desired effect as they repeated the offence shortly afterwards" (LGR 3/1/16, Annual Report, Grootfontein, 1933). This had the effect of leading more and more magistrates and police to the conclusion that the "only solution" was to force the Bushmen to resettle on the other side of the Police Zone.

Chapter 12

Beyond the Police Zone: Disrupting the Labor Supply

Even beyond the Police Zone, Bushmen were not exempt from police harassment. On the contrary, there, where the glare of potentially embarrassing publicity was absent, justice was even more roughshod. A major stimulus for police patrols into the area beyond the Police Zone was the alleged Bushman raids on black migrant contract workers in transit to and from their homes in Ovamboland, the Kavango River area or even further afield in Angola and Northern Rhodesia (now Zambia). This issue had started to emerge during the German era, but it became a critical point of concern especially after World War I. Such attacks discouraged inexpensive migrant labor, which constituted the very basis of the South African "Native Policy" (Gordon 1978b; Moorsom 1977).[1] So seriously did the South Africans take this threat that when the governor general of South Africa, Lord Buxton, toured the territory in 1919, it was arranged for him to have a special audience with some Bushmen at Grootfontein. The press report deserves to be quoted extensively, first, because it is a major South African policy statement on Bushmen and, second, because it demonstrates the ideological and often rather burlesque qualities of ceremonial as "invented tradition":

> For the prosperity of the country the Ovambo and other natives must be encouraged in every way to come from the distant parts to work in . . . South West Africa, and these murders by Bushmen can do enormous harm. It was particularly fortunate that the Governor-General was able to address an unusually large group of Bushmen at the Residency in Grootfontein.

Although at present working on farms, the call of the wild will inevitably drag these savage people back to their old haunts in the impenetrable north, and so his Excellency's words will spread through the vast desert lands to all three tribes of Bushmen. . . .

The group of Bushmen stood in a semi-circle in the Residency garden, and although their faces were mostly passive, it was not difficult to see that they understood the full meaning of the Governor-General's speech by an almost alarmed change of expression.

The Government would do its best to look after the Bushmen and see they got justice and fair treatment. It was better for them to come to work on the farms. . . . They must not steal cattle or sheep from the farmers. The Bushmen should work to purchase cattle and sheep, which would then belong to them.

Then, speaking gravely and firmly, the Governor-General said: "I hear that some Bushmen have been killing Ovambos . . . such deeds cannot be allowed, and if they continue the Bushmen will get into very serious trouble. . . ."

The German soldiers treated the Bushmen as wild animals, but in their wonderful way they immediately got to know the difference between the German officers and the Union people, with the result that the Grootfontein Patrol is respected and unmolested even in the wildest parts of the north. But whether the Bushmen can ever be tamed and become useful citizens is a doubtful question. (*African World* 1919/20:204)

The first report of an attack on migrant workers South Africans received was in October 1918 when two blacks were killed twenty-five miles from Karakuwisa. A patrol consisting of Lieutenant Burger and one native and two white constables was immediately dispatched. They succeeded in making seven arrests. However, one Bushman was shot, two witnesses absconded and two of the accused died in Grootfontein prison before they could be tried. The headquarters of the South African Military Constabulary raised nagging questions about the shooting because when it occurred there could not have been the slightest proof that the Bushman who was killed had committed the alleged murder. In fact, as the bodies of the alleged murder victims were never found, there was no evidence that a murder had even been committed (ADM 116-3823/8). There is no evidence that the matter was taken further.

These events raised questions of policy with regard to the extension of law beyond the Police Zone. Waters, the government legal adviser, felt that the administration should move slowly, apart from which, "the vendetta between Bushman and Ovambo is of old standing and probably there is not much to choose between the two sides" (ADM 116-3823/8, Waters to Gage, 30 January 1919), whereas the secretary of the protectorate felt that the area could not be excluded from criminal jurisdiction

Bushmen listening to the phonograph of the Denver African Expedition in northern Namibia in 1928. The photograph reinforces the distinction between modernity (the phonograph) and primitivity (the Bushmen). (Photo courtesy of State Archives, Windhoek)

(ADM 116-3823/8, Sec. to Gage, 27 February 1919). Eventually, the issue was forced. On a tour of the Kavango, Magistrate Gage was told by Chief Njangana (of the Djiriku) that he would not send any more workers to the Police Zone because of Bushman attacks on returning workers. Gage also met a party of Barotses that had originally numbered thirty-one. They claimed to have been attacked by Bushmen at Gatsamas water hole, where they had lost all their possessions. Seven of their party had been killed and three others wounded. Later he met a second and a third "batch," all of whom reported that they had been attacked. In total, twenty-five Barotses were said to have died. The chief felt that rifles would not deter Bushmen, who would then simply hide and attack at night, in which case the rifles might be abandoned and end up in the possession of Bushmen. In all, an estimated 15 to 25 percent of all workers were killed or died on the return journey, and this manifestly influenced the labor supply function of the Kavango area, which, although small at that time, was believed to have great potential (ADM 116-3823/8, Gage to Sec., 7 October 1919).

Action was called for, and Gage proposed that the Blockfontein police station be reopened in order to maintain good relations with the

Kavango people, who, he hoped, would not lose their confidence in the ability of the settlers to protect them. Second, Gage felt that failure to take action would be construed by Bushmen as a sign of weakness. Gage's proposals were turned down on the grounds that the small number of laborers did not justify the cost (ADM 116-3823/8, Gage to Waters, 7 November 1919). Instead, when the attacks increased in number, it became policy to send out an occasional special police patrol. There were "several" alleged murders of Kavango laborers, but none were investigated because they were reported too late for police action. Moreover, it was widely believed that there were numerous unreported murders (SWAA, A13/26, Annual Report, Grootfontein, 1923).[2]

For all their vaunted, self-proclaimed legal positivism, the courts were apt to stress economic factors when sentencing Bushmen caught by the police. In *Rex v. Thuantha et al.*, the learned judge came down hard on the Bushmen, who he believed were "savages who know no law and are comparable with children who are *doli incapaces* [incapable of guilt]. [A practice like] waylaying much needed supply of native workmen cannot be allowed to continue. A beginning at punishment must be made. A commutation might be misunderstood" (*Rex v. Thuantha et al.* 1920 SCC).[3] The judge ordered the hapless Bushmen to be publicly hanged in the presence of fellow Bushmen, who were to be trucked into Windhoek to witness the event in the hope that the hanging would be a deterrent.

The special patrols were generally a frustrating experience for the constabulary, as there was little likelihood of arrests. Police patrols were to engage in "clearing of Bushmen, pontoks [residences] must be burnt . . . this is essential. . . . [Otherwise] we shall have a recrudescence of murders and the labour supply will decrease and possibly vanish" (SWAA, A50/26, 9 March 1926).[4]

The magistrate's words had a prophetic ring to them. From a labor supply point of view, 1926 was a bad year. In March, a Kavango was killed. "This was just before the annual tide [of workers] should have begun to flow and effectively dammed it back. Tidings of raids travel fast and gather size as they go." Later, in his annual report, the Kavango native commissioner pondered the serious "riddle" of why labor was not forthcoming from the Kavango region despite inducements like new boreholes along the labor route and the serious famine in the Kavango and the substantial increase in wages in the Police Zone. "From the plentiful supply of labour at a fee of 7/-, it has dwindled to a trickle at 22/6 'with extras.' The Government has sacrificed an income of several hundred pounds a year, the mines are short of labour and the farmers are worse off than they have been for many years." Yet an answer to the riddle is suggested earlier in the same report. The influence of Bushmen in determining the labor supply function of the Kavango region was consistently overlooked and the reluctance of Kavango workers to participate in wage labor was usually attributed to their relative affluence, "laziness" or low morals (Gordon 1977, 1978a). Certainly, Bushmen appear to have been "not backward in helping themselves to what they desire," and it seems that they even attacked a party that had a rifle (but no ammunition) (SWAA, A3/36/1, 13 September 1926).

Head Constable Sargent was compelled to undertake two special patrols on the labor routes that year. On his first patrol, Sargent encountered very few Bushmen and, apart from razing a few *werfts* and arresting four Bushmen, returned to Grootfontein, the major labor-processing center, empty-handed. He concluded that patrols were useless and that workers should be released from their jobs at staggered intervals so that they could be provided with a small escort of police, or the mines should provide an armed foreman. On his second patrol, he managed to capture three males, eleven women and ten children in an ambush. In an extraordinary statement, reflective of the informal retributive system, he added: "As there was nothing against these Bushmen having killed any natives, I did not feel justified in shooting them as we could easily have done" (SWAA, A3/36/1, November 1926). These words were accepted without comment.

Harassment of Bushmen who lived beyond the Police Zone, especially those unfortunate enough to live on the labor supply route, continued for a number of years. The major labor routes followed traditional trade routes of Bushmen, and frequently the migrant workers would encounter Bushman trading expeditions en route to either the Kavango or the Police Zone. These trading expeditions were still taking place after World War II when some Kung complained that they were being molested and occasionally robbed by Okavangos on their way to the river to trade (Schoeman n.d.[a]: para. 20).[5]

Bushman raids continued despite special police patrols and the fact that the labor organization had started to send workers back in large groups accompanied by armed guards. In August 1927, the Kavango native commissioner complained, "It is becoming almost the exception rather than the rule for any returning labourers to get safely through" (SWAA, A50/26). Gabillet, the officer in charge of the Kavango, became so paranoid when he heard a rumor that a band of Bushmen was going to attack his camel post that he impressed a number of blacks, armed them and launched a preemptive strike against the alleged band of marauders. Led by a guide to Mpungu, he surrounded a Bushman camp at dawn and called on them to surrender. They acknowledged the call by letting loose volleys of arrows and then "savagely attacked with knives." One of Gabillet's blacks was killed, so Gabillet's party opened fire and killed four Bushmen. They also managed to capture five males, one youth, nine women and ten children. Gabillet concluded his report with the words: "Trust that it will now be clear . . . that some drastic action should be taken against this vermin which not only seriously threatens the safety and welfare of the Europeans at this station, but renders the Tsumeb road very gravely dangerous to every native using it" (SWAA, A50/26, 3 October 1927). An official in Windhoek, clearly cynical, wrote in the margin of this sworn statement: "Wonderful self-restraint and damn bad shooting on the part of the Bushmen."

The magistrate of Grootfontein thought that a solution to this problem might be for the Northern Labor Organization[6] to recruit Bushmen as contract workers. This brought forth the following strongly worded reply:

> It is very difficult to place Bushmen as labourers with farmers and in the case of half-bred Bushmen from Ovamboland we have had complaints from former employers about these boys. It is maintained that Bushmen need not be imported into the Police Zone as they give sufficient trouble already without costing rail-fare etc. to bring them to the place of employment. The Organization therefore would not like to try and recruit Bushmen. (SWAA, A50/25, Schonfelder to Mgte, Grootfontein, 23 October 1927)

And so Bushmen beyond the Police Zone were spared the indignity of contract labor, despite the cry that the labor shortage was critical. Perhaps there is more to it than meets the eye? Consider the following telegram sent a few years later: "Suggest deserters . . . be paraded under escort in mine compound and tell all other Okavango that every kraal head along the River now ordered capture natives stop Tell them also about possible attack by Bushmen stop consider Tsintsabis police be temporarily increased by five to six Bushman trackers" (NAT 29, 24 September 1938).[7]

It can thus be seen that Bushmen performed the very valuable function, from the settler point of view, of discouraging and apprehending deserters. This policy functioned not only on the Kavango labor route but also on the Ovambo route. It was not an occasional policy but one with a long, continuing history (see, e.g., SWAA, A521/52, 6 March 1928; A521/13[4], 22 December 1947). As soon as there was an increase in the number of desertions, Bushman trackers were hired, not only for actual tracking, but also for the psychological impact in deterring potential deserters.[8]

After 1927 the number of Bushman attacks decreased considerably as a result of the sinking of boreholes along the route and armed guards' accompanying worker parties. Labor route policy was now set. Most of the workers who did not use the services of the armed escort were assumed to be deserters and, because they traveled in very small groups, were the most vulnerable to Bushman attack. Thus there was no justification in increasing the number of police patrols (SWAA, A50/26, 3 March 1930).

The labor guards appear to have done a good job of terrorizing Bushmen. The Northern Labor Organization had much trouble with their armed escorts, who were often sacked at one end of the route only to be rehired at the other. For instance, one guard came across a group of Bushmen eating an eland. He scared them off with his rifle and took the meat and a six-year-old child. Bushmen pursued him for a day and fired several arrows. "We have tried to explain to the Bushman child," wrote the secretary of the Northern Labor Organization to the post commander at Nurugas, "the mistake that was made by our foreman, and have given him some beads and tobacco to take to his people in lieu of atonement. We would be obliged if you would keep the child there at your station and advertise widely the fact that his parents are wanted to fetch it again. . . . Please explain . . . the presents sent to them [3 packets of beads and 5 pounds of tobacco] are a token that we want them to be friendly" (SWAA, A50/26, Schonfelder to Post Commander, 21 January 1931).

The raids on these heavily laden returning migrants, resplendent with their tin trunks and occasional donkey, were not simply an exercise in "primitive redistribution," although, to be sure, the booty gained on such raids was rapidly dissipated in the exchange networks; rather, the motive of vengeance appears to have weighed heavily. Workers on their way to the Police Zone frequently raided Bushman settlements in search of food. Father Wust reported the experience of a church brother who had allowed some Okavango migrant workers to accompany him on the journey to Grootfontein. The brother watched incredulously as Okavango workers systematically pillaged all Bushman properties they came across. Meat, fruit, hides and even items that they could hardly use were taken. The Bushmen responded by saying that they would seek retribution when the Okavangos came back and were *not* under the protection of a white man (Wust 1938:258). Two points can be drawn from this case: first, that such behavior was obviously intimately associated with Bushman attacks on returning labor migrants and, second, that the extension of white rule enabled blacks to exploit Bushmen to a degree that had not been possible previously.

That Bushman attacks on laborers were more reactive than active is also suggested by the fact that it was practically impossible to arrest Bushmen in the Kaukauveld. Punitive expeditions would depart up to

Bushman prisoners eating in the stockade of the Otjiwarongo Gaol, under supervision of the black police warder, circa 1930. (Photo courtesy of State Archives, Windhoek)

six months after the crime had been reported. The question should thus be, Why were there not more raids on the workers? The policy of providing armed escorts to workers traversing the Kaukauveld led to further abuses, which included the kidnapping of youngsters. Yet when the administration was aware of these abuses, it did not take them seriously.

By 1937, shortly before the Northern Labor Organization switched to motorized transport, a final series of events was deemed to require official correspondence. Bushmen had started congregating at some of the boreholes and acted as unsalaried caretakers of these pumps. The Northern Labor Organization had no cause for complaint except that on occasion, Bushmen used too much water. These Bushman "settlers" were said to have given up part of their roaming life. Their settlements were surrounded by palisades (for protection against animal and human predators), and they had small gardens that were cultivated with hoes traded from the blacks. They grew mostly maize, millet and tobacco. Their gardens were cleared in depressions in the ground and contained rich, moist soil. They were surrounded with simple fences to protect the crops from game (SWAA, A50/26, Schonfelder Memorandum, 1 Feb-

Bushmen captured by the South West African police on the Kavango River in the late 1930s. The clothes they have been provided as protection against the cold are old burlap bags; their chains are thinner than those used by the Germans. (Photo courtesy of SourceWust, 1938)

ruary 1939). All of this suggests a knowledge acquired through friendly interaction with the Okavango workers. The Northern Labor Organization had reason to be pleased with these developments because not only did the organization get free caretakers for the pumps, but also Bushmen often cared for injured or ill labor recruits for weeks on end. These settlers also engaged in extensive trade, often functioning as the middlemen between Bushman relatives who lived in remote areas and the labor recruits. The major trading items were hides and ostrich-eggshell necklaces.

However, at the Kanovlei borehole, some Kavango complained that Bushmen had robbed them after they had gone to a Bushman *werft* (located some distance away from the borehole) to trade meat for mangetti nuts. The native commissioner investigated and reported that the "allegations were refuted by the Bushmen who were not in any way hostile." Addressing the broader issue, he continued: "It may not be policy to order the Bushmen to leave Kano Vley as they would then perhaps make their way into the Police Zone and squat on the native reserves and farms where . . . they would not be welcomed by the natives or farmers . . . [on the other hand] attempts to get these Bushmen to do light work on the roads for payment have been unsuccessful to date" (SWAA, A50/26, Eedes to CNC, 16 August 1937).

Chapter 13

Extending Administrative Control: Bushmen "Reserved"

Much of Bushman land was also expropriated by the state for use as game parks and native reserves for other Namibian indigenes, primarily Herero speakers, who were displaced from the central highlands by white ranchers. How did Bushmen get on with their reserve peers? This chapter examines the dynamics of life in these and other "reserves," both "native" and "game."

Native Reserves

In deciding what administrative system to use for governing its newly acquired mandated territory, in 1921 the South Africans set up a Native Reserves Commission, charged with the task of examining "the general administration of native locations in the territory, their size and conditions prevailing therein and the availability of native labour in such locations and reserves" (cited in Werner 1982:29).

As a working principle, the commission adopted South African–style segregation. The question was where indigenes were to be located, as most of their traditional areas were already occupied by white settlers and no administration bent on trying to obtain white support was going to remove settlers. At the same time, the proposed reserves had to be within close proximity to provide a ready source of labour for settlers. Such considerations led to the pattern of establishing at least one "native reserve" in every magisterial district. Other "reserves were selected for Native occupation as they were out of the way. Their situation, it was considered, would lead to avoidance of friction which was continually occurring between the Native and the Europeans" (cited in Olivier 1961:116).

The "troublesome Natives" were, of course, Herero, and the "out of the way" reserves they were allocated, Aminuis, Epukiro, Waterberg East, Otjituo and Eastern, were all located in the Kalahari Sandveld, in areas generally felt to be unsuitable for settler ranching because of a general scarcity of water, inadequate pasturage and distance from markets (Wellington 1967). These areas were also known to have been historically occupied by Bushmen.

In 1923 Aminuis, Epukiro and Otjituo reserves were proclaimed. They were followed a year later by Waterberg East. Their size was periodically increased as a result of continued Herero protestations. All expansion was into Bushman territory. By the 1950s Herero reserves extending into the Kalahari covered 2,462,803 hectares (Werner 1982:30).

Historically, Herero have always been vocal in their distress at their assigned "homeland." In 1924 Herero Chief Kutako protested vehemently to the South African administration: "We are a big nation and as such we shall not develop in a country like this where there is only deep bore-hole water. In fact it is a desert where no human being ever lived before. It is a country only good for wild beasts—We are the original inhabitants of South West Africa and we know the best and the worst of the whole country. . . . We are human beings and we do not want to be changed into wild beasts" (cited in Wellington 1967:279; First 1963:114).

As numerous commentators have pointed out, the landmass might look impressive on paper, but its inadequate water supplies made it unsuited to pastoralism. Nor was the administration particularly generous in providing wells.[1] Rhetoric notwithstanding, Herero moved to their allocated reserves. According to Werner, by 1928, 43 percent of all Herero speakers were resident on reserves and by 1949 this had risen to over 50 percent (Werner 1982).

By its very nature, pastoralism is predatory. Herero have always, like good pastoralists, valued their cattle highly and been swift in retribution for any harm done to their herds. Being compelled to farm in these marginal areas raised the relative worth of their cattle and made retribution even more severe, especially in the minimal presence of any overarching governmental controls. Bushmen have always been afraid that Herero would penetrate further into their hunting grounds and take possession of their land (Köhler 1957:49). In 1926 a Bushman headman crossed the border from Botswana into the Epukiro Reserve and gave warning that Bushmen would not tolerate any further encroachment either by man or beast (SWAA, A50/25, Gobabis, 26 May 1926).

Encroachment did not occur only from the west, however. In 1917, Tawana from Ngami were given permission to use the Nyae Nyae area for winter grazing, on condition that they maintained good relations with the local Bushmen and did not engage in hunting. The Tawana sent their herds out under the care of Herero. Some Bushmen lost their lives resisting this incursion, which resulted in various police patrols' being dispatched from both Grootfontein and Maun. One patrol, led by Sergeant Brooks in the winter of 1935, found 138 Herero at Gautscha and Gora with over 800 head of cattle, 9 horses, 98 donkeys and 400 sheep and goats that belonged to Muruwera of Mahupa. The Herero claimed to have been doing this winter trek for the past thirty years. Brooks threatened to shoot the cattle if they were not immediately removed. In 1937 a beacon was put up marking the border (SWAA, A50/101), but it is obvious that it was difficult and, indeed, rare for either the Namibian or the Botswana police to patrol this area.

In the Herero reserves the general pattern of Bushman-Herero interaction consisted, at least initially, of Bushmen moving to the Herero settlements during the dry season, where, in return for doing various domestic chores like collecting firewood and water, herding and milking, they were given a small amount of tobacco and food (especially milk), depending on availability. Such ties were usually established with people with whom there was already some preexisting relationship, generally past dealings with relatives or because of trade. Indeed Bushmen still bring hides and skins to Herero for trade. Sometimes these sojourns were extended to beyond the onset of the rains, when Bushmen were generally expected to leave for the bush and return the following season to the same family. Where this relationship has developed into one of all-year permanence, and when the year has been good, Bushman servants may be rewarded with a goat or a calf at the end of the year.[2] In essence, this process of sedentarization was a logical extension of hunting-and-gathering strategies.

Notwithstanding the striking similarity of stereotypes and the fact that whites were reputed to pay more than black ranchers, several officials noted that Bushmen often preferred to work for blacks. This was not to say that blacks did not exploit Bushmen, but simply that they tempered it with flexibility and less social distance, epitomized best perhaps by the fact that Herero employed kinship terms in addressing Bushmen and served as foster parents (*Grootmaak ouers*) to young Bushmen.[3] Young Bushman children were frequently left with Herero until they were adult, when they would usually return to their natal group. Marriage between the two groups was rare. When a child was born as the result of an informal liaison, it might be defined as a Herero (or Tswana) if its parent's family were wealthy and decided to adopt it.

Herero/Tswana abuses of Bushmen were checked and controlled some-what by fear of possible Bushman retribution. The former had a healthy respect for the Bushmen's poisoned arrows (*Rex v. Tjamp and Kutha* 1936 SCW) and believed that "if you kill a Bushman, you won't live." Moreover, Bushmen supposedly possessed certain magical powers that enabled them to turn into animals.

The use of kinship terms and acting as foster parents also offered scope for exploitation. Kinship terms indicate a paternalistic and author-itative relationship in which Bushmen are condemned to being perpetual children or junior kinfolk. Cases of abuse of foster children are also evident. It was a common practice for Herero police constables to adopt the children of Bushman parents who had been jailed, and often such abuses came to light only because they were within the observational sphere of the white constabulary. In one such case, a constable forced his Bushman foster daughter to be a prostitute, charging 3 shillings for "carnal connection" (*Rex v. Link* 1919 Gobabis). In another case, an inquest into the death of a sixteen-year-old Bushman revealed that he had "deserted" his Herero foster-father-cum-master and was so soundly thrashed that he died. The white constable supported his black colleague by claiming that "he gave Willem a lot of trouble by running away from his work." The district surgeon found that death had been caused by peritonitis and pneumonia. The foster father was not charged or disci-plined (LGO N5/1–2, Inquest: Oesib, 1925). Oral testimony suggests that such cases were by no means so rare as the written records would indicate.

Like all colonizers intent on legitimating their territorial claims, Herero tended to play down any "Bushman troubles" they might have had: "We have never had any trouble with 'wild' Bushmen," the Reserve Board of Otjituo claimed in 1948. The board was, of course, exaggerat-ing. Lebzelter (1934b:18) described a continuing war between the Otji-tuo Herero and the Kung, in which the Herero would attack on horse-back, striking the Kung from the saddle with their lethal knobkerries. Complaints did surface, however, when Herero lost cattle and were unable to apprehend the culprits or recover the cattle. Thus in May 1927, Headman Hoveka of Epukiro Reserve led a deputation to Win-dhoek to complain about Bushman depredations in his reserve. Bushmen had allegedly been constantly raiding Herero cattle, and an eighteen-strong Herero commando unit had set out on horseback to recover the cattle but lost a man to a poisoned arrow. Hoveka twice apprehended the Bushman culprits, but on each occasion the reserve superintendent had released them because of insufficient evidence, despite the fact that they had admitted their guilt.[4] The alleged troublemakers were all Bushmen who had lived among Herero for some time and then moved

to other parts of the reserve. This suggests that Herero-Bushmen relations were not that satisfactory from the Bushman perspective. In conclusion, Headman Hoveka asked for government compensation for the
losses he and his people had sustained and requested permission to catch
and kill the offending Bushmen, as the government was apparently
incapable of dealing with them. Because Bushmen were "snakes," he
wanted them removed from his reserve (SWAA, A158/7, Magistrate
Gobabis, May 1927; A50/25, Deputation to Magistrate Gobabis, May
1927).

There is a problem of locating cases dealing with Herero-Bushman
conflict, because police rarely patrolled the native reserves (SWAA, A3/
50, 21 September 1928).[5] Special police patrols were mounted to the
reserves only after numerous representations were made by irate Herero.
When Herero did exact justice on their own accord (as was usually the
case), they seldom reported the case to the reserve superintendent. Thus,
for example, the superintendent of Otjituo reported on one futile patrol,
"I am inclined to believe that the Hereros suspecting the Bushmen of
being the thieves attacked them and probably inflicted casualties and for
that reason have conveniently lost all sense of direction" (SWAA, A158/
10/1–6, Grootfontein, 26 June 1925). Nor would Bushmen be inclined
to report abuses because they were sufficiently intimidated by Herero.[6]

The Etosha Game Park

For most of the years between the two wars, the Etosha Game Park
was under the aegis of the warden, Captain Nelson, or, after 1928, the
native commissioner of Ovamboland, who served as part-time warden.
Nelson's policy was to "advise Bushmen on the boundaries to seek work
or leave the vicinity of the farms. . . . I also informed them that they
would not be interfered with in the Game Reserve providing they did
not poison the waters or trespass on occupied farms" (SWAA, A 511/1,
Nelson to Sec., 5 October 1922; see also ADM 5503/1).

Four years later Nelson concluded that his policy had been successful:
The practice of not punishing Bushmen for killing game had reduced
stock-theft losses on neighboring farms, and the presence of Bushmen
in the park had not resulted in a decrease of game there or even of game
being frightened away. Bushmen were able to move in and out of the
park with ease, and many of them did so, as they made good farm
servants "and are most reliable herds [herdsmen]." Unfortunately, tuberculosis and venereal disease were rampant and this meant a low rate of
reproduction (SWAA, A50/67/2, 10 August 1926). Policy until the
creation of a Department of Nature Conservation after World War II
thus amounted to tolerance and, occasionally, active encouragement of

Bushman resettlement into the park,[7] including both Heikom and Kung (Farson 1941:77).

In general, Bushmen were appreciated in the Etosha Game Park. As Hahn[8] put it in a pamphlet for the Wembley Exhibition in 1935:

> In the precinct of these places a study can also be made of the wild Bushmen resident there. They form part and parcel of this sanctuary and afford an interesting study for those anxious to acquaint themselves with their life and pursuits. For small quantities of tobacco these Bushmen will keenly collect firewood, help visitors to establish their camps and are most useful and clever in erecting "skerms" for close-up game photography. (15 October 1935, NAO 33/1)

But the Bushmen, apart from helping to sustain the image of "wild" Africa, were also appreciated for their economic role: They were useful informants against any white poachers, stray stock and Ovambo labor deserters. They were obliged to assist in keeping the water holes open and were available for cheap piecework labor, like combatting veld fires and constructing roads, whenever called upon. Indeed, to reiterate, seen within a wider perspective, the game reserves with their "wild" Bushmen formed a convenient form of social control for recalcitrant migrant workers because the system discouraged desertion.

Native Reserves Beyond the Police Zone

Generally it appears that Bushmen got on well in Ovamboland. In times of drought, Bushmen often moved in and lived with Ovambo families, usually those with whom they had previously established trading ties (South Africa 1931; Heintze 1972). When old Bushmen could not fend for themselves, they too would attach themselves to an Ovambo household (NAO, Annual Report, Ovamboland, 1939). After such a move, the men would generally assist their hosts in moving their livestock to outlying cattle posts during the winter months (NAO, Annual Report, Ovamboland, 1933). Stock theft by Bushmen was unknown, and they would often return strayed cattle (Schoeman n.d.[a]). Indeed, as Schoeman later noted, a surprising number of Bushmen had settled down in Ovambo-style houses and had fields and cattle.

Perhaps the best social indicator of discrimination involves sex. Ovambo intermarriage appears to have been quite common with Heikom Bushmen, but not so common with Kung. It was not only a case of Ovambo men marrying Bushman women but also the other way around, and there was no stigma attached to the offspring of such unions.[9] It was not just commoners who intermarried. Paramount Chief Martin of the

Ondonga, Chief Kathikua, and the father of the former Ngandjera chief, Tshanika, were all "half-blooded" Heikom, according to Hahn (SWAA, A50/188/5, Annual Report, 1939).

Hahn sharply contrasted this near-idyllic situation with that of the Heikom living immediately south, in the Police Zone:

> The Heikom have perhaps suffered more than any other Bushman tribe. . . . Their various family clans or groups have become disintegrated and have been pushed further and further north . . . latterly by our own settlement schemes. Their hunting grounds and *veld kos* [plant foods] areas have either been completely taken from them or have shrunk to such an extent that in very many cases the wild or semi-wild Heikom today finds it almost impossible to eke out an existence. . . . It is surprising that these people do not indulge in more cattle and stock thieving. (SWAA, A50/25[1])

The situation of the Kung living closer to the Kavango River was, to a degree, slightly different from that pertaining in Ovamboland; this is usually attributed to the relative natural affluence of the Kavango River region. As one native commissioner put it: "The natives are themselves too lazy to proceed outside the 'inhabited' areas to gather fruit, and rely on the Bushmen to bring it in. In return for this service, the Bushmen are allowed to reside on the outskirts of the inhabited area during the reaping season, and greatly assist to finish off the meager crop of grain" (South Africa 1934:45). Of course, it might not have been so much a matter of laziness as of fear of possible Bushman attack, which occurred frequently at times. Annual reports for the interwar years contain no reference to Bushmen living permanently attached to black settlements in the Kavango Reserve. In 1939 the mission doctor, A. Krause, characterized Bushman-Kavango relationships as symbiotic. Bushmen came at the harvest and assisted in the gleaning. When there was a drought or food shortage on the river, the Kavango people sought food from their "little friends." There was no sign of violence (Krause 1939:81). But the situation was changing: By 1945 Bushmen were reported to have "learnt to rely on Ovambo and Okavangos in times of shortage and have, in consequence, acquired the habit of eating cereals, which is obtained in exchange for ostrich eggshells, *veldkos* and honey" (SWAA, A50/188/10, Annual Report Okavango 1945). Four years later the medical officer was able to discern a definite process: "Seemingly more and more Bushmen migrate to the banks of the Okavango every year, to assist the natives in the harvesting season in exchange for food, tobacco, beads, etc. The influence of the easier existence . . . [is] appreciated by the Bushmen who will stay for longer and longer periods every year" (SWAA, A50/ 67).

Details on the nature of these relationships are scarce. What data we have must be seen in the context of the Okavango. For example, a survey of 364 households, conducted in the Sambiu "tribal" area as late as the early 1960s, found that the households were composed of eighteen different "ethnic" groups. Only 98 households were classified as Sambiu, whereas 156 were classified as belonging to the four other "recognized tribes" of the Kavango, namely, Kwangari, Djiriku, Mbunza and Mbukushu. The other 110 households consisted of thirteen "foreign tribes" (Bruwer 1966a). This is consistent with the historical record. Most of the so-called Okavango tribes settled on the southern banks of the Okavango River only after 1900, as the area was regarded as the domain of Bushmen (Gibson 1981).[10] Indeed, the Okavango is the only area in Namibia where place names derived from Kung words are still to be found (e.g., as in "Djiriku").

The dominant economic-political structure that emerged with black settlement of the southern banks of the Okavango was a form of slavery, or bondsmanship, as Bishop Gotthardt preferred to call it (Gotthardt, in SWAA, A403/1).[11] Some estimates of slavery ran as high as 50 percent of the adult population. As Gotthardt explained the system, each headman had a number of *wapika,* or subjects, who in turn had their own *wapika.* Each subject was supposed to work and assist his master, and the master was supposed to provide his or her subject with fields for planting. Many Okavango chiefs and headmen had Bushman hunters working fulltime for them and would entrust firearms to them (Engelbrecht 1922; Wust 1938). "Foremen" were officials appointed by headmen to oversee wards. The foreman Langhans, who was located twenty miles from the Kavango on the Omuramba Omatako, had a Bushman bodyguard of between fifteen and twenty men (SWAA, A3/36/1, 1924). Typically, these Bushmen resided about a mile away from the kraal of their "patron," just outside what was ethnocentrically defined as the "inhabited" area. Bushmen were also employed as cattle herders. Cattle theft, however, was common, according to the native commissioner, because the Kavango did not attach as much value to their cattle as did the Herero, nor did they employ enough herders.

The conclusion reached in the 1945 annual report seems to have been the norm: Bushmen "are not molested or harassed by the natives and are not interfered with by the Administration unless they commit the more serious crimes" (SWAA, A50/188/10, Annual Report, 1945; also NAR 11/7, 19 January 1938; A50/67/2).

Chapter 14

Reaction and Counterreaction

> The biggest native difficulty in this district is the labor-evading, game-destroying, stock-thieving Bushman who roams all over the district causing trouble. He is a slippery customer and very difficult to lay by the heels for offenses committed.
>
> —*Magistrate Outjo*

Bushmen did not mutely accept police and other settler activities. On the contrary, especially in the Nurugas area, the scene of most of the "Bushman trouble" during the German era, Bushmen were, according to settlers, becoming rather audacious. Evidence of this buildup in fractiousness was visible some time before the farmers started to complain vociferously. In 1925, the magistrate expressed concern at the large number of squatters in the district, which was, he felt, leading to increased poaching. The coming of the squatters was facilitated by the fact that many farm owners were leaving their farms in the care of indigenes so as to take up work themselves or were the owners of several farms. In the Nurugas area, nine of the sixteen farms were unoccupied. In such circumstances police had difficulty in differentiating between squatters and servants (SWAA, A50/6, 8 October 1925). In 1926, eighteen Grootfontein farms had resident indigene families of more than ten members (the legal maximum) and these were mostly in the Nurugas area, where Bushmen were indigenous to the locale and thus difficult to move (SWAA, A50/6).

By 1927, Bushmen were fighting back: Farmer Weinrebe of Nuiseb complained that a Bushman had openly challenged him, and that a party of 100 had attacked his kraal at night but had been driven off with rifle fire. The Bushman who had issued the challenge was allegedly the same one who had stabbed the local police constable, van Heerden, and wounded farmer van Zyl of Nuitsas. A patrol sent out to investigate this event found, except for between ten and fifteen foot tracks, no evidence of an attack (SWAA, A50/26, 25 August 1927). After the Weinrebe case, Grootfontein police were inundated with complaints from farmers in the area (SWAA, A50/26, 8 January 1928), capped by a strongly worded petition that pointed out that these depredations were "scaring away potential settlers." The petitioners pleaded for more police to constantly harass Bushmen, all Bushmen to be relocated east of the Omuramba Ovambo and Omuramba Omatako, cattle theft to be made a capital offense and captured Bushmen to be deported for life to the southern Guano Islands, off the Namibian coast (see Appendix). In forwarding this petition to the administrator, Magistrate Scott cautioned that farmers could easily take matters into their own hands (SWAA, A50/26, 27 October 1927). He was, no doubt, speaking from experience.

An official inspection of the Nurugas police station lent credence to the farmers' claims. Subinspector Mason found that Bushman crime had "increased in leaps and bounds," as evident from the twenty-three unsolved cases for the year—seventeen stock thefts, three malicious damage to property cases, two assaults, one escape and one attempted murder. His recommendations were draconian. The number of white and black police was to be increased until such time as all "Bushmen were dead, in gaol, or were outside the Police zone." More pertinent, Mason felt that local police lacked individual responsibility since they had not attempted to kill the culprits when they fled. Such action was warranted by the First Schedule of the Police Act, which stipulated that killing a fleeing person or someone who is resisting arrest was "justifiable homicide": "All members of the force know this, yet they seem to fear the consequences of doing their duty. In the interests and honour of the Force to which I belong, I am prepared to tell the men that I want the criminals [dead or alive] and I will shoulder the responsibility and should there be trouble in regard to native policy, the Administration can deal with me as it thinks fit" (SWAA, A50/26, 19 December 1927).

Magistrate Scott also investigated the situation and found the fears of the farmers borne out by the facts: Weinrebe of Nuiseb had lost thirty-five cattle since August 1927; Thomas of Buschfeld, forty-four; and van Zyl of Nuitsas, twelve, including six that had been left to rot. "All the farmers were unanimous that the Bushmen were becoming more audacious every day and would fire without provocation on both Europeans and natives." Recently, they had shot at police trackers and whites. Their depredations had not eased off since the first rains, probably because cattle were easier to kill than game. Most of the crimes were said to have been committed by vagrant squatters or by ex-stock-theft convicts (SWAA,

A50/26, 1 December 1927). Scott joined Mason in calling for tougher measures, suggesting that (1) Bushmen should be killed if they attempted to flee arrest; (2) it should be an offense for a Bushman to be unemployed in the Police Zone; (3) it should also be an offense to carry bows and arrows in the Police Zone; (4) in all of the above, Bushmen should be subject to arrest without warrant by any peace officer or private individual and (5) on *werft* raids, any bows and arrows found that could not be traced to individual owners should result in all the males of the *werft* being held jointly responsible (SWAA, A50/26, 10 October 1927).

Later he suggested further countermeasures: more "Bushman messengers" to be employed by the police, which should be expanded, and native constables to be armed when on Bushman patrols. Moreover, it was difficult to secure convictions under the Stock-theft Proclamation, and the Vagrancy Proclamation was wholly inadequate: "It is absurd to order a Bushman to go and work for anyone as he runs off as soon as he gets to the farm." To stiffen these laws, penalties should be increased from three to twelve months' imprisonment, and the sentence of employment be made permissive instead of peremptory. With such changes, the police would be "able to round up a good many of the beggars." Although hunger was not a compelling factor, emergency food supplies should be made available to "wild" Bushmen at Karakuwisa during times of drought (SWAA, A50/26, 1 and 29 December 1927).

Many of Scott's recommendations were implemented. Six extra Bushman "messengers" were hastily engaged. Horses were brought in to replace the unwieldy camels at Nurugas and the number of police strengthened. Informal policy also changed. For example, with regard to imprisonment, the chief native commissioner suggested that Bushman prisoners serving sentences over two months be sent to jail in Windhoek (SWAA, A50/26, 28 October 1927). Scott replied that he planned to send to Windhoek Bushman prisoners serving sentences of even less than two months and "when these Bushmen are released from there it might be possible to obtain employment for them in Windhoek or further south and so relieve the situation here" (SWAA, A50/26, 10 November 1927). Only the second part of the proposal was rejected on the grounds that Bushmen would "pine away" and potential employers would be hesitant about hiring them because of their reputation.

Tightening the Legal Noose

Most important, the laws were changed. Proclamation 11/1927 sought to prevent squatting by limiting the number of "native families" allowed to live on a farm to five. Similarly, the Vagrancy Proclamation was amended (by Proclamation 31/1927) to increase prison terms from three to twelve months. More critical, in terms of securing convictions, the words "judgement of the magistrate" were changed to "opinion of the court." Most draconian of all, the Arms and Ammunition Proclamation was amended (by the Government Notice II of January 12, 1928) to include Bushman bows and arrows under the definition of firearms, thus making their possession illegal without a license issued by the local magistrate.

These measures, according to Scott, had the desired effect. In his annual report for 1928, he was able to state that a large number of Bushman stock thieves had been "rounded up." The vagrancy law was of the greatest assistance in dispersing Bushmen when there was insufficient evidence for securing conviction. Repeat offenses, which tended to occur when the Bushmen were released from prison, were countered by imposing longer sentences and encouraging Bushmen to move away from Grootfontein. The increased police contingent was able to "continually harass the various bands and now there was only one band left."

The "bow and arrow" law raised important legal questions.[1] Its purpose, as Scott explained it, was to force Bushmen "to enter regular service on the farms . . . or else to take up residence beyond the Police Zone" (SWAA, A50/26, 21 March 1928). Despite the attorney general's opinion that possession of "Bushman bows" was discriminatory as there was no such thing as a Bushman bow, and despite questions from various magistrates on how to differentiate between, say, a Herero bow and a Bushman bow, the legislation has remained unchanged. Possession of a Bushman bow requires a license, but no fees for bow licenses were ever fixed, nor have any Bushmen ever applied for licenses, although one farmer did apply on behalf of his Bushman laborers and was turned down. Whites apparently do not require licenses and have not been prosecuted for being in possession of "Bushman bows," as in such cases they have been defined as "curios."

But what of Scott's proposal to establish a food-supply depot for Bushmen beyond the Police Zone so that in time of drought they would not have to trek to the farm areas and steal stock? In 1933 there was such a terrible famine that over fifty Bushmen from Karakuwisa trekked to Nurugas and tried to obtain employment on white farms. Since these farmers were adequately supplied with labor and there was a danger of cattle theft, police allowed the Bushmen to squat at the police station. Police reported that there was no food in the Sandveld, and most Bushmen were forced to subsist on the gum of thornbush. Surprise raids on their *werfts* disclosed no food and no *veldkos*. Kemp, the South West Africa Company employee stationed at Karakuwisa, reported that Bushmen were begging for food and that the Grootfontein farmers could suffer depredations. The magistrate refused to consider food aid because he believed that if rations were issued "it will simply encourage the Bush-men to rely on this" (SWAA, A50/26, 6 May 1933).

How successful were these measures to control Bushman depreda-tions? The Grootfontein magistrate's annual reports tell the tale. By 1929 the "gangs of Bushmen were finally broken up" and there was no Bushman trouble because "they seem to dread long terms of imprison-ment and hard labor . . . they only come near the [Police] Zone [now] for water." Police policy of inducing Bushmen to work on local farms after release from jail also served to discourage Bushman resistance. But by 1930 there was a reported increase in stock theft, up to fifty-three from thirty-three, not in the Nurugas area, but in the area to the north and west of Tsumeb. Most of this stock theft was allegedly committed by Bushmen resident on farms. As the police commandant explained it:

> Bushmen released from gaol have no doubt given their friends full details of prison life, and the bodily labour which they had to perform and it was evident that the impression made in their minds has undoubt-edly had the desired effect. Wandering Bushmen were seldom heard of and appear to have trekked into the Sandveld beyond the Police Zone. They seem to have realized that the police had the position well in hand, and were being aided by members of their own tribe as trackers. (SWAA, 29 December 1930, LGR 3/1/16)

By 1931, however, the Nurugas Bushmen had "recommenced oper-ations," and in 1932 it was obvious to the magistrate that severe prison sentences were no deterrent. In 1933, 111 cases were reported. To cope with this increase, the magistrate reduced the long sentences and im-posed lashes in all instances, but again to no apparent effect. In 1934, probably on account of the good rains in December 1933, the number of stock thefts dropped to 98, with "the Bushmen beyond the Police Zone [being] most persistent." In 1935 the number of stock-theft cases dropped further, to 73, because of the continued good rains and the fact that many of the Bushmen left the Police Zone rather than surrender their "illegal" bows and arrows. In 1936 all Bushmen in the Tsumeb district were reported to be working for white farmers and in the following year, only 21 cases of stock theft were reported. The last year for which I could find reports, 1938, showed only 28 cases.

In summary, the original police strategy was to arrest "all and sundry in the neighborhood of the crime" (ADM 3823/8, Gage to Sec., 9 October 1919). The policy of increasing the size of the legal stick with which to batter Bushmen into submissive labor continued until 1935 when the police changed their official policy. In 1947 Chief Inspector Naude, a long-serving officer and avid amateur "Bushmanologist," provided a valuable historical perspective of an insider on police policy toward Bushmen. It is worth quoting in extenso. Initially he said:

> Specific cases were rarely dealt with, as this was impossible and a general clean-up was usually indulged in, which in a number of cases led to clashes in which some of our men and Native Affairs officials as well as animals were killed and dangerously wounded by poisoned arrows.
>
> The net result being that a number of Bushmen were arrested for all sorts of contraventions and escorted to the nearest Court, a considerable distance from their werfts, leaving the women and children behind to fend for themselves, only to be sentenced to 7 or 14 days on petty charges, amongst other for wandering about without a pass, which it is perfectly obvious they could not have, as they had nowhere to get it from.
>
> The net result of such action was to antagonize them further, with the result that they regarded all white men with suspicion and the natives, especially the Hereros, as oppressors, whom they sought to avoid and against whom they were ready to defend themselves if cornered.
>
> In short, we learned by experience that our methods, instead of bringing them within the scope of the Administration's Native Policy, drove them into the bush, and under cover; consequently we could not procure the result we aimed at, namely that of domesticating the Bushman. . . . About 1935 we decided against these organized patrols and adopted a policy of befriending them through our police patrols, who were instructed not to arrest them for all sorts of petty offenses, but to instruct them to reside at water-holes beyond the Police Zone or occupied area. (SWAA, SW51/47, Circular to all District Commandants, 3 April 1947)

From Object to Subject in Bushman Banditry

Clearly, ecological factors played an important role in determining the pattern of raids on livestock and migrant workers. Data from court records show a close correlation between frequency of stock thefts and lack of rainfall. This was true for the annual cycle as well as for longer drought cycles. In the annual cycle, October was the peak month for stock theft because it was just before the rains when the veld was dry. Game was not only scarce at this time, but it was also easier for farmers to track lost or stolen livestock so they were more aware of thefts during this period. A further inducement to stock theft during this period was that it was also the most uneconomic period in the ranching cycle, and thus farmers were frugal in providing meat to their work force. In the longer cycles, it is clear that drought brought larger than average numbers of Bushmen to farms and that stock thefts thus increased. Indeed, even attacks on Kavango laborers coincided with periods of drought and famine.

Perhaps the most remarkable feature of the pattern of stock theft and social banditry was the general adaptability of Bushmen to changes in the environment and settler reprisals. Bushmen would, for example, steal horses belonging to Herero residents in Epukiro Native Reserve, use the horses in hunting and then kill them so that Herero were unable to use them in tracking the Bushmen. Bushmen were also frequently aware of changes in local police strength, and this had a significant impact on raiding. For example, Captain Swemmer, the Grootfontein police commander, complained that the Bushmen squatting at police stations at Otjituo, Nurugas and Auuns were not working but observing police movements, which they then reported to their bandit friends (ADM 13/36, 25 October 1919). And the well-known bandit Zameko was aware that the police post at Epukiro had been closed down shortly before he "declared war." This also accounts for the resurgence of Bushman banditry during World Wars I and II, when most of the rural police stations had only a token staff. Typically Bushmen stole from three to seven head of cattle, although on occasion they would snatch up to sixty head of sheep, herding these to distances of up to eighty miles from the farm. They were also quite capable of waging wars of attrition against unpopular farmers. Thomas, the manager of farm Foxhof, reported that over a period of six years his flock of 1,500 sheep had been reduced to 70 (H.J.K. 1921), and this was clearly not only the result of disease and other natural causes of attrition.

During the initial period of colonialism, a herd of varying size might be driven off, but this pattern gradually changed to an occasional slaughter, with the meat being carried off to the encampment. Given the environmental and social constraints, such behavior was appropriate. To drive a herd of livestock into the Kalahari not only left a highly visible trail but also slowed down the speed of flight from expected pursuers. Killing one beast at a time, in contrast, minimized the possibility of discovery. Numerous stock-theft cases involved a number of cattle or sheep that were killed at irregular intervals of about a month. Police observers were, at times, amazed at how quickly meat or artifacts stolen from whites were dispersed or consumed, in short, placed into the exchange network (Wiessner 1982). This should not be surprising: It is an inevitable result of the fact that the police saw possession of such articles or any quantity of meat as tantamount to proof of theft.

Settler observation that Bushmen were becoming "increasingly shy of contact with whites" (H.J.K. 1921; Engelbrecht 1922) actually noted an adaptive response to punitive measures. When forced to move away, the Bushmen sometimes fled to Botswana (Hermans 1977). However, at

other times their behavior could only be described as downright audacious. Farmer Friederichs complained that after the court case in which
he was accused of inciting his "tame" Bushmen to kill a cattle thief, "the
Kalahari have become so bold as to stone one of my cattle herd[er]s who
attempted to prevent them driving off my animals so that he had to leave
them in their hands whilst going for assistance" (ADM 3360, 27 February 1923). Farmer Weinrebe complained that Bushmen had sent him a
challenge, telling him exactly when they were going to raid his cattle
kraal. They then engaged in some psychological warfare and built large
bonfires around his kraal. Bushman action often involved more than just
a few isolated individuals; indeed there is clear evidence that there was a
larger common consciousness of their oppression by settlers. Describing
one of his efforts to arrest some Bushmen on the outskirts of a farm,
Lieutenant Hull found that "during our absence Ackermann's tobacco
garden had been looted and destroyed by another party of Bushmen. No
doubt that the so-called tame Bushmen are in league with the cattle
stealers and should be removed from their present abode. They have
given warning to wild Bushmen as to the movements of white men"
(ADM 273, 24 December 1915). Bushman solidarity was frequently
expressed in the following manner: "Immediately the police took action
and arrested a number of Bushmen . . . all the Bushmen in the employ
of the complainant deserted his service, leaving him and his wife to do
the caring of their stock themselves" (South Africa 1923).

Perhaps the most important reason for Bushman shyness, but one
that settlers did not believe Bushmen capable of, was the desire to escape
colonial domination. In 1920, Deputy Police Commissioner Kirkpatrick
visited farmer Thomas in the Nurugas area, where he met a Bushman
woman who had given birth to three boys while resident on the farm
and had killed all three of them: "She says she will not bring up boys in
order that they have to work for white men! She has no grudge against
white people, but she adopts the idea that Bushmen should not work for
white people and is not going to have any child of hers so doing" (H.J.K.
1921:177).[2]

Sometimes one suspects a sophisticated appreciation of the situation
that was not always immediately apparent, for example, farmer Metzger
complained that he had over seventy Bushmen squatting on his farm
who had refused to budge because two of them had been state witnesses
in a recent court case and friends of the convicted had apparently sworn
vengeance. Metzger appealed to the government for help in providing
rations for them, for fear that otherwise they might engage in stock theft
(SWAA, A50/25, 14 June 1935).[3]

The major reason for Bushman success in maintaining their banditry
for so long lay in their ability to split up into small groups and survive off

the land. In their Kaukauveld heartland they were the rulers: Few outsiders could permanently penetrate it, even with camels, and hope to capture them. "Both Bechuanas and Hereros are afraid of the Natives on the hinterland who threaten to kill them should they trespass on what they call their veld. The position would be reversed did they carry arms," wrote the Gobabis magistrate (SWAA, A396/7, 22 July 1925).

Chapter 15

Bushmen "Tamed": Life on the Farm

It is the mediocre citizens who set the general tone of the colony. They are the true partners of the colonized, for it is the mediocre who are most in need of compensation and of colonial life. It is between them and the colonized that the most typical colonial relationships are created. They will hold on so much more tightly to those relationships, to the colonial system, to their *status quo*, because their entire colonial existence—they have a presentiment of it—depends thereon. They have wagered everything, and for keeps, on the colony.

—*Albert Memmi*

Debate and argument about the successful transformation of Bushmen into "useful" workers continued.[1] Although some farmers and officials were sympathetic, Paul Barth spoke for the settler majority. The Bushman, he wrote, "with his wrinkled skin, bloated stomach, and sly, cunning eyes, looks like a beast of prey himself . . . they seem to be dying out and no-one will be any worse for their loss, as they are destroyers rather than producers" (Barth 1926:150).

The secretary for South West Africa concurred: "The only solution for the Bushmen, if there is one, is their absorption in other tribes or apprenticeship to farmers who will give them a square deal and get the children to settle down as stock-herds, otherwise they must gradually die out" (SWAA, A198/26, 1 June 1938). Children as apprentices not only provided cheap labor but in effect served as hostages and thus guaranteed the continued good behavior of "wild Bushmen."

The point about complaints by farmers is that they protested too much: Farmers derived considerable benefits from exploiting Bushmen. Indeed, in many cases, it was this exploitation that ensured the economic viability of their farms. Bushmen were taken into employment by farmers for a variety of reasons, but the chief one was undoubtedly economic. As the experienced Grootfontein magistrate put it:

> Mr. H. will get value for every penny he spends on the Bushmen, in fact, I believe he will get more value by employing Bushmen than if he were to employ other natives, because Bushmen are usually satisfied with wages in kind such as tobacco, beads, material, etc., and there need be no cash disbursements. A Bushman has no sense of value of these articles and will render the service required by his master for them without considering their intrinsic value. (SWAA, A50/67, Mgte Gtftn to CNC, 15 April 1939)[2]

Another important reason for hiring Bushmen was for protection. Settlers believed that "tame" Bushmen would deter "wild" Bushmen from raiding cattle on the farm (SWAA, A50/26, Hulsmann to Volkmann, 14 March 1939).[3] Moreover, if stock theft occurred, "tame" Bushmen were used to track and punish the raiders (*Rex v. Hans and Josef* 1922 SCW). Additionally, Ovambo contract farm workers were especially prone to deserting in the northern districts like Grootfontein. Grootfontein was the depot for contract workers en route to and from their reserves, and there was a constant flow of Ovambo speakers in this region. It was thus relatively easy for contract workers to trade identity documents or work their way home or south, where they could pose as passless Ovambo speakers and get repatriated home. Moreover, police were strikingly unsuccessful in apprehending these deserters. Bushman deserters, in contrast, because of their more parochial social boundaries, were relatively easier to track down because they had usually left relatives on the farm[4] (NAO 24/8, NC Ondangua to CNC, 18 February 1947).

But perhaps the most important reason for hiring Bushmen as workers was to prevent "trouble," especially if the farm was in an area that traditionally belonged to Bushmen. Missionary Vedder, influential doyen of Namibian ethnography, unblushingly advised farmers on how to neutralize resistance to such land theft:

> If a farmer buys a farm from the government, and if a Bushman band lives on this hitherto uncultivated land, it depends as a rule upon the attitude of the farmer how his future will shape itself. The farmer in himself is not disliked by the Bushmen, for on occasion one can get much from him which otherwise must be dispensed with, e.g., tobacco and matches. In addition, the farmer will cultivate only a small portion of the land. The loss of a piece of land does not greatly disturb the Bushman, since his hunting territory is great . . . nor does the fact that he runs cattle on the land make very much difference, for the Bushman has no use for the grass, and the wild game of the veld will still have

enough. But there are three things which arouse the anger and vengeance of the Bushman. One must not forbid him to use the water, to
hunt, and to gather veldkos. Whoever does so declares war against him,
and the challenge is accepted. The history of many a farm is witness to
this. There are many farmers who wish to have no other laborers on
their farms than the young men of a Bushman band resident on the
land. Theft seldom occurs, and the people do not desert from their
work. The old Bushmen are happy that their young people can bring
them tobacco, matches and similar things. They themselves like their
old Bushman life without disturbance. But other farmers dare hardly
go about without fear of the poisoned arrow, for in sheer ignorance,
they have declared war against the Bushman either by trying to drive
them away from the farm, or by forbidding them the three main sources
of life. For this reason, the Government, when it sells a farm in the
country of the Bushman, should make it a condition of sale that the
Bushmen living on the land must not be denied rights of water, hunting
and veldkos. This condition would really be of importance for only a
relatively short period. Once the younger generation of Bushmen is
accustomed to work, and the older generation has died out, the matter
will have adjusted itself. (Vedder 1937:435–436)[5]

Some farmers did not have Bushmen resident on their farms when
they moved in, nor did they have access to other labor. In such cases, the
temptation to engage in "manstealing" was especially strong, if there
was a Bushman band or two within range. The Boltman brothers, who
farmed south of Gobabis, were well-known exponents of this art. On one
occasion they captured twenty-eight Bushmen and forced them to work
on their two farms. They did not report this matter to the police, even
when some of the Bushmen deserted. Instead, they recaptured and
chased them back to the farm by driving them in front of their horses
(SWAA, A50/27, Station Commander, Pretorius, 16 April 1926).

A manstealing cause célèbre was *Rex v. Brand and two others* 1929
SCW. Three young white Gobabis district farmers rode out and captured
approximately fifty Bushmen. After setting fire to their huts, the farmers
chased the Bushmen through the night in front of their horses to the
farms, where the Bushmen were allotted among the farmers as laborers.
A police constable who passed through the area a few days later con-
doned the manstealing by arresting and jailing some of the Bushmen for
being in possession of *löffelhund* (jackal) skins. After serving five days in
jail, the Bushmen were returned to the farmers. The court held that
manstealing could not be proven because the Bushmen could have easily
escaped and found the accused guilty on an alternative charge of assault
and fined them 5 English pounds.[6]

Although the use of small children as labor hostages was more
common than generally believed (see, for example, Sangiro 1954; Wendt

1981),[7] no statistics on the number of "apprentices" were recorded. Moreover, not all farmers went to such extremes, and there were cases of Bushmen actively seeking employment on some white farms. Indeed such behavior not only was a recognized foraging strategy but more often than not was a way of seeking protection from police or other human predators (Bleek 1922:50; SWAA, A50/26, Hulsmann to Volkmann, 14 March 1939).

Once Bushmen were recruited, they had to be retained and prevented from deserting. Some techniques used by farmers have been alluded to, especially the crucial role of children. A vast area of manipulation involved the legal system. Bushmen could not be forced to enter into service contracts, but if they refused, could be charged under the Vagrancy or Masters and Servants Proclamation. The contract system was easily abused. It often happened that none of the farm workers were present at the attestation of their contracts by police, nor were they aware that their contracts had been renewed. Their employers simply kept their contracts and paid them every two months (*Rex v. Halberstadt* 1917 SCC).[8] Twenty years later a senior police officer complained that the Masters and Servants Proclamation (1920) was frequently abused by "a certain class of farmer" who encouraged Bushmen to settle on their farms so that they could be used for cheap labor, receiving little or no wages. These Bushmen frequently deserted and the farmer would then charge them with desertion, which meant that a special police patrol had to investigate. This situation had reached such proportions that he felt compelled to suggest that Bushmen be specifically excluded from the Masters and Servants Proclamation, unless the contract was validated by an authorized officer and included the provision that Bushmen be allowed to return to the veld periodically to collect *veldkos* (SWAA, A50/67/2, Naude to Police Commissioner, 15 July 1938).

As Bushmen were usually employed on outlying farms, they were subject to two special forms of control. First, there was peonage: The farm owner would supply the Bushmen with goods against a future wage and because this debt was never quite wiped out, they were obligated to remain (see, for example, *Rex v. Voswinkel* 1918 SCC). Second, Bushmen subject to the personal abuse of the farmer were unaware or unable to obtain legal redress except by accident.[9] A single example must suffice.

A Grootfontein farmer suspected a Bushman of stealing, so the Bushman was "tied with a riem [leather thong] around his neck and made to run before the farmer's horse for 4 km. He was then laid over a cart and thrashed, after which he was hauled up by his neck until his feet only touched the ground and was found in this situation when the police came to investigate the theft. The farmer received a 5 pound fine or 1 month imprisonment" (South Africa 1925).[10]

More often than not, farmers saw reporting offenses committed under the Masters and Servants Proclamation as a waste of effort because they might have to travel over 200 kilometers, pay hotel expenses and leave their farms unattended only to see the offender being fined a pound or sentenced to a month in jail, which they regarded "as a holiday." Thus it was not only banditry that flourished in such circumstances of under-developed communications but also informal retributive justice from the settler farmer.[11]

Descriptions of life on the farms for Bushmen during this period are rare. According to the retired German officer, Volkmann, the major role changes involved women. "How different is the life of a Bushwoman in the farm location. She gets plenty of good food without any extraordinary exertion together with sugar, tobacco and clothes. She has only to fetch wood and keep the fire going." Small wonder, he concluded, that women did not want to revert to a hunting and gathering life again (SWAA, A50/26, Volkmann to Sec., 1939).

Typically, to judge by annual returns from various police posts, the foodstuffs provided to the Bushmen workers were not as bountiful as Volkmann implied. It was often suggested that the poor quality of rations was the major reason for Bushmen deserting. At Sandfontein, in the Gobabis district, for example, rations consisted of mielie-meal and mielies. Families still had to resort to the collection of *veldkos* because "farmers . . . very seldom ration their laborers with meat, a delicacy which the Bushman cannot do without" (South Africa 1939). As a magistrate put it, "The average Bushman in employment is not over fed, and many persons consider a supply of milk, some tobacco and *veldkos* [which the Bushman has to provide for himself] as sufficient" (South Africa 1927).

In 1938, Professor Maingard reported on the bad health conditions of farm Bushmen in the southern Kalahari. In doing so, he was essentially summarizing what was contained in various administration reports. Tuberculosis and venereal disease were prevalent, and nasal catarrh and conjunctivitis were common. There was definite evidence of malnutrition, which led to a greater susceptibility of these people to disease: "On the farms the diet consists chiefly of mielie-meal and coffee, with separated milk, a little tea and sugar, and occasionally, a little goat or sheep flesh. It is no more liberal in quantity than it is in quality. Typical diet on the farms is as follows: eight beakers full of mielie-meal per family per month and an oil tin of separated milk per day. It is not surprising that malnutrition is rife among them" (Maingard 1937:293).[12]

Bushman "wages, if they receive any at all, are always less than those paid to Hereros or Ovambos and their food rations too are less and of inferior quality" (SWAA, A50/67, Hahn to CNC, 5 September 1940). Indeed, one can be more specific: Typically their official wages were half those paid to other workers, including contract workers. When Ovambo were paid 8/- per month, Bushmen were getting 4/-, Bushmen youths 2/- and Bushman females 2/6 (see Radel 1947:460; SWAA, A521/13). These wages were not raised for at least twenty-five years (from 1920 to 1945), so in effect there was a decline in real wages. Not surprisingly, the districts of Grootfontein, Gobabis and Outjo paid the lowest wages in the territory (Radel 1947:45–78), and this correlated with a high percentage of Bushmen in the rural labor force. But even these wages can be deceptive because they were often never paid, as some farmers deducted grazing fees and the value of any livestock lost (SWAA, A521/13, 31 March 1937).

Farmers rationalized low Bushman wages on two grounds: poor physiques and unreliability. Both call for comment: With regard to physique, it seems problematic whether physique was that important in serving as a herd boy; moreover, the question of how farm food affected physique, although arguable, is obviously significant. Bushman unreliability was typified by Bushmen leaving with or without permission during the rainy season and returning when open water and *veldkos* became scarce. Such behavior can hardly be called unreliable, as it was wholly predictable and did not disrupt the round of daily labor as much as it could. The agricultural cycle for a dry-land irrigation farming system in the northwestern Kalahari went through the following sequence. The harvest time peaked in May, and labor was usually required also in April and June. July to September was a period of relative leisure, after which labor was extensively required for the preparation of fields, which were usually completed shortly after the first rains (Leser 1982:147). At no time did the departure of Bushmen during the rainy season create major economic loss or discomfort to the rancher; their temporary absence was more than offset by the fact that during times of labor intensity, the whole Bushman family, the aged, women and children included, provided the needed labor at no or relatively little cost to the rancher.

A common justification used by farmers and officials for low wages was that Bushmen did not appreciate the value of money. They were not interested in receiving cash "because they do not accumulate it. They are more interested in trifles like bright buttons, beads and pebbles," wrote Meintjes in 1939 (SWAA, A50/67, Meintjes Memorandum), and spent their wages on tobacco. In this situation it was easy for officials to blame the victim:

> Many of them are, however, undernourished—generally because they are too lazy to work. Because of this trait they are not usually well paid on the farms as they do not make good reliable servants. They are also inclined to over-indulge in the use of tobacco. They are so prone to this

failing that there are some farmers who obtain their services for nothing more than tobacco and some food. It is admitted that many of them are not worth much more than that. (SWAA, A50/188/11, Native Affairs, Annual Report, 1946)

The number of Bushman workers increased as the number of whites' farms increased. By 1939 Meintjes could report that "now there is hardly a farm in the district where Bushmen farm laborers are not to be seen." They were mostly in the eastern and northern portions of the district, "proving it seems that they yielded to the domination of the white man only when there was practically no further escape" (SWAA, A50/67, Meintjes Memorandum, 1939).

In this process of encirclement it was widely reported that Bushmen "only take employ where they grew up" (SWAA, A50/67, Mag. Gobabis, 20 April 1928; also LGR 3/1/7, Tsumeb, 1945 and *Rex v. Kahoekaboud et al.* 1923 SCW), thereby underlining the importance of traditional Bushman land tenure systems. The point about the maintenance of the traditional hunting-and-gathering life-style in such a truncated form was that it was economically rewarding to the farmer. It subsidized, reproduced and underwrote his farming techniques and profits.

The incorporation of Bushmen into settler agriculture was aided by activities of missionaries. Again missionary policy was not monolithic. By all accounts the influence of the Catholics was minimal, whereas that of the Lutherans was significant.

Missionary Efforts: The Roman Catholics

Of the various missionary groups, the Catholics have had the least immediate influence on the future of Bushmen, if only because of the Catholics' relative lack of resources. After World War I, the work of proselytizing among farm Bushman laborers was continued by Fathers Jaeger of Grootfontein and Schulte of Tsumeb and, judging by alarmist Rhenish missionary reports, was quite successful. However, the large infusion of dour Afrikaner Calvinist farmers in the Gobabis and Grootfontein districts soon made farm visits rather difficult.[13]

At the same time, clergy were reassessing their relationship to Bushmen. In 1938, the long-serving Kavango priest, Father Wust, pointed out how unpredictable Bushmen were and that it was very difficult to generalize about them: "The Bushman is the unlucky child of the moment. He acts according to his moods—today like this, tomorrow like that. Sometimes he is a courageous hero and soon again the poorest coward, then again a harmless child or the cruelest most unscrupulous villain. He can live with hunger and thirst like no other, but no other person can beat his greed and eat as much as he can" (Wust 1938:258; see also Gotthardt 1933:82–83).

Assessing the mission's chances of gaining Bushmen converts, he wrote:

> If the Bushman would settle down, our reform work would not be so difficult. Under present circumstances a regular influence over the Bushmen is impossible. If we could get the Bushmen to settle down and to learn agriculture we could prevent them from dying out and educate them in the Christian faith. The duty of the government should be to save the Bushmen from dying out. I am convinced that the German [?] government, backed by all the informed Germans, would do everything to prevent the demise of this race. . . . On top of it one would not need an endless amount of money to do it. With small means, one could complete a huge service of love. (Wust 1938:329)

Unlike Lutherans, Catholics did not have the ear of the government and unlike that other long-term resident, Vedder, Wust did not try to advise farmers on how to deal with Bushmen who found their lands settled upon by whites. Instead, he raised the basic question: "Even the Bushman has a right to his land. One can only expect him to share it with those who are in need. But no power in the world has the right to disown the Bushman completely and to finish him off like it has been done" (Wust 1938:258). Such searching points obviously did not sit well with those in power, and the Catholics found it better simply to try to consolidate their position in the Kavango.

Missionary Efforts: Lutheran Proselytization

In 1926, and again in 1930, the Reverend Ponnighaus made strong pleas at the annual Lutheran missionary conference for a Bushman Mission. It was scandalous, he cried, that the Rhenish Mission, which had been in the country for eighty years, had no specific mission among Bushmen, who were the oldest and most interesting people on earth. Moreover, both Dr. Fourie, the medical officer for the Mandate (and local Bushman expert), and the secretary for South West Africa acknowledged that the Rhenish Mission had first claim to missionizing the Bushmen. It was important to convert them before the Roman Catholics got to them. Bushmen had to be shown the way to eternal salvation before they became extinct. Ponnighaus concluded his paper, "I ask urgently and from the heart that this matter be taken into consideration, that we propose a future deliverance [and] that we get an American mission interested" (Elok Archives, unsorted).

Perhaps the most dramatic result of Ponnighaus's plea was the work of the Reverend A. Unterkötter of Tsumeb. His numerous publications provide invaluable insights into how he saw his own efforts: The lengthy drought from which the country was suffering was said to be God's way of ensuring that Bushmen came into contact with the Gospel. The drought caused numerous Bushmen to give up their independent existences and squat on farms near water holes. These refugees told Unterkötter: "Messenger of God, you have come to us and cultivated in our hearts a desire for heavenly food. Will you desert us now and forget us and let us starve of hunger for God?" (Halfstuiver-Vereeniging 1935:4–5). "They cried like children because they could not hear God's word" (Unterkötter 1935:30). "Need and hunger sowed the desire for God's word" (Unterkötter 1955:5). Unterkötter and many of the readers of his numerous articles and pamphlets were undoubtedly touched by this plea. With Unterkötter they could share the "pleasure for a Missionary to watch how ready these happy Bushmen are to learn God's word" (Unterkötter 1955:9), beguiled, no doubt, by Unterkötter's portrayal of the missionary situation: "In Bushmanland, there where the Hyenas, Jackhals, Lions and Leopards say good night to each other, on the outermost border of the congregation, the doors for evangelization are wide open. The crop is large, but few are the laborers" (Unterkötter 1955:2).

Working with a succession of evangelists, Unterkötter managed to get more than 2,500 Bushmen into baptism training in less than six months. His method of proselytization was simple: "First we tell them the history of creation so that they can see God's love in Jesus which is what the Bushmen are also looking for in order to be saved . . . [and then we] close with a light song" (Unterkötter 1935:24). Despite such startling successes, there was much work to be done because the number of Bushmen was not 8,000, as officially estimated, but more in the region of 50,000, Unterkötter assured his readers. Fortunately though, some of the local farmers were most helpful. For example, farmer Friederichs, who spoke Bushman fluently, personally prepared over fifty Bushmen for baptism. Later, to his chagrin, Unterkötter discovered that many of these Christian converts were backsliding, which he attributed, not to the irrelevance of what he might be preaching, but rather to the work of the Roman Catholics and the devil. The devil was especially fond of working through the local Bushman sorcerer, and thus the sorcerer had to be neutralized. Unterkötter realized the multifaceted role that sorcerers played in Bushman communities and tried to isolate the sorcerer socially, despite the sorcerer's plea that he was Catholic and wanted to be left alone. To ensure isolation, Unterkötter stationed an evangelist near the residence of the sorcerer and "broke" the sorcerer (Unterkötter 1938).

By 1937, Unterkötter was running into problems with his Bushman Mission, especially after the death of his ace evangelist, Ari, so he took his sabbatical in Germany and was prevented from returning by the outbreak of World War II. In 1947, he returned to Tsumeb and found few Christian Bushmen. He attributed this to poaching by the Roman Catholics, who were bribing the poor Bushmen with more tobacco. His sober conclusion: "The Bushman Mission was a straw fire which burnt out quickly" (Unterkötter 1955).

Some missionaries were uncomfortable with the way in which Unterkötter was exploiting the image of Bushmen. The Reverend A. Wulfhorst wrote from Ovamboland criticizing Unterkötter's stress on the "virginity" of the missionary effort among Bushmen (Wulfhorst 1937). Indeed, one cannot help wondering if publicity was the dominant purpose of Unterkötter's mission. Not only did he solicit overseas contributions, but he even managed to persuade the black congregation in Luderitz to open a special fund for the Bushman Mission. It was not an accident or even God's work that resulted in Unterkötter's taking up his Bushman Mission but, rather, a deliberate political decision. In this crass ideological exploitation of Bushman, which Unterkötter did so masterfully, we have to consider the role of academics as well.

Chapter 16

Academics on the Attack: Ethnological Influence on Bushman Policy

In 1935, at hearings of the South West Africa Constitutional Commission, Vedder, by then head of the Rhenish Missionary Society, successfully argued that two Bushman reserves should be created, one in the north for the Heikom and one in the northeast for the Kung:

> Their language alone justifies the preservation of this primitive race.
> . . . You have reserves for game, you have reserves . . . for the Hereros,
> the Ovambos, and the Okavangos, but you have no reserve for Bush-
> men, yet historically and scientifically Bushmen are entitled to far
> greater consideration than any other of our native tribes. . . . The
> difficulty today is, however, that his lands are gradually being taken
> from him . . . he has been prohibited from trapping or shooting in parts
> which he regarded as his own for generations. (*Cape Argus*, 3 September
> 1935)

Historical Roots of Bushman Reserves

Vedder was not the first academic to suggest the creation of a Bushman reserve. Lebzelter had echoed Muller and von Zastrow in suggesting that the area beyond the Police Zone constituted a de facto reserve for Bushmen, and "Kung . . . will be able to continue living there in peace as there is no hope that this area will ever be usable for farming or as cattle ranges" (Lebzelter 1934b:80).[1]

There was a clear recognition that existing Bushman policy was not working,[2] but the commission's Bushman reserve recommendations received a mixed reception. They found ready support in the scientific community and some bureaucratic championing. Some suggested that the northern Heikom reserve in the Etosha Game Park was already a de facto reserve and the only hindrance to its proclamation was a lack of money (Offe 1937). But at the apex of the civil service there was obstinate resistance. When the Permanent Mandates Commission in Geneva asked the administrator's representative, the secretary of the territory, F. P. Courtney-Clarke, whether Bushman reserves were going to be created, the response was clear:

> Courtney-Clarke—It was impossible to keep them in reserves. As nomads they would require very much land.[3]
> M. van Asbeek—If ever there was a case of a sacred mission (Article 22) it was the present one, where it was a question of safeguarding a native population from complete extinction and defending it against the ills by which it was overwhelmed.
> Courtney-Clarke—Vedder's idea is impractical.
> Mssl. Dannevig—Had the impression that the Administration thought the Bushmen would gradually disappear, because they were an extremely backward people, who made difficulties for the settled population.
> Courtney-Clarke—The Administration did not wish the Bushmen to be exterminated, but considered that the creation of reserves for Bushmen for the benefit of ethnologists was not a practicable solution.[4] He thought that the best solution was that they should be gradually absorbed into the other tribes. (SWAA, copy of minutes in A50/67/2)

The notion of Bushman reserves solely for the benefit of ethnologists was grounded in what some administrators and journalists felt was crass academic and scientific exploitation. Already in 1929 the traveler W. J. Makin had complained:

> As is usual with any disappearing race, the Bushmen have now become an absorbing ethnological study to many pundits in the professional world. Every year white men come to the edge of the Kalahari desert, camp out there with an array of cameras and scientific impediments, and try to entice the nomads of the desert to visit the camp. Tobacco is scattered as lavishly as crumbs to ensnare birds. And the few Bushmen who are in touch with civilization, a type that like a nameless dog will hang about the place where a bone may be flung at them, come into camp and are scientifically examined. (Makin 1929:278)

Such intense scientific interest was not surprising, given the fact that Hedley Chilvers had already reckoned Bushmen as one of the Seven Wonders of southern Africa (Chilvers 1928).

A delegation of Bushmen, led by Donald Bain, on their way to the parliament in Cape Town. As part of his campaign to save the "living fossils" of the southern Kalahari, Bain exhibited Bushmen at the Empire Exhibition in Johannesburg and brought them to Cape Town to ask the government for permission to kill game for food. *Source: Illustrated London News,* 29 May 1937. (Photo courtesy of the Illustrated London News Picture Library)

The Wider Context of the Proposals

Despite the veto by senior officials, Vedder's proposals generated apparent wide support, not only from some influential farmers,[5] but also from South Africa's fledgling scientific community, the members of which eventually succeeded in outmaneuvering the administration's bureaucrats. They had the advantage of widespread public awareness created by a remarkable public campaign launched by the prominent big-game hunter, Donald Bain, to create a reserve for the last of the South African Bushmen in the vicinity of the Kalahari Game Park. In his quest, Bain teamed up with his natural allies, academics.

Bain invited expeditions from the Universities of both Cape Town and the Witwatersrand to visit his Kalahari camp to study Bushmen he had collected for display at the Empire Exhibition. An edited volume resulted from this visit (Rheinhallt-Jones and Doke 1937). Academics and scientists formed committees in Johannesburg and Cape Town to support the Bushman cause. They enthusiastically went about canvassing support. Professor Maingard, for example, raised the question of a Bushman reserve with the Historical Monuments Commission, where "there was a difference of opinion about whether the Bushmen should be regarded as human beings or as fauna. If they were regarded as fauna, the reserve could be proclaimed (laughter)" (*Cape Argus*, 26 February 1937).

When Sir William Clark, the British high commissioner, attended a meeting of the Inter-University Committee for African Studies, he found general agreement on the need for a standing committee on the Bushman question. This committee was to approach the Carnegie Foundation for funds and was to consist of both academics and relevant civil servants (Boydell 1948:110–111). Eventually the committee was composed of Sir William Clark as chairman, Senator Rheinhallt-Jones (director of the South African Institute of Race Relations); Douglas Smit, the secretary for native affairs (also representing the South West Africa [SWA] administration); Mr. Priestman, the resident commissioner for the Bechuanaland Protectorate; and Professors Clement Doke, a linguist, and Isaac Schapera, a social anthropologist.[6]

The outbreak of World War II provided the South West Africa Administration with a convenient excuse for opting out of this collaboration with academics. The administration had never been enthusiastic about the idea of the committee but felt that, in terms of international relations, it had to be involved. It was later to use the supposed activities of the committee as a convenient excuse to defer action on the Bushman "question." The administration, like its colonial counterparts elsewhere, was suspicious of academics.

The Ineffectiveness of Anthropologists

The resentment of the administration toward academics was clearly expressed. When Smit reported on the committee's functions to Courtney-Clarke (the secretary for South West Africa), he did so in the following terms: "The suggestion is a result of the agitation set afoot by Bain and supported by many influential people that we should provide a big reserve for the Bushmen, but we have not been very sympathetic because we feel that it would serve no useful purpose owing to the fact that the Bushmen wander about to such an extent" (SWAA, A198/26, 7 August 1937). Courtney-Clarke replied that he agreed that the Bushman reserve idea was impractical, unless the "whole of Bechuanaland was reserved" and that, besides, it had been tried in the old days in the Cape Province where it had failed.

Part of the administration's ill-feeling toward academics can be attributed to previous experiences with that category. When South Africa took over the territory in 1919, it invited various scientists to undertake research there and even sponsored some of the projects. The Bushmen were the first group to be investigated by an expedition from the South African Museum, but the relationship turned sour when the administration thought that it had been financially shortchanged. The next anthropological researcher to be sponsored was Agnes Winifred Hoernle, who was commissioned to study the recently rebellious Khoi. Hoernle felt compelled to mention in her report the difficulties and widespread social disorganization that she had encountered. The administrator wrote across her report, "This is politics not anthropology." The next academic to apply for funding from the administration was Clement Doke, the Witwatersrand University linguist. Initially he was turned down because of lack of funds, but his persistence led to his university principal, J. H. Hofmeyr, writing to his cousin, Gysbert Hofmeyr, the administrator. This intervention resulted in Doke's obtaining some research funds to study the Kung language. Fifteen years later, when Doke was appointed to the standing committee, Courtney-Clarke recalled this episode and thought that Doke had "taken the administration for a ride."

Resistance to anthropologists was widespread among district officials. Thus Harold Eedes, the Kavango native commissioner, after lamenting the inability of Bushmen to be reliable workers, intoned, "It is unfortunate that, owing to their laziness and destructive customs, the Bushmen living in the Prohibited Area can only be regarded as useful for purposes of anthropological study" (SWAA, A50/26, Eedes to CNC, 16 August 1937).[7]

Academic input on how Bushmen were treated was thus minimal or problematic. Part of the problem was that scientific orthodoxy was so strong that on occasion facts were deliberately trimmed to fit it. If one labels someone a Bushman, one does not simply give that person a distinctive identity, one also makes a value judgment about that person and indicates how that person is expected to behave. In 1936 Professor A.J.H. Goodwin, the pioneer Africanist archaeologist, was moved to complain that "the Bushmen . . . have suffered severely from the beliefs of the man in the street. To most men, the Bushmen are an extinct race, aboriginal to South Africa: very primitive and apelike; a product of the Kalahari Desert, which has forced them to develop a heavy protruding rump; whose average lease of life is about a century, but who are nevertheless unable to count above two" (Goodwin 1936:41).

C. H. Hahn might have been the first European to express surprise at Bushman copper mining ability, but he most certainly was not the last. In January 1925 a young Clement Doke visited the Kung in Grootfontein: "I was under the impression that these people were almost extinct, and very difficult to locate, but I had my eyes opened regarding them, for during my brief travels in but a small portion of their country I personally came into contact with over 200" (Doke 1925:39).[8]

Doke's analysis and policy prescriptions were unlikely to impress hard-nosed practical administrators: He found the "Qhung" to be a fascinating little people who were "consistently dirty." He pronounced them "to be a decadent and not a primitive race [since] they shew traces of a higher civilization [in their beadwork]" (Doke 1925:42). He complained about their unreliability:

> The Bushman knows no law. He knows no discipline. He is a law unto himself. No Missionary society has yet attempted to reach the Qhung. One hopeful feature is that individuals have been taught to work, and I have even seen women harvesting in the fields. . . . From my short stay among these people, I am convinced that they would respond to the Gospel appeal; and their evangelisation is to me the only hope for their civilization, and the only solution to the difficulties of contact experienced to-day. (Doke 1925:44)

Similarly, the director of education, Ainsley Watts, in his 1926 master's thesis, provided a vivid demonstration of the scientific molding process: "Interspersed among the Berg Damara were what Alexander calls Bushman-villages, but the inhabitants could not have been Bushmen, because they neither build huts nor form villages. At one of these villages a demonstration was given of the methods employed by these so-called Bushmen to kill the gnu and ostrich. A feather frame is used to disguise the body, a long neck and head of an ostrich is mounted on a stick" (Watts 1926:44–45).[9]

Academics and intellectuals were hardly different from Goodwin's man in the street. Thus Charles Templeman Loram, leading liberal on the South African Native Affairs Commission, referred to the Namutoni Bushmen as having a "brutal and stupid communal life . . . practically devoid of ideas. . . . The Bushmen have no sense of right and wrong; every conception of law and order is lacking in them" (Loram Papers).

During the interwar period anthropologists studiously avoided trying to explain or understand what was happening to the Bushmen. Often explanations by nonanthropologists were at once more fantastic and accurate. Typically they revolved around sex. The South African blue book on how the Germans treated the natives of South West Africa attributed the chief cause of the decline in Bushman numbers to the "Germans persist[ing] in taking Bushwomen from their husbands and using them as concubines" (South Africa 1918:148). Venereal disease seems to have upset a number of authors, for example, E. F. Potgieter, who, in trying to maintain the myth of Bushman isolation, was forced to conclude that "nobody knows how the Bushmen became infected, and even the best experts on this race are surprised at the special vulnerability of the Bushmen to such disease" (Potgieter 1937:11).[10]

Perhaps the most important intellectual to have given these myths a scientific credibility, and thus helped to sustain them, was Heinrich Vedder, missionary, ethnographer, historian and politician: "From the earliest times [the Bushmen] were despised, hated and fiercely persecuted by all other natives and the only dwelling places left to them were inaccessible hiding places. . . . Distrustful of everyone who belonged to another tribe . . . they avoided all contact with the outer world, and they live even today, their miserable Bushman life, just as their ancestors have lived it for centuries" (Vedder 1938:78).

Similarly, other German ethnologists who worked on the Bushmen, like Paul Glass and Viktor Lebzelter, found it easier to talk about these unpleasant processes when they had been sanitized by time and located in another country. They did not analyze the policies applied to the Bushmen by either the Germans or the South Africans while they were doing research.

Lebzelter was inclined to attribute population decline to the ravages of World War I and the declining water situation. He did, however, emphasize malaria and tuberculosis and, to a lesser extent, cold-related diseases as the Bushmen's greatest enemies. These, coupled with a high infant-mortality rate, he said, had led to a steady population decline (Lebzelter 1934a:80). The traveler W. J. Makin (1929:280) was more forthright: "The peculiar diseases of the white man are more powerful in death-dealing than machine-guns and bullets," he wrote, especially "syphilization."

German scholars were not alone in blaming the victim and ignoring the wider sociopolitical structure. In his classic *The Khoisan Peoples of South Africa*, published in 1930, Schapera, undoubtedly the finest ethnographer of southern Africa, had this to say about Namibian Bushmen: "Their numbers seem to have declined a good deal within recent years. The official estimate for 1913 gave the Bushman population . . . as 8,098, which may be contrasted with the 1926 figure of 3,600. Allowing for probable inaccuracies in the two estimates, there does nevertheless appear to be an undeniable decrease. This may be attributed largely to the ravages of disease, especially malaria" (Schapera 1930:40).

Even after there had been a sea change in attitude toward Bushmen, leading liberals in South Africa, like Leo Marquard, stuck close to the firmly entrenched official mythology: "There are about 5,000 Bushmen in South-West Africa, and these people, as elsewhere, are unable to adapt themselves to European civilization. They have steadily retreated before the Europeans. . . . Very occasionally they become servants of European farmers, but . . . European civilization does not seem to be able to influence them in any way" (Marquard and Standing 1939:251–252; cf. Dungan 1927:17–18).

Despite efforts by ethnologists like Lebzelter (1928) and Vedder (1937, 1938) to humanize these myths, their exertions had little impact on academics, administrators or farmers. This is not surprising, given the lowly definition Bushmen were accorded by the government. Eric Louw, the South African representative to the 1934 session of the Permanent Mandates Commission of the League of Nations, asserted that "nothing more could be done with the Bushmen than to punish them when they made depredations." They were "parasitic," "like wild animals," "a low type" and a "deteriorate race" (cited in Dowd 1954:69). In short, they were untamable and hence impossible to educate, a conclusion endorsed as late as 1958 by a government commission on education (South West Africa 1958)! Even practical academics were not impressed. Thus, in a doctoral thesis on rural labor problems, written during World War II in an internment camp where he enjoyed the enforced company of many German farmers, Rädel was able to conclude that

> it should not seem at all strange that the Bushman vanishes when there is enough game to hunt in the vicinity and then returns and resumes his work as if nothing had happened. Even though he is a tenacious hunter, he does not have much stamina for manual labor. This is partly because he is not used to it, and partly because of his small stature. He is not good at working with cattle because it is out of his range of experience. Because of his nomadic existence he is most suited for sheep or cattle herding. (Rädel 1947:194)

Part 4

Bushmen Iconified

Chapter 17

Creating Bushmanland: Anthropology Triumphant?

By the end of World War II the overwhelming majority of Bushmen had became part of Namibia's invisible rural proletariat, eking out an existence on settler farms. A survey conducted at the end of 1947 showed that 65 percent of the 179 farms in Grootfontein and 52 percent of the 135 Gobabis district farms had Bushman residents. These farms averaged 12.2 and 12.7 Bushman residents respectively. Some farms exclusively employed Bushman labor (LGR 3/1/7; LGO 3/1/60).[1]

As if to signal that this "problem" was "solved," public and government attention shifted from a concern with Bushmen within the Police Zone to those living beyond it, that is, the "wild" Bushmen "out there." Its culmination was to be the creation of a Bushman reserve, which later formed the nucleus for the Apartheid-inspired Bushman homeland. What were the socioeconomic factors responsible for this change in emphasis? Apart from the economic implications of this changed policy for the powerful farming lobby, other settler factions were also developing considerable interests in such a change. The Bushman's economic role in the wider Namibian social formation had increasingly been supplemented, but not replaced, by an emergent ideological role.

This chapter will show that contrary to their customary modesty as to their impact on policy, academics, especially anthropologists, have had a major role in shaping Bushman policy. And this has occurred despite the fact that historically in most settler-dominated colonies the role of anthropology in policy-making has always been meager. Among the practical minded settlers anthropology was seen as a deviant discipline— a waste of time because any good settler "knew" what blacks needed. Anthropology, especially when practiced by foreigners, was a waste of time, "spoilt" the natives, caused "trouble" and was treated with a high degree of suspicion (Gordon 1988, 1989). This paranoia was exacerbated by the tense international situation as South Africa tried to incorporate Namibia into South Africa in the face of vociferous international opposition. The fear of international embarrassment meant a virtual embargo on any social research, especially if it were done by foreigners with liberal credentials. A confidential memorandum written by the Ovamboland native commissioner concerning the activities of the Loeb Anthropological Expedition, which General Jan Smuts, the South African prime minister, had personally invited to study the Ovambo,[2] conveys this sense of administrative outrage well:

> When Mr. Rodin arrived here he was entertained at the Mess, and enquired whether his coloured servant could use the shower bath. I understand that Mrs. Loeb is teaching an Ovambo to type in Grootfontein, and that the instruction takes place in her bedroom at the hotel. . . . I think Dr. Loeb should be summoned to Windhoek, or to Swakopmund, when he can be given advice, and instructions by a senior official as to the attitude foreign visitors are expected to adopt towards Natives in South Africa, more particularly in the Native Areas of South West Africa. (SWAA, A198/3, 8 December 1947)

Only foreigners with impeccable conservative credentials were given research clearances, and then significantly their research was not on the larger, more politically sensitive, groups or problems, but on Bushmen. The most famous research expeditions after World War II were undertaken by the Marshall family. The Marshalls were seen by officials as being relatively harmless wealthy conservative amateurs who had some influence in the United States.[3] But even they were not exempt from harassment, being carefully vetted by the South African Embassy, and their movements in Namibia were constantly monitored. Despite these administrative precautions, rumors abounded and questions were raised in the settler-run Legislative Assembly. On 27 May 1958, Grammie Brandt, the member for Grootfontein, asked the administrator twelve questions about the Marshall expeditions, including the following:

> (6) Is the Administration aware of any social fraternisation between the Europeans of this expedition and the Bushman community; (7) Are films and tape recordings made by this Marshall and are they censored before they are sent overseas; . . . (10) Does the Administration intend establishing a Bushman reserve in this area; (11) If so, is it the result of the influence and business of this Marshall expedition; (12) Will the

Ngani, a Heikom who spoke nine languages and mixed a good cocktail. He was attached for many years to the F. P. Courtney-Clarke (secretary of South West Africa) household and later served as interpreter for the various Marshall expeditions. (Photo courtesy of A. Courtney-Clarke)

needs of Europeans for land be considered before this Bushman reserve is established? (South West Africa 1957:88–89)[4]

By allowing research on Bushmen, the South Africans could claim that they were not against research per se and, moreover, were doing their bit for promoting science, given the importance of Bushmen for international science. The research field was well established. Indeed in 1957 the prominent anthropologist Martin Gusinde concluded concerning Bushmen, "It is gratifying to be able to report that the culture and racial type of this desert people . . . can, on the whole, be regarded today as sufficiently investigated" (Gusinde 1957:296).

Another factor contributing to this focus on Bushman was the intellectual climate at Afrikaans universities, where Bushmen have a central role in the *volkekunde* (ethnology) discourse. Their role in the *volkekunde gestalt* is important if only because many whites who were to influence Bushman policy were trained at Afrikaans universities and this shaped their explanations for Bushman behavior. The tone of *volkekunde* research was set by E. F. Potgieter in his euphemistically entitled study *The Disappearing Bushmen of Lake Chrissie* (1955). Potgieter apologetically claimed that "it was found that amongst these people there is today a marked lack of the type of social activities which are of importance to the anthropologist in the field" (Potgieter 1955:x).[5] The implications of this study, which dealt with the last small band of Bushmen in the Transvaal, are spelled out in Coertze's influential introductory text, *Inleiding tot die Algemene Volkekunde:*

> Exaggerated conservatism as psychological phenomenon must not however be confused with cases where a people are intrinsically [innerlik] incapable of undergoing change in a fixed direction subject to stimuli derived from foreign cultures. In the case of the Bushmen, we find, for example, that despite close contact with whites on the one hand and Bantu on the other, *they became neither Bantuized nor westernized.* Where it did occur, it only went to a certain level after which they die out and disappear. The intrinsic bondedness between their life-style on the one side and their inherited racial characteristics on the other side meant extinction for them. This phenomenon is exemplified by the Bushmen of Lake Chrissie (Potgieter 1955). Here it was a case where the Bushmen were apparently intrinsically incapable of adapting to changed living circumstances. The challenge of new conditions of living was too big for them, not simply because they were conservative, but because they had an *inherent incapability* of meeting new challenges. (Coertze 1963:47 [emphasis added])[6]

The Decisive Discourse

The origin myth of Bushmanland attributes its creation to the government Commission for the Preservation of the Bushmen, which was chaired by the famous Afrikaner author and anthropologist P. J. Schoeman. In accounting for its own lineage, the commission (also referred to as the Schoeman Commission) displayed a fatal ignorance of history: "It was not until the Bushmen became more accustomed to Europeans through official feeding schemes, etc., that it became apparent that disease was rife amongst them and that they were in danger of extermination. The appointment of this commission was a direct result of a report received in 1949 from the Regional Medical Officer of the Okavango" (Schoeman n.d.[b]: para. 28).

This version is not only simplistic but also wrong: For a start, there was the ever-present white-farmer lobby. In 1946, a deputation of the Grootfontein Farmers' Association visited the administration to discuss the "Bushman problem." They requested that a few boreholes be sunk for the Bushmen well beyond the Police Zone, where a white official would also be stationed. This was necessary because Bushman stock-raiding patterns had changed. Stock thieves were no longer local "tame" Bushmen but "wild" Bushmen from outside the Police Zone. The administrator pointed out the difficulty of keeping Bushmen on reservations but agreed on humanitarian grounds that something should be done. One consequence was the appointment of the Commission for the Preservation of the Bushmen. And just to underline the importance of the farming lobby while the commission was engaged in its activities, an articulate spokesman of the ruling Nationalist party in the Legislative Assembly succeeded in having a motion passed that called on the administration to place all "vagrant" Bushmen in a special reserve for the following, rather contradictory, reasons: Bushmen were the first representatives of Homo sapiens; after this bow to misplaced humanism, he continued that they were largely a "bastard race" and rife with venereal disease. More important, vagrant Bushmen were a threat to farmers because apart from depleting the farmers' livestock, they were responsible for most veld fires and the killing off of the territory's game. In addition, Herero were employing Bushmen to do their work for them and thus Herero managed to do even less work (*Windhoek Advertiser,* 31 March 1951). It is not coincidental that these calls came when large tracts of the Kaukauveld were being opened to white farmers in the wake of World War II and that farm labor was a major concern, leading to its own round of expert commissions (South West Africa 1950a; 1950b).

International considerations were also important. The administration was aware of and sensitive to the attitude of the United Nations and most certainly did not want to further antagonize world public opinion unnecessarily.[7] Support for the idea of a Bushman reserve was also forthcoming from other commissions. The "Report of the Game Preservation Commission" (South West Africa 1949: para. 32), for example, recommended that "Game Reserve No. 1 be abandoned as such, and if, as appears to be the case, it is unsuitable for land settlement purposes, it might possibly be converted into a Bushman Reserve."[8]

Welfare officer from Otjituo Reserve providing maize to a group of "indigents." He is carrying out post–World War II program of "enticing" "wild" Bushmen from the Kaukauveld. Note that no females are present. (Photo courtesy of State Archives, Windhoek)

Feeding Schemes and Kavango Guards

The feeding schemes to which Schoeman referred also have a history. The police had been experimenting with them at least since 1935. Nevertheless, in 1947 the scheme was expanded and paid Kavango "Bushman guards" were placed at water holes where Bushmen congregated during the winter months. Apart from maintaining law and order and reporting all incidents of interest to the native commissioner, a guard's duties included protecting Bushmen against other blacks; protecting game—especially giraffe—from Bushmen and keeping the Kurung-Kuru–Tsintsabis Road open by maintaining the water holes. Later, once they had gained the trust of Bushmen, guards were to encourage them to plant millet and raise goats. For this latter purpose Bushmen were supplied with seeds and lent implements and goats.

This scheme was part of a new approach that sought to "befriend" rather than "scare off" the Bushmen. Police were issued small supplies of tobacco, salt and mielie-meal to be used "as necessary" when making contact with "wild" Bushmen. It was hoped that such an approach would lead to a decrease in stock theft. The 1947 territorial budget contained a new item: a sum of 500 pounds (Item M of Vote 12) for "water provision and relief to Bushmen . . . with the object of endeavoring to bring them under control and eventually congregating them in a Reserve on their own southwest of Otjituo." In 1948 the Bushman budget was increased to 1,000 pounds (Vote 12L) "to provide relief to Bushmen with the object of gaining their confidence and inducing them to give up their wandering habits."[9] This budget allocation remained virtually unchanged in subsequent years and was chronically underspent, underlining the low priority given to Bushmen by the field administration. Moreover the administration failed to attract suitable Kavango recruits for the guard positions and then only visited Bushman posts at irregular intervals. This led to abuse of power, manifested in sexual assault of Bushman women and children. Adults were also forced to participate in illegal giraffe hunting. Complaints of this nature were frequent enough for the native commissioner to remark, in 1955, that Bushman guards "can easily fall into the habit of 'living like lords' and doing nothing much in the interests of the administration. They hold a position of authority over the Bushmen such that the way is open to the less scrupulous of them to use the Bushmen in their own interests" (cited in Olivier 1961:217). Nevertheless the number of Bushman posts gradually increased to sixteen in 1962 (Grobbelaar 1967:3), after which it declined as bureaucratic attention shifted to Bushmanland proper.

The Commission for the Preservation of the Bushmen

This then was the immediate social context in which the (Schoeman) Commission for the Preservation of the Bushmen was established in October 1949.[10] The other member was Major Naude, formerly of the South West Africa Police, and a young native affairs clerk, Claude McIntyre, was seconded to serve as secretary. The commission undertook some tours and produced an interim report in September 1951 (Schoeman n.d.[a]) and its final report in 1953 (Schoeman n.d.[b]).

Given the background of suspicion against academics, the appointment of Professor Schoeman to chair the Commission for the Preservation of the Bushmen might appear surprising. It was not: He was available, having recently resigned his chair at Stellenbosch, where he had been actively involved in developing a cohesive doctrine of *Grand Apartheid* and had unsuccessfully contested a parliamentary seat as native representative. In addition to his academic respectability,[11] as an Afrikaner, he could be counted on to "know how to behave." Given this background, it was inevitable that the commission would come up with a recommendation for a special Bushman reserve, if only to maintain the logical consistency of the Apartheid ideology. Schoeman himself was a prominent writer of hunting tales in Afrikaans and was given a contract by the

"Wild" Bushmen exhibit at the 1952 van Riebeeck Festival in Cape Town. One of the highlights of the celebration of 300 years of colonial settlement at the Cape of Good Hope was this exhibit. P. J. Schoeman (at right), chairman of the Commission for the Preservation of the Bushmen, brought the Bushmen from Namibia. (Photo courtesy of the *Cape Argus*)

well-known Afrikaans weekly *Die Huisgenoot* to describe his experiences with the Bushmen. The dominant theme of his writings reflected Afrikaner experience: The Bushmen wanted a home of their own.[12]

The "all important question," he felt, was could

> Bushmen adapt themselves to a new way of life . . . work on a farm . . . pastoral life? . . . Judging by their historical past, the one and only answer would be: No. . . . The Bushmen seem to lack something . . . some inner or spiritual ability. . . . And yet one cannot deny the fact that their will to survive is as strong—perhaps even stronger than that of any other race or tribe. . . . As an idealist I would like to see the Bushmen living their own lives in one or more reserves of their own— with a Chinese wall around them. But unless the Administration is prepared to supply them with food, they will, I fear, be a continual nuisance to both the Natives and the European farmers, and they will gradually exterminate all the big game. (Schoeman, Memorandum n.d.)[13]

There were major differences in the recommendations of the interim and final reports. The interim report called for creating two reserves: one for the Heikom Bushmen, adjoining the Etosha Game Park, where they had "traditional hunting rights," and the other for the Kung in Game Reserve No. 1, with headquarters at Karakuwisa. In the final report, these recommendations were substantially changed. The Heikom were no longer to have a reserve, and the Kung Bushmen reserve was to be at Nyae Nyae, not at Karakuwisa. It is difficult to explain this volte-face, except to note that Schoeman had accepted employment as chief game warden of Etosha while he was chairman of the commission and that not only was Karakuwisa part of a game reserve but it also had potential to be developed by European ranchers. In contrast, Nyae Nyae was isolated from markets, and its belt of *gifblaar* (*Dichapetalum cymosum*) made cattle ranching singularly unattractive in that part of the Kalahari.

The future of the 500 Heikom living in the Etosha Game Park was dim, as the final report urged their expulsion. They were to be given the choice of moving to Ovamboland or, because the commission found them to be such good workers, allowed to enter the service of "selected farmers" who were all located south of Windhoek to deter them from deserting and returning to Etosha (Schoeman n.d.[b]:para. 47). The rationale for this was that over 70 percent of Heikom wore " 'white' clothing and regularly begged for tea, coffee and sugar. . . . These recently acquired needs will gradually convince them to work on farms in the vicinity"(para. 24).

This maneuvering must be seen in the context of a fight for survival within the world of bureaucratic politics. Given the division of land in Namibia in which all prime land went to white farmers, Nature Conservation was left to fight in bitter rivalry with the Department of Bantu Administration for the bits of land unwanted by white farmers. Many areas were transferred back and forth between these two departments.[14] More than grass got hurt in this battle of bureaucratic elephants. The Bushman became a convenient scapegoat.

Conservation officials brought a new sense of order: Bushmen remaining in the Etosha Game Park were forced to move to the rest camps, "where proper housing, medical care and work opportunities were available. They became our trackers, builders, camp workers and later our road grader and bulldozer operator" (de la Bat 1982). In short, they were a ready supply of cheap labor. It is said that the first task of the newly formed Game Catching Unit was to round up Bushmen living in the park. Three hundred "unemployed" Bushmen were given the choice of moving to either Ovamboland or the white farms (Olivier 1961). The press dutifully reported this event with suitable hyperbole:

Only recently have the South-West African authorities had to stop Bushman remnants near the Etosha Pan from hunting, as zebras and wildebeeste were threatened with total extermination at their hands. At first the Government decided to ship them regular food supplies in the form of meat, but as this scheme proved impractical the Bushmen were removed from the barren territory. All of them, numbering about 500, have now been taken from their remote homeland to be absorbed as herdsmen and farm labourers into the economy of the country. (Holz 1956:11)

Reasons given by old game rangers for their removal included: They kept dogs (as they had in the 1930s); they did not behave in a "traditional" manner; they were not "real" Bushmen; worst of all, they had started to "beg."[15] The obvious point that needs to be made here is that all these allegedly nontraditional practices are common foraging strategies. Perhaps the reason for their eviction was precisely because they were adapting too well! Moreover, park Bushmen had started to raise livestock on their own initiative. Bushmen were careful stock owners and quite aware of natural dangers. So successful did they become that in 1947 the game warden was compelled to restrict further the number of livestock to five large and five small stock per Bushman. Not only were they "adapting," but they were thriving and engaging in entrepreneurial activities such as training oxen to pull wagons and selling these oxen to Ovambo workers returning to Ovamboland (NAO 24/8).

However, for the Kung, who were the largest group of "wild pure" Bushmen, the commission urged the creation of a special reserve in the Kaukauveld because Kung were in the process of drifting toward white farms and "if this is allowed to continue, the group is in very grave danger of extinction" (Schoeman n.d.[b]:para. 51). To counter this, a full-time official should be placed near Gautscha Pan in an effort to attract Bushmen from outlying areas such as Mpungu, the Kaudum and Karakuwisa, the native reserves and areas in the west (where they might be a nuisance to white farmers or laborers). Schoeman spelled out the process by which this was to occur:

There should be no undue haste about this development; it will have to keep pace with the "taming" of the Bushmen. First, those in the immediate neighborhood of the pans should be persuaded to settle down to farming. When they have done so, their vacated hunting grounds will attract the next lying bands. When these have moved in, they, in their turn, should be similarly persuaded and so the process will continue with ever increasing momentum until all the Bushmen are settled. (Schoeman n.d.[b]: para. 56)

Action to establish the Gautscha reserve was slow.[16] But was the delay in the implementation of the Bushman reserve proposals merely the result of bureaucratic muddles? These proposals were not acted upon until 1959 because it was only then that the economic aspects became even more pressing than quasi-scientific considerations. An undated memorandum by the chief Bantu affairs commissioner provides the following insight:

> It is being found that the Bushman farm laborers are deserting . . . from the Gobabis district to go to Bechuanaland. To replace this labor, farmers have to place orders for [Ovambo contract migrant] labor and the waiting period is now four and a half years. The reason for the desertions appears to be that the Bechuanaland authorities have appointed an official to deal with Bushman affairs over there, and apparently offer them protection. It is feared that unless similar steps are taken immediately we will lose many of our Bushman laborers as well as others. The matter of creating a Bushman reserve is thus seen as exceptionally urgent.
>
> It is not only the farm labor question which makes the creation of this reserve so urgent, there is also the question of control of our eastern border with Bechuanaland where the penetration of Bechuanaland natives to hunt game still continually occurs and which usually resulted in the deliberate setting of . . . veld fires. (Olivier 1961:140)

This quotation is important because it stresses the importance of placing the Bushmen within the regional political economy. What is left unsaid is often as important as what is said: The commission made no mention of the Bushmen already "tamed" and working on settler farms, even though they constituted the vast majority of Bushmen. Presumably, the commission assumed that their future had already been settled. This chapter has set the stage for understanding the bureaucratic and policy uses of Bushmen and how policy ostensibly meant to *increase* the self-sufficiency of "wild" Bushmen paradoxically increased their dependency upon government welfare payments.

Chapter 18

Bushmen Obscured: Farms, Parks and Reserves

The major impetus for the creation of a Bushman reserve thus came from settler farming interests. Academics, by highlighting the "wild" Bushmen who would be "saved" by the reserve, detracted attention from the plight of the Bushman majority, who continued to battle for survival as workers on settler farms. Table 18.1 provides details about the substantial percentage of Bushmen in the rural labor force.[1]

The post–World War II period ushered in massive expansion of white ranching land. By 1955, for example, the number of white ranches in the Gobabis district had increased from 135 to 256. The percentage of Bushmen as farm workers tended to remain constant, as most of this new expansion was into areas traditionally accepted as belonging to Bushmen. Bushmen preferred to work on farms that encompassed their traditional land areas.[2] They tended to cluster in groups the size of the "traditional" hunting band (see Table 18.2). It is also characteristic of an impoverished rural proletariat (Iliffe 1987). Many Bushmen in the Gobabis district, according to Köhler, had migrated in from the north to relieve the labor shortage, having "been persuaded by the example of the others" (Köhler 1959a:25), which can hardly be regarded as a sufficient explanation. A Gobabis Legislative Assembly member stated that Bushmen "were a dead loss to the country. They were of no social importance and were, moreover, an economic drawback" (*Windhoek Advertiser*, 31 March 1951). Despite rhetorical assertions like that, the practice of "blackbirding" (abduction of workers) was common. Neither the law[3] nor the administration had much deterrent value in limiting this form of labor recruitment because few settlers were brought to court,

Table 18.1   Percent of Bushmen in the Rural Labor Force (selected years)

| | Grootfontein | | Gobabis | |
	Percent	Total	Percent	Total
1936	34.3	3,934	—	
1939	36.8	1,329	24	1,329
1947	40.2	1,392	34.2	882
1951	33.9	2,436	—	
1955	24.5	1,154	32.1	1,142

Sources: Various magistrate's annual reports; Oswin Köhler, *A Study of Grootfontein District* (Pretoria: Government Printer, 1959); Oswin Köhler, *A Study of Gobabis District* (Pretoria: Government Printer, 1959).

Table 18.2   Bushmen Resident on Settler Farms

| District | Number of Farms with Resident Bushmen | Group Size | | |
		<30	30–50	50+
Tsumeb	134	94	28	12
Gobabis	381	343	33	5
Grootfontein	447	430	15	2
Outjo	191	185	4	2
Otjiwarongo	81	80	0	0

Source: François Marais et al., *Ondersoek na die Boesmanbevolkingsgroep in Suidwes-Afrika* (Windhoek: Direktoraat, ontwikkelingskoordinering, 1984), p. 40.

except as an infringement of the Masters and Servants Proclamation, which provided a maximum fine of 5 pounds or one month in jail.

Even relatively isolated Nyae Nyae, where the Marshalls had started to do fieldwork, was not immune (Marshall 1976:60). McIntyre, erstwhile secretary to the Commission for the Preservation of the Bushmen and soon to be first Bushman affairs commissioner, reported on a visit there in October 1955 and noted some of the consequences of blackbirding:

> At Gam . . . I met some 30 women and 3 men. At first they were not very communicative until I was recognized from a previous trip then they complained bitterly of the loss of their men-folk through (highly illegal) recruiting by farmers for work in the Police Zone. . . . At Nama and Gautscha Pan I was immediately recognized and assailed by wailing women demanding the return of sons and husbands who had been similarly removed. . . . Food supplies in the vicinity were exhausted [and] the whole band should . . . have trekked . . . but they were waiting . . . in the hope that the men who had been taken away would be returned. . . . I was . . . shewn girl wives with children and aged women whose supports . . . had been removed by force by farmers from the Police Zone. Within the last fortnight since the Marshall expedition had left, another four Bushmen had been removed from the band by farm-

ers. One of these Bushmen was a cripple. They asked me to ensure their return. In every case, they said, the farmers had promised to return their men within three months but some had been gone a year now and they did not know what to do. . . . The Bechuanas at Gam told me that at least a hundred Bushmen had been removed during the last year. All were emphatic that the Europeans came from South West Africa. (SWAA, A659, McIntyre to CNC, 11 November 1955)[4]

Lorna Marshall provided the graphic sequel: "Sometime later, these families tried to run away from the farms to return to Nyae-Nyae. They told us they were followed by two white men and a white woman on horseback with guns, led by a 'tame' Bushman tracker. These people forced some of the Kung to return to the farm. Under a barrage of threats and with pointed guns, they seized some of the Kung children. In the fracas, others of the Kung got away" (Marshall 1976:283).

Life on the Farms

What was life like on the farms? The Reverend Weineke, a Lutheran missionary, visited a Bushman *werft* on a farm:

The men are still at work so that only the women, children and old people were there. They sat in a circle in front of the half open huts which we could hardly call huts. They consisted of sticks and roots stuck in a semi circle in the earth and joined at the top. This structure is then covered with a superficial covering of grass so that one can see through the walls in all directions. Rags and tatters lie on the sand which is the floor. Tin cans hang on the poles, these are the cooking and household implements. I saw four huts like this and in front of each sat women and children. We greet them and put out our hands. They laugh friendly and stretch out their dirt encrusted hands. Some women have tokens of clothing on. Two women have only loin cloths. An old shrivelled grey haired lady quiets a baby. In the center of the encampment burns a fire with an old rusty tin on it. (Weineke 1956:6)[5]

Two decades later, despite the fact that farmers were forced to treat their workers better following the abolition of the contract labor system in 1973, the situation was virtually unchanged. A report by a Dutch Reformed Church missionary on the situation of Heikom farm workers in the Grootfontein, Tsumeb and Otavi districts noted that "drunkenness, sexual alienation, labor shyness, stock-theft, lack of interest in their work and 'apparent' aimless trekking from one employer to another are but some of the daily problems encountered" (Swanepoel 1978).

Wages were still low, although Swanepoel gave no figures, and child labor was still practiced. Swanepoel's church did manage to inspire a few scattered farm schools for Bushman children. But these schools, with their inappropriate curricula, serve two unarticulated sociological functions: They stabilized Bushman labor by catering to a desire of Bushmen, and they ensured that labor did not leave, as children were in effect hostages at boarding schools.

Some farmers began to construct housing for their workers, but the overwhelming majority of Bushman workers still lived in self-made tin shanties. Sanitation facilities were nonexistent, and as a consequence, some farmers were forced to regularly deworm their Bushmen workers in an effort to save their cattle from becoming infected with measles! Materially,

> the Haikom possesses only the barest necessities. Furniture consists of a few old tins to sit on and here and there is a type of chair. Tables are scarce. They sleep usually on the ground—very often outside around the fireplace. Their eating utensils are mostly a pot or a tin and a wooden paddle to stir the porridge. Spoons are also used, but they usually eat the porridge with their hands out of the pot or bucket. They drink their tea or coffee out of tin mugs—bought or home-made. . . . Clothes are kept in suitcases, tin trunks or any hollow thing. Cupboards are almost totally absent. Water is kept in tins, buckets and plastic cans. Eating utensils are not treated very hygienically. The dogs and fowls sometimes empty the pots when the people have finished. Dogs and fowls are generally kept and on some farms the employer gives them cattle and goats as part of their compensation. They then also get grazing rights for these animals. Problems usually arise when the employee resigns and must find other employment and grazing for his animals. The consequence is that a herd can never be built up. It is less of a problem for them to eat the animals or to sell them. (Swanepoel 1978:8–9)

Life on the Native Reserves

The logic of Apartheid called for the establishment of large homelands for indigenes. The core "native reserves" had been established in 1922, and these were gradually expanded. Then in 1964 the Odendaal Commission called for creation of a Herero homeland of around 5,900,000 hectares by consolidating the Epukiro, Waterberg, Eastern and Otjituo reserves and extending them to the Botswana border in the east and including the Rietfontein Block Farms in the southeast. At the same time, to raise sufficient land in the Kavango homeland, the government merely extended the boundaries of this homeland a great distance to the south. Sandwiched between these two homelands was the 1,800,000-hectare homeland for Bushmen (South Africa 1964). As most of the land involved in this reshuffle of the Apartheid poker game was state land, there was little vocal opposition to this de facto greatest theft of Bushman land in the history of Namibia. Whereas Bushmen living beyond the Police Zone had previously had a reasonably free existence as a result of the government policy of laissez-faire, benign neglect, they now found themselves forcibly incorporated into homelands of others, especially Herero.

In this chapter I consider their experiences on the Herero reserves and later "homeland" because Herero pose the most direct threat to Bushman lands. Like pastoralists elsewhere, Herero have displayed their ability to restock after natural and human-caused disasters, and despite unsatisfactory structural conditions, their stock multiplied. In 1925, shortly after the creation of the reserves, there were 13,801 head of cattle in the Epukiro, Waterberg East and Otjituo reserves. Thirty-two years later the total had increased to 105,153 (Werner 1982:11).

Given the lack of water, the need to remain near the homestead for dairying purposes and the rate of increase of stock, it is not surprising that already by the 1940s, officials, and some Herero, were voicing concern about overgrazing and desertification (Wagner 1952). Whereas the administration argued for culling, Herero argued for an increase in the number of water points.[6] The dangers of such a strategy are obvious. Goldschmidt recently commented: "Perhaps the most obvious solution to the problem of arid-land pastoralists is to dig wells to provide water. The evidence suggests that this solution universally not only fails but exacerbates the pastoralists' situation" (Goldschmidt 1981:104).

The danger of Herero pastoral expansionism onto Bushman land is still very real. In January 1983, forty-one Herero illegally entered the proclaimed Bushmanland from Botswana with over 3,200 head of cattle. They claimed to be fleeing from Botswana because of mistreatment. Specifically they were not getting a decent price for their cattle and half of their crop was allegedly taken away (*Die Republikein*, 21 January 1983). These Herero were repatriated, but it appears to be just a matter of time before commercial ranching penetrates Bushmanland.

By and large the Herero people in the deep Kalahari were humane and treated Bushmen reasonably well within the limits of their self-imposed caste system, but this did not negate the general pattern of antagonistic and exploitative Bushman-Herero interaction that has been observed on all Herero reserves and is consistent with the historical pattern. Fear of possible Bushman retribution, however, has decreased as more and more Herero have been able to purchase firearms, ostensibly as protection against SWAPO insurgents. The role of the government authorities in regulating abuses continued to be minimal and mostly accidental.

Perhaps the most significant case to emerge from chance discovery involves the Waterberg Massacre. In *Rex v. Majarero and twenty-three others* 1947 SCW, twenty-four Herero were found guilty of cold-bloodedly massacring thirteen Bushmen: two males, four females and seven children. The reason for the massacre was that a Herero had been killed by a Bushman arrow while he was on a fifteen-man mounted commando trying to recover some cattle allegedly stolen by two Bushmen. The next day, a commando of between twenty-six and forty-five Herero, mounted on horses and donkeys, set out to exact retribution. They managed to surround the band of fleeing Bushmen, and while those on horseback patrolled the periphery to prevent escape, the donkey brigade dismounted and went in for the kill on foot. Using clubs and assegais, they ripped open stomachs and severed hands. In this well-planned and cold-blooded atrocity, not a single Herero was wounded. Three Bushmen males managed to escape.[7] In passing sentence, the judge commented on the unsatisfactory nature of the evidence given by the Herero, and two of the accused were later convicted of perjury.[8] Outraged Herero promptly but unsuccessfully appealed the seven-years-imprisonment sentences. A year later, that great champion of African liberation Chief Hosea Kutako led a deputation asking for the release of the incarcerated Hereros, on the grounds that they had already suffered enough for their misdeed.

The horrifying aspect of the Waterberg Massacre was that in 1983 few knowledgeable Herero were able to recall these tragic events. It was as if they had been expunged from the collective memory.[9]

Of the various "ethnic groups," Herero may truly be said to have gained the most in the recent political dispensations handed out in the "canned bully beef barrel" politics of the territory. With their vocal opposition to the government's plans, they have successfully managed to retain possession of all their reserves, while at the same time extending their control over the eastern Kalahari.

Chapter 19

Bushmanland Fabricated

On Christmas Eve 1959, Claude McIntyre, the ex-secretary of the Commission for the Preservation of the Bushmen and newly appointed Bushman affairs commissioner, set up camp at Tsumkwe.[1] His policy was enunciated by the administrator on his first visit to the reserve, who told the assembled Bushman crowd in no uncertain terms:

> The area in which you live is very valuable for farming purposes and many Europeans and Natives would be very glad to be given a chance to farm there. These Europeans and Natives could soon turn this wild, uninhabited land into an area to support many people. They would achieve this by their knowledge and by their hard work. These two factors—knowledge and hard work—are the essentials for any people to survive in the world today. Without them any people must eventually starve and die.
>
> The Government takes great interest in you as one of its peoples and wants to give you a chance to become civilized and to lead normal happy lives. . . . But this depends on your own efforts. . . . You must become like other people—self-supporting. . . . It would be very wrong of the Government to allocate land to people who cannot use it properly. . . . Therefore the Government might consider bringing Bushmen from other clans. . . . Your Commissioner will then be responsible for their welfare and progress. When this takes place I ask you to live in peace and to forget your old tribal boundaries. (*Bantu* 1961:627–628)[2]

McIntyre interpreted these policy directives to mean that Bushmen had to be taught industriousness, which he attempted to do by keeping them continually busy (South Africa, Department of Welfare 1962:16). He also felt that a "great advance for these Bushmen [will be] in their recognition of personal property. That is the basis of all civilization" (*Cape Argus*, 15 April 1963). McIntyre focused on agriculture. In order to attract Bushmen to settle at Tsumkwe, rations were made available for the aged and infirm and large gardens were established. Tsumkwe was to show steady, and at times dramatic, growth: From 25 in 1952 to 120 in 1961 (Marshall 1976:158). In 1965 it stood at 550 and five years later it reached 700. By 1974 over half of the 2,000 Ju-/wasi of Bushmanland were living at Tsumkwe on government subsistence (Jenny 1982:32), and in 1980 the figure had risen to 1,090 (Marshall and Ritchie 1984:44).[3]

The penetration of the contemporary cash economy into Tsumkwe was swift and its consequences far-reaching. Shortly after it established its Tsumkwe Bushman Mission in 1961, the Dutch Reformed Church Mission erected a small trade store, which reinforced the local need for cash. By 1971, the store had grown so large that the government-controlled Bantu Investment Corporation (later renamed First Development Corporation, or ENOK) had to take it over. At the same time Europeans started complaining about the cash-induced drunkenness and prostitution. Within a year articles purchased from the store had started displacing bride service (labor to pay bride price) as a mode of legitimating marriage among local Ju-/wasi.

Despite pleas from the highly influential Odendaal Commission that the Bushman affairs commissioner be a skilled and sensitive person, the position became a revolving door, with a high turnover of commissioners who saw the posting as an isolated and dead-end position. Most commissioners lasted for less than two years. Previous skills were hardly relevant. Given this situation and lack of interest from the "center," development and implementation of even a small project was difficult. Instead it was easier simply to dole out rations and welfare for "needy" cases. Very little development, in most conventional senses, appears to have been initiated by McIntyre's successors. For example, almost all of the forty-four boreholes in Bushmanland were sunk under the auspices of Nature Conservation rather than Native Affairs, according to the senior nature conservator stationed at Tsumkwe. In short, Bushmanland represents a classic case of what Jeremy Beckett called "welfare colonialism" (Beckett 1985).

Despite the administrative efforts to provide food, livestock, plowing services and occasional jobs at Tsumkwe, the settlement is characterized by overcrowding, conflict and a host of other social problems like alcoholism, malnutrition, exceptionally high infant-mortality rates, apathy and general alienation (Gordon 1984b; Marshall and Ritchie 1984; van der Westhuizen et al. 1987). Environmental degradation accentuated the need for alternatives to foraging. A common refrain heard was "hunger has grabbed us."[4]

Despite this dismal record, such is the importance of Bushmen— and surely it can only be ideological—that Bushmanland has attracted many distinguished visitors, from the United Nations secretary-general

Former foragers collecting rations at Tsumkwe in 1978. Is this the triumph of welfare colonialism? (Photo courtesy of South African Museum)

to folksinger Ivan Rebroff.[5] The ideological importance of Bushmen is brought into focus when the activities of missionary societies are considered. A brief analysis of missionary activities provides a pertinent commentary on the situation in Tsumkwe.

Who Saves Whom? The Role of the Missions

In the 1950s and 1960s Bushmen were, comparatively speaking, neglected by the Lutherans. Perhaps it was realized that scarce resources could be spent more profitably elsewhere. Possibly, the fact that most of the farmers in the northern districts were by then Afrikaners, who were hostile to "foreign" missionaries, also influenced the Lutherans.[6] In addition, the public-relations value of Bushmen had been eclipsed by the "most primitive" Asmat of Netherlands New Guinea, where the Lutherans had opened a new mission. This is evident if one pages through back issues of *Berichte der Rheinische Mission*. In their time the Bushmen enjoyed a disproportionate amount of publicity and photographs in this publication, but by the 1950s and 1960s they had been largely displaced by the Asmat.

By far the most significant mission action was, however, that launched by the Dutch Reformed Church (DRC) Mission. In the early 1960s, when the DRC's activities in Nigeria were about to be curtailed because of its association with Apartheid, the DRC decided to enter the already over-crowded mission field of Namibia. A Missionary Planning Commission was established, and one of its key members was J. P. Bruwer. Not only was he an ex-missionary, but he was also one of the few ethnographers to have worked in Namibia. Well-connected, including service on the Executive Committee of the ultrasecret Broederbond (Wilkins and Strydom 1978), Bruwer was to become a member of the Odendaal Commission, the body that had developed the blueprint for imposing Bantustan homelands on Namibians. After that he was appointed first commissioner general for the native peoples of Namibia and, as such, had personal access to the South African prime minister.

Like the Lutherans before them, the DRC decided to focus on Bushmen. They obtained an inordinate amount of publicity from their Bushman Mission. Most articles in the local Windhoek press that dealt with Bushmen also dealt with the activities of the DRC Mission among them. What these articles romanticized was not so much Bushmen as the glamor of missionizing (and an appeal to send contributions).

Hot on the heels of the government's establishment of a Bushman reserve, the DRC announced that it would be opening a Bushman Mission among the "primitive Bushmen of the Kalahari Desert" because the reserve would "provide an opportunity for doing missionary work among them on an organized basis for the first time" (*Cape Argus*, 3 October 1960).

A year later, a young, inexperienced, idealistic missionary, Ferdie Weich, pitched his tent at Tsumkwe.[7] He sank his own borehole and by 1964–1965 had built a small school, clinic and trade store. He rapidly became a folk hero to many Afrikaans-speaking students, and many of them spent their vacations helping him. Reflecting on his experiences in 1964, he noted that the Bushmen lost interest very quickly as a result of their "instinctual nomadic lifestyle" (Weich 1964).

The church celebrated its first ten years in Tsumkwe with the publication of an informative brochure, but no converts. By this time, Weich was working full-time on translating the Bible into Ju-/wasi, under the sponsorship of the South African Bible Society. Given the small number of Ju-/wasi, let alone the number of Ju-/wasi readers, and the fact that all schooling was in Afrikaans, this project must surely rank as one of the more eccentric examples of idealism. Another missionary, the Reverend J. M. Swanepoel, ran the mission, and his style was almost the antithesis of Weich's laissez-faire approach (see *Die Regte Mense*, various issues, 1982). Swanepoel immediately set about organizing film evenings and weekend camps for Bushman schoolchildren. He brought in evangelists from the (revivalist) Dorothea Mission and boosted mailings of the quarterly newsletter to friends of the mission from 500 to 1,200.[8]

At the end of 1972, the South African Bible Society decided to withdraw its support of Weich's Bible translation, and the Dutch Reformed church was left with the problem of having two missionaries at Tsumkwe, both of whom wanted to stay. Eventually, it was decided to retain Weich with permission to devote one day a week to Bible translation. Swanepoel accepted a position in South Africa and later Grootfontein.[9]

Of Breakthroughs and Mass Conversion

Finally in 1973 after years of unsuccessful proselytization, there was a "Breakthrough Amongst the Bushmen" (*Die Suidwester,* 12 September 1973) following an intensive three-week campaign conducted by the Dorothea Mission, which worked through two sets of interpreters. *Die Suidwester* described what happened. A Bushman named Bo was bound by his hands and feet and brought before the Bushmen at a service. He was then released and dressed in white clothes. "The demonstration made a big impression. More than 200 Bushmen were baptized" (*Die Suidwester,* 15 May 1973). For baptism, each male was given a new white shirt and a pair of blue trousers and each female received a new dress. In a press statement, the mission secretary explained that "these Bushmen were confirmed after intensive catechism and serious discussions which demonstrated that they were in earnest about their new religion [however], the Church did not want to impair the Bushmen's own identity and as far as possible, Bushmen will be trained to do religious work among their own people" (*Windhoek Advertiser,* 24 October 1973). In a press interview, the secretary enthused:

> This breakthrough can lead to progress for the Bushmen. Viewed from an economic and hygienic point of view, they will be much better off.
>
> We want to emphasize one thing, that it is not our aim to change the culture of these people.
>
> While we will do everything in our power to enrich their standard of living and spiritual life, we want, above all, to see that they remain Bushmen. Thus, we also intend to create a pure Bushman congregation there. (*Die Suidwester,* 23 September 1973)

Despite all the publicity given to this mass conversion, by February 1974, when Weich returned to Tsumkwe from vacation, he found a palpable spirit of rebellion among his congregants. Not only had church attendance dropped to about twelve, but also a Bushman deputation had been to the Bushman affairs commissioner to request the removal of the mission from the reserve. The mission never recovered from the psychological trauma of rejection, and church attendance declined consistently.[10]

In a bid to rationalize its resources, the Dutch Reformed church withdrew Weich from Tsumkwe in 1975 and stationed him in Grootfontein so that he could work among farm Bushmen.[11] Church prospects, however, improved markedly the following year. Not only did the white congregations of Grootfontein and Tsumeb agree to underwrite the missionary effort in their farming district, the Gobabis church members did the same. More important, it was the year that Omega base was established in the western Caprivi to house and train Angolan Bushman refugees and the Dutch Reformed Church Mission was allowed to proselytize there as well.

Cooperation between church and state should not be underestimated. Why, after all those years, did the DRC Mission decide to work on the Grootfontein and Tsumeb farms? Part of the answer, surely, is that such activities were seen as part of the counterinsurgency strategy adopted by the South African army. Most of the work of the church was in the northern parts of the district—precisely those areas that SWAPO guerrillas penetrated during the rainy seasons. Because SWAPO was portrayed as a bunch of godless Communists, then, clearly, if one had devout Dutch Reformed Bushmen in the vicinity, they would be able to provide valuable tracking and observational services to the South African Defence Force. No wonder the Afrikaans-speaking farmers in the area were supportive of the mission's activities, even ferrying workers to church meetings and accommodating university students who spent their June–July vacations (an off-season for guerrillas) on the farms, proselytizing Bushmen farm workers.

Weich did not find the change to working with predominantly Heikom Bushmen very satisfying and soon transferred to the Cape and was replaced by Swanepoel. Two years later, in 1978, it was decided to reopen Tsumkwe Mission with a permanent missionary. This decision was made because the South African army intended resettling 4,000 to 5,000 Bushmen in Bushmanland by the end of 1979. By reopening Tsumkwe the army hoped to "prevent competition which would confuse the Bushmen." Swanepoel undertook this task but within a few months was asked to leave by the government because he was allegedly overinvolved in the 1978 ethnic political elections.[12] In his stead, the redoubtable and experienced Weich was recalled. He found the situation much changed as a result of the large influx of cash and liquor, but the Lord was providing new opportunities, as the army was concentrating its Bushman settlers at strategic points on an ethnic basis—farm workers at one camp, Angolan refugees at another—and this sedentarization was providing him with an opportunity to preach to people who would not otherwise have had the benefit of missionaries.[13]

By 1982, Weich had to cope with three different language groups at fifteen posts, most of them army bases. At the same time, he was uneasy about the pervasive air of uncertainty, as the following extended quote from his annual report discloses only too well:

> Furthermore, there is the presence of the Military here. Many of the Bushmen are here because the Military is here. Many of the points where people live have been placed on the map by the Military. But above everything which there is and which is being done is written: "Temporary." And who can answer the question: "How long?" The Military may stay here for years, but they may also leave within a few years. And when they are gone what will happen? Who will maintain the water installations? If not, where will the people move to? Will they stay in this area? If they stay, how will they survive? And if they move away, who knows where, what will we do? There is the possibility of independence. Is it coming? And if it is coming, when? What does the word mean? What will our position be? Will the whites stay, or will they trek? Will the Military stay or will it be drastically reduced? If the Military leaves, what about the economy of the country? To what degree does the present wave of affluence depend on cash brought in from outside by the Military? And if the wave of affluence subsides, if the policy towards the Bushmen should drastically change, how will they live? Will this area even be able to exist as a Bushman area or will they migrate to the cities and towns and wash up against their outskirts like jetsam?

There are, of course, no answers to these searching questions.

Chapter 20

Denouement: Captives of the Image of Wild Bushmen

The first South African cabinet minister to visit Tsumkwe was told by Ju-/wasi in no uncertain terms that "Times are difficult. The season is dry and game is scarce. We cannot go on living like this. Teach us to do something ourselves like the Bantu . . . so that we can live like other people. . . . [Another said:] We live like the wild animals of the veld. We have no home because we are harassed everywhere" (*Die Burger*, 13 August 1960). Like other oppressed, Bushmen constantly pondered the cause of their oppression. Inevitably their conclusion was that it was because they did not own cattle (Silberbauer and Kuper 1966).

Veteran filmmaker of Bushmen John Marshall understood this issue all too clearly and with remarkable energy created a Bushman Development Foundation to help Ju-/wasi realize these aspirations. His efforts, however, ran into a bureaucratic brick wall because the Department of Nature Conservation had persuaded the local Ju-/wasi to have the habitable portion of Bushmanland declared a game park. Nature Conservation was strongly opposed to stock farming in Bushmanland, as this would destroy the "pristine" image of the game park. Bushmen would be allowed to stay in the park, provided they lived "traditionally" (as defined not by them but the local white nature conservator).[1] Eventually, in the face of international opposition, Nature Conservation compromised and had Bushmanland declared a zone for trophy hunting of lions and elephants by rich foreign sportsmen. This controversy must be located within the broader sphere of bureaucratic politics.

The Rise of Nature Conservation and the Demise of Bushmen

As the fortunes of the Department of Bantu Administration went into decline because of the international public odium attached to the emblematic "Department of Apartheid," the star of Nature Conservation rose. With the completion of tarred roads linking Namibia with South Africa in the 1960s, mass white tourism became feasible. The dominant "parks" ideology at that time laid heavy emphasis on parks as a place for "beer and braais" (barbecues), especially because land previously used for such leisure activities was being increasingly taken up by mainline activities like farming. The department's approach was to make these "national treasures" available to the ordinary white, so there was a strong emphasis on, for example, caravan parks. Increasing white affluence in Namibia and especially South Africa encouraged travel as a leisure activity. Several writers, most notably Henri Lefebvre (1971), have stressed the critical importance of these leisure activities for the reproduction and maintenance of inequality within the larger society. Travel of this genre allows for time-outs from the rat race, from the contradictions and tensions inherent in southern African society, and thus allows, paradoxically, for reinforcing the system.

With the collapse of white agriculture in Namibia (Moorsom 1982) and the tenuous situation of fishing and mining, the new economic development buzzword became "tourism." Until 1980, Nature Conservation was part of the white ethnic administration, but then it was incorporated into the national government. This change of status allowed it to move into the black "homelands." As de la Bat put it, "There are large areas with tremendous conservation and tourism potential which are yet unexploited and need to be developed" (de la Bat 1982).[2]

Tourism was seen as a panacea: It was believed to be an industry that could be developed rapidly and without large investment. The drumbeat of *tourism* had an almost cargo-cult-like air: All the believers had to do was provide the facilities, and tourists would drop in to save the economy of the country.

By the 1980s, too, the emergent urban-based alienated white petite bourgeoisie had became more sophisticated in its tastes and conscious of growing environmental problems. Adjusting the sails of tourism, Nature Conservation began to explore the viability of elite expeditions to "natural and wild" parts of Namibia in addition to its mass-tourism strategy. And it is this strategy that sets the context for the Bushmanland game park controversy.

Why then did the Ju-/wasi originally agree to the nature conservationist's proposal? One of the primary reasons was the fact that Ju-/wasi felt that this would discourage, even prevent, the influx of their more sophisticated, landless, and culturally distinct Bushman brethren from Angola or from the white farms in the old Police Zone. In addition, the game conservator, who had been in Bushmanland longer than any other white official, was more dynamic than the various Bushman affairs commissioners and capable of getting things done, like sinking boreholes, which Ju-/wasi appreciated.

The new threat was inspired largely by the fact that Bushmen were heavily recruited into the South African Defence Force (SADF) and the army needed a place to resettle discharged soldiers. Indeed the "prae-torianization" of Bushmen represents a cultural pinnacle in the manipulation of Bushman imagery by Western society.

The "Praetorianization" of the Bushmen

Recruitment of Bushmen into the SADF started in 1974 when the army established a base in the Caprivi, appropriately named Alpha, in order to train Bushmen as trackers in the low-intensity war against SWAPO insurgents, who were fighting for the liberation of Namibia. The following year the western Caprivi witnessed a large influx of Bushmen refugees fleeing from the ravages of war-torn Angola, and Omega base was established to provide them with food and shelter. By 1978 Omega housed some 3,000 Bushman refugees. Interviews conducted by SADF ethnologists with these refugees provided an interesting profile: They were, comparatively speaking, a settled people. Seventy percent were said to have had fields that they cultivated regularly. Close to 73 percent claimed that they had owned livestock, and over 50 percent stated that they had previously lived in brick houses (R. D. Coertze, personal comment). According to a most recent army version of their past, Vasekele[3] Bushmen had lived peacefully in southeastern Angola until the late 1960s, when guerrillas started abducting and impressing them into their army. The remaining Bushmen fled and joined the Portuguese counterinsurgency units. Then, during one of South Africa's raids into Angola in 1975, South African Bushman trackers met up with fleeing Vasekele Bushmen soldiers and their families. "It took little persuasion to encourage the *Vasekele* to join" (*Paratus*, February 1983:28). Most Vasekele saw their sojourn at Omega as temporary and wanted to return to Angola when circumstances permitted (Marais 1984).

These refugees formed the core of the white-officered 201st Battalion. They joined up "not only because of the absence of employment in this virtually underdeveloped area but also because they fear that if the guerrillas are victorious they will be massacred for having supported the Portuguese in Angola" (*New York Times*, 24 February 1981).[4] Given the general psychological climate pervading Omega, it was difficult to talk about Bushmen "volunteering." The relatively high salaries and services received for signing up easily created the delusion that it was an act of "free choice." Certainly their decision to join was not a well-informed choice: "Lt. Wolff admits that the Bushmen have 'no political sense' and

know little about the causes in the war which they are helping to fight.
. . . 'They do ask what is going to happen to them' in the future. . . . 'At
this stage I can't tell them anything,' he says. 'I'm here for the fighting
part, not the talking'" (*Christian Science Monitor*, 19 March 1981). A year
later, the army acknowledged that Bushmen refugees had very little
choice in the matter. They had either to sign up or leave the region
entirely (*Star*, 24 November 1982). No matter how "adult" Bushman
might be, in terms of international law, they had unwittingly become
mercenaries because by no stretch of the imagination could they be
regarded as Namibian or even South African citizens.

The SADF proudly proclaimed that it had abolished race discrimination. Black and white soldiers ostensibly received the same wages and
opportunity for promotion (but obviously Bushmen were handicapped
because they lacked the requisite educational qualifications). But on a
symbolic level the racist structure remained. The battalion insignia was
a pied crow. "The black portion of the bird represents the Bushman
population, whereas the white breast represents the white leadership
element (thus the Bushmen accept that the whites take the lead in the
development process). The crow is the first bird let out of Noah's ark
that did not return—this symbolizes the fact that the Bushmen too, will
not return to their previous customs," the commanding officer of the
201st Battalion explained (*Paratus*, 1978). And of course the symbolic
nuance of naming their base Omega was not lost on whites, who saw it
as symbolizing the end of the Bushman's nomadic ways (*Die Republikein*,
4 July 1978).

By 1981, Omega housed half the estimated population of the western
Caprivi, about 850 Bushman soldiers, 900 women and 1,500 children
(*Christian Science Monitor*, 19 March 1981), and most of the rest lived in a
squatter camp immediately outside the army camp. Omega had an estimated monthly cash flow of R 300,000, whereas annual military expen-
diture at the camp was put at R 1.75 million (*Star*, 24 November 1982).
The camp had all the classic characteristics of a total institution (Goffman 1961). Not only were all the men in the army, but children went to
an Afrikaans-language military school, where they were taught the white
South African syllabus. White officers' wives, aware that Bushman women
felt rejected, did their bit for the *Volk* by arranging "absolutely essential"
activities to keep the women occupied (*Die Burger*, 12 July 1981).

Bushman dependency on the army was recognized: "In the operational area they are more reliant on the presence of the South African
Defence Force for their daily needs than any other group" (*To the Point*,
12 September 1980), whereas the *Eastern Province Herald* (2 February
1980) observed: "Virtually the entire Bushman population of the Western Caprivi is supported by the military. If they go, the entire socio-

economic structure will collapse" (see also *New York Times,* 24 February 1981). Such dependency was necessary, according to one commanding officer, for the army to have "saved them as a tribe from extinction" (*Star,* 9 September 1981).

Given their power, how did the army perceive its wards and their tasks? Officers adduced *hate* as the major reason for Bushmen joining the army. "A Bushman's hate for SWAPO will give you the shivers . . . they hate SWAPO because they enslaved them and took their daughters for prostitutes," said Commandant Botes (*Sunday Tribune,* 1 March 1980).[5] A subsidiary myth used to support this belief was that "since earliest times they have been despised and persecuted by the other tribes" (*Eastern Province Herald,* 8 February 1980), and that "traditionally they were the drawers of water and hewers of wood for the blacks" (*Die Burger,* 8 February 1980). Officers were aware that the category of Bushman encompassed a wide diversity of physical types. They recognized, for example, that "the other Bushman tribe is taller, and darker, and although they claim to be Bushmen, could easily be mistaken for Africans" (*Eastern Province Herald,* 21 August 1980). Yet, despite all this alleged oppression, "nothing will anger the proud yellow man more than if you tell him he's a black. He's a Bushman, nothing else," explained Commandant Botes (*Sunday Tribune,* 1 March 1980). Given the well-documented phenomenon of ethnic-identity switching in situations of oppression and the remarkable ethnic diversity in the Kavango area (see, e.g., Gordon 1978a), it was rather surprising that Bushmen did not engage in such behavior if they were as oppressed as the army alleges.

Another reason given by officers for Bushmen signing up was that they had nothing much to do: "Traditionally the man here is in heaven. The only thing he does is plough fields. The women do all the work. It's taken years to teach the man to do his part. But we are gaining. We do it through school—agriculture is a compulsory subject" (*Star,* 9 October 1981).

But there were other factors as well in their recruitment. Bushmen were highly valued as trackers because in settler mythology they had a reputation for being the best trackers in the world (*Die Huisgenoot,* 14 April 1978). Their field craft was legendary in the SADF. According to the second-in-command at Omega: "If a patrol has a Bushman with it, then it is unnecessary to post guards at night. The Bushman also goes to sleep. But when the enemy is still far away he wakes up and raises the alarm" (*Die Burger,* 6 January 1982). Their reputation as trackers also meant that they were recruited for psychological purposes: It was hoped that Bushmen would inspire fear among the guerrilla forces but that they would also boost the morale of the SADF. They were living talismans: "With the Bushmen along, our chances of dying are very slight,"

Christmas in the Kalahari, military style. Omega military base, early 1980s. (Photo courtesy of author)

one trooper said (*Time*, 2 March 1981). Bushmen had become prisoners of their own reputation.[6]

The press were enraptured by "these beautiful people" (*Pretoria News*, 26 February 1981), and delightful vignettes of the problems of "guided culture change" were the order of the day. Usually they involved the Bushman's alleged special aptitude for mathematics, their legendary athletic prowess and their love of singing. Charming stories were recounted about the many married youngsters at the primary school because, as Commandant Botes explained, they married at ten and babies were usually born when the mother was about fourteen (*Die Volksblad*, 15 July 1981). They were "very emotional," and wives did not want their husbands away on patrol for longer than a month. Likewise, a widow was never a widow for longer than a month (*Die Volksblad*, 3 July 1981). Despite this, Botes assured the press, Bushmen were rather prudish. Adultery was not tolerated, and polygyny was for those who had nothing to do (*Die Volksblad*, 15 July 1981).

Officers relished their paternalistic attempts at "upliftment,"[7] which they rationalized by arguing that it would enable Bushmen to protect and be proud of their identity. To this end, for example, the school curriculum was modified to allow schoolchildren to spend a few days in

A Bushman soldier with an officer of the Pied Crow Battalion at Omega in the 1980s. Photograph emphasizes difference in stature. (Photo courtesy of State Archives, Windhoek)

the bush every year, in the belief that they would then maintain their basic "hunting culture."

Generally, officers accepted as inevitable the extinction of Bushmen and argued that their program was aimed at smoothing the way for Bushman assimilation into the emergent black rural proletarian culture (see, e.g., *Armed Forces*, 1980). The program, which was based on the premise that Bushmen should become like whites, involved adult education, religious training courtesy of the Dutch Reformed church, some agriculture, hygiene, sewing and baking, "while the importance of neatness is also continually stressed" (*Paratus*, 1978). Very little attention was given to what would happen after the SADF left.

This involvement in guided cultural change was actively encouraged: "The Defence Force does not only make war. On the contrary, the task of civilizing . . . is probably greater than the military function" (*Die Volksblad*, 15 July 1981). Although the SADF has a large ethnology section, drawn mostly from ethnologists trained at Afrikaans-language universities, its "civilizing" program seemed, at best, ad hoc, naïve and contradictory. Lieutenant Wolff, "the only white soldier fluent in the Bushman's language . . . is adamant that the South African Army is not Westernizing the Bushmen, who are no longer nomadic, but live at Omega" (*Daily News*, 24 February 1981). "Our aim is not to Westernize them, but to make them a better Bushman," he was widely quoted as saying (e.g., *New York Times*, 24 February 1981).

Encouraged by its success, the SADF started applying the Omega model to Bushmanland in 1978. It settled Bushmen "according to a socio-economic scheme and as far as possible in family groups at certain 'growth points,'" ostensibly to protect them from SWAPO. Yet "Bushmanland," as even a neophyte geographer knows, was of minimal, if any, strategic value in the struggle for Namibia. So enthusiastic was the SADF about Bushman recruits that it lowered its minimum educational requirements for them. In 1982 the Bushmanland unit was given battalion status. Whereas other "population groups" each had a single battalion, Bushmen had two! Bushmen had the dubious distinction of becoming the most militarized ethnic group in the world (Lee and Hurlich 1982).

Originally, the SADF had its base at Tsumkwe, but it was soon forced to move away because of water scarcity and increasing social tensions between the local Ju-/wasi and the Angolan Bushman soldiers brought in to form the nucleus of the new unit. Conflict between the different Bushman groups in the army was such a problem that each group was segregated into a different camp.

The SADF's high salaries (R 500 per month plus rations) and civic actions in the fields of health and education quickly resulted in the majority of Bushmanland's population's becoming dependent upon them. Ominously for the local Ju-/wasi, the Angolan soldiers named their main base, Luhebu, "our home" (*Paratus*, August 1979:6).

The SADF expected to have some 1,200 troops in Bushmanland by 1987, including 800 with their families, creating a military-dependent population of some 6,000. The impact of this large-scale influx on a fragile ecosystem is disconcerting, yet for all the Department of Nature Conservation's concern about such matters, it raised no public voice in criticism.

What alarmed Ju-/wasi was the fear that the SADF was going to use Bushmanland as a resettlement site for its redundant Angolan refugees and mercenaries. Predictably, the SADF decided that for "security reasons" Bushmanland had to be "developed."[8] What was this aid package that catered to the perceived "vacuums" in development? Rather conventional straitlaced projects. First, agriculture—gardening plots measuring 30 meters by 100 meters were allotted to male relatives of soldiers, but they were forfeited if the recipients did not work them. Second, there was medical care. Pre- and postnatal clinics "are in the offing and the need for geriatric care is also being realized." Third, "education is the modern day assurance of survival and as such enjoys high priority" (especially as the army enjoys a surplus of teachers doing national service). Last, permanent housing that would "encourage a general standard of community welfare and hygiene. The Bushman was also encouraged to see his investment of a salary in a permanent housing structure as an investment" (*Paratus*, February 1983:27–31). So successful was the Bushman "experiment" that the army sent recruiting teams armed with video presentations to the Bushman farm schools. The favorite game of these farm schoolchildren became "army army." In all this, the critical question of what would happen when the South African army left was conveniently left in abeyance. Indeed the general commanding the South West African Territorial Force found the question to be a nonissue (*Star*, 24 November 1982).

The grip of praetorianism on pariahs is viselike. With independence under a SWAPO government inevitable, Bushman soldiers were given a choice of remaining in Namibia or of following their masters back to South Africa. Most chose the latter. Five days prior to Namibia's independence on 19 March 1990, the South African Defence Force resettled 3,915 Bushmen at Schmidtsdrift, near Kimberley, in South Africa, at a cost of R 5.5 million (*Vrye Weekblad*, 30 March 1990).

The above data run counter to most of the established ethnographic record. If I am accused of "quoting out of context," then I would submit that given the frequency and consistency of these reports from a wide variety of press sources, they represent fair comment and reflect the weltanschauung of the army. Those misrepresentations by the army and press formed a crucial part of the ideological justification of their policies, yet few South African anthropologists publicly challenged them.[9]

Part 5

Have We Met the Enemy and Is It Us?

Chapter 21

On Vulnerability and Violence

One night while collecting "Bushman stories" around the camp fire, P. J. Schoeman, *volkekundige* (ethnologist) and chairman of the Commission for the Preservation of the Bushmen (1951–1954), was told by his principal informant: "You made us a race of nomads and refugees. Our pregnant mothers gave birth to their children while they were fleeing from you" (Schoeman 1957:12). Yet Schoeman ignored this crucial topic.[1] Later, when his informant told him that Germans and Afrikaners had shot Bushmen like wild dogs and wolves, Schoeman replied: "Only those of your people who murdered and stole cattle, Xameb. We must cover the truth with sand" (Schoeman 1957:206). Twenty years after that book's original publication in Afrikaans, Schoeman wrote an article entitled "Orphans of Africa." Bushmen were dying out, he said, as there were only some 2,000 in Botswana, about 100 in the Kalahari Gemsbok Game Park and between 8,000 and 10,000 in the Kavango region. They had become extinct in South Africa as a result of a "tragic reciprocal misunderstanding."[2] In Namibia their numbers were diminishing because of their lust for tobacco. Unable to restrain this craving, Bushmen trekked up to the Kavango River, where they sold their wives to black migrant workers returning from the mines for tobacco. These migrant workers would eventually infect *all* the women with venereal disease with fatal results because Bushmen would flee rather than see a white doctor (Schoeman 1971).

This study has stressed the interplay among policy, economics and academics as they meshed to shape a future for those labeled "Bushmen" in Namibia. Its special moral concern has been that of anthropological silence or, worse, denial. Genocide is a topic that surprisingly we anthropologists seem to lack a capacity to recognize even though it is widely recognized that forager groups are especially vulnerable to this scourge

(Kuper 1981).[3] This strange neglect arises, I suspect, from our inability to *see*, coupled with an inadequate theoretical framework with which to plumb the depths of violence and its associated terror.[4]

It is still very much an issue. A recent article by Solway and Lee (1990) argued that tales of Botswana Bushman oppression were largely a figment of the colonial authorities' imagination and served as a convenient justification for establishing colonial overrule.[5] Descriptions of servitude by Bushman and black alike, the authors asserted, are exaggerated. Solway and Lee (1990) were puzzled by the incongruity between the overstated degree of inequality described by Kalahari residents and the relative ease with which Bushman "serfs" disappear into the desert, leaving their "masters" high and dry. They concluded that "in no instance in which hereditary serfdom has been asserted by Kgalagadi has it been observed in practice." Similarly Wilmsen (1989a) had Bushmen and Herero speakers happily interdigitating before the detritus of the capitalist world system swamped them, but even after the deluge he portrayed a relatively peaceful scene.[6]

On a rhetorical level the Botswana situation shows remarkable similarities to that in Namibia, but in the latter there is certainly substance to the rhetoric. To be sure there are important differences. The evidence that Herero speakers were inhabiting the western Kalahari is by no means as clear as that asserted by Wilmsen (1989) for Botswana. On the Herero reserves were also found small numbers of Bushmen, and there the rhetoric of servitude was common coin. Like their Botswana neighbors, few people in Namibia could actually provide specific instances of violence. This image was however contradicted by court and archival records. Thus before one even addresses the issue of violence, the problem of how to reconcile informants' accounts with the court records must be dealt with. The point about the various cases discussed in this book is not that violence was an everyday occurrence or that it had to occur in the presence of anthropologists to be significant. Writing about such acts in violence-torn Lebanon, Michael Gilsenan put it well:

> Like miracles they occur only rarely and are exceptional. . . . The moment comes out of the blue, though it does not surprise because its density and concentration are taken to be expressive and a manifestation of more general and universally operating schema of what life is. . . . As the holy man's act of grace witnesses to the wider plan of things, the hidden reality behind the worlds appearances, so the [white or black] lord's act expresses the nature of the reality of those same appearances. (Gilsenan 1986:29)

There is irrefutable evidence that violence is indeed a feature of life in the northeastern Kalahari. The more important question is, what is it that makes this area so conducive to acts of savagery by both blacks and whites?

Frontiers and Other "Rough" Situations

Formal and informal policy resulted in Bushmen's having three options: resist, flee or acquiesce, which were practiced in varying mixes. That Bushmen were active in banditlike resistance activities during the period from about 1906 to 1939[7] should surprise no one, for geographically the area was well suited to banditry: It was remote and inaccessible, and travel over the thick sand was notoriously slow and cumbersome. Indeed, as Eric Hobsbawm observed: Hunter-gatherers supply a disproportionately large number of social bandits when their society is incorporated into larger economies based on class conflict (Hobsbawm 1969:14).

> [Bandits consist] essentially of relatively small groups of men living on the margins of peasant society, and whose activities are considered criminal by the prevailing official power-structure and value-system, but not (or not without strong qualifications) by the peasantry. It is this special relation between peasant and bandit which makes banditry "social": the social bandit is a hero, a champion, a man whose enemies are the same as the peasants, whose activities correct injustice, control oppression and exploitation, and perhaps even maintain alive the ideal of emancipation and independence. (Hobsbawm 1973:143)

Clearly the Bushman material straddles the conventional wisdom on banditry. In one sense the Bushmen were social bandits, but in another, they were not. Namibians have a great need for the elaboration of a mythology of heroic resistance to the colonial incursion. There is more than enough evidence to suggest that Bushmen have the makings of being canonized into political heroes. Yet why has this not occurred? An answer must surely consider the related issue of the demise of Bushman banditry.

According to Hobsbawm, banditry goes into decline when the area undergoes "modernization . . . the combination of economic development, efficient communications, and public administration, [which] deprives any kind of banditry, including the social, of the conditions under which it flourishes" (Hobsbawm 1969:15). But such a technological deterministic explanation does not go far enough. Bushman banditry was of a terminal type. They were never able to make the transition from social banditry into revolution or common criminality because they were locked into a system of social arrangements that made them "natural" bandits. These factors included, most important, their mode of living, which called for a comparatively low labor demand, whereas band social organization enhanced their spatial and social flexibility, manifested in their relative autonomy and ability to live off the land. Commoditized social relationships with other sections of the emergent Namibian society were tenuous at best.

Their strength (and weakness) lay in their not being irreversibly ensnared within the capitalistic world market system. At the same time, with the decline in the ivory-hunting market, Bushmen were undergoing a process of marginalization, and this was exacerbated by the German ban on firearms in 1892. These events, coupled with settler expansion, shaped the form of Bushman banditry. Bushman marginalization was of such a nature that band/gang/horde solidarity was never strong enough to counter a social system and ideology that bred informers at a remarkable rate. The major factor responsible for the decline of Bushman banditry was simply that the government recruited more and more Bushmen as trackers and police messengers (see, e.g., Marshall 1976:283). Many Bushmen joined the police for the rewards of money, guns, horses, power and women it offered. It was the efforts of these trackers that led to the demise of Bushman banditry and to Bushmen's being irrevocably associated with the coercion of the oppressor in the minds of other oppressed groups.

Another option for Bushmen was to flee beyond the Police Zone. One consequence of movement into this ecologically fragile area was that, in order to survive, many Bushmen were forced to engage in banditry against black migrant workers who, until the introduction of motorized transport in the 1930s, had to walk along the dry river beds en route to their homes in the north. Contrary to popular belief, the Kalahari is not simply an open expanse of vacant land. Large parts are waterless and other parts are claims in a complex system of land tenure (Wilmsen 1989b). Many Bushman refugees were thus forced to congregate on the emerging public thoroughfares. The state deliberately fostered and used the image of "wild" Bushmen in an effort to deter black labor desertions. Another consequence of this population pressure was that more Bushmen were forced to settle in the Ovambo and Kavango "native reserves." This was a development of no small consequence. By 1945, for example, the Kavango native commissioner estimated that up to a third of the total Kavango population consisted of Bushmen. Bushmen living in such areas inevitably attached themselves to black households, where their status approximated that of villeinage. Their assistance in black agricultural activities resulted in more blacks' being released to participate in the state-controlled migrant-labor scheme.

The third option was to remain on the settler farms and become, in effect, a rural (lumpen)proletariat. Most of the farms on which Bushmen worked bordered on the Police Zone, an area notorious for its high labor desertion rates. The presence of large numbers of low-paid or unpaid, potentially "wild" Bushmen on these farms served to deter other workers from absconding and moreover had the effect of depressing wages for other workers as well.

The Role of Firearms in Bushman Conquest

Although it is commonly assumed that firearms played an important role in "opening up of the frontier" and "taming" Bushmen, the situation is much more complex than most historians believe.[8] First, one needs to consider the efficiency of firearms. The most commonly used firearm was the flintlock (von Moltke n.d.[a]; Lategan 1971, 1974). The Thirstland Trekkers, for example, still used flintlocks until the end of the nineteenth century because of a shortage of percussion caps. Flintlocks were notoriously unreliable, averaging a misfire in every 5 shots and wildly inaccurate beyond a 50-meter range, even when used by an expert marksman. A statistician calculated that in one of the Eastern Cape frontier wars, it took at least 80,000 bullets to render 25 enemy hors de combat, whereas in more favorable conditions of a European war the ratio ranged from 1:250 to 1:437 (Shineberg 1971:80) Perhaps one can understand why many of the Great White Hunters let their camp followers face charging elephants with flintlocks while the hunters lay inebriated in their wagons (Chapman n.d.).

Flintlocks were replaced by percussion-lock rifles, which gradually found their way into South Africa after 1840. They were certainly more reliable, as they had an estimated misfire rate of 4 or 5 in 1,000. But they were still unwieldy weapons to operate. Thirstland Trekker and big-game hunter Jan Harm Labuschagne's description of the complex gymnastics involved in loading from the saddle has been preserved in Lategan 1971:

The powder-horn had already been replaced by a flask, from which the precise amount of powder for the charge could be measured. It had a catch at the neck, which was pressed down with a finger to open the slide; at the same time the thumb closed the mouth of the flask and this was now inverted, allowing the neck-measure to fill with powder. When the catch was released it snapped shut, thus sealing off the correct amount. Labuschagne relates: "To load during the chase was an art . . . the hunter always held his gun in his right hand; in order to load, he had to lower the gun by the stock until the muzzle was within easy reach of his left hand, which still held the reins. The gun powder was now measured out from the flask, which hung on the left side, and poured down the muzzle of the gun, something that required the greatest dexterity, considering that the rider was never still in the saddle for a moment. The bullet was taken from the pouch and inserted in the muzzle. Now the ramrod was drawn and used to ram the bullet down on to the powder. It was easier to put the ramrod into the barrel than to replace it in the groove under the barrel. When the ramrod was replaced, you pulled back the cock to the half-cock (safe) position, and if the exploded percussion cap remained in position, it was flicked off with the finger. Then you took a fresh cap from the cap-pouch . . . pushed it on the nipple and pulled the cock back into the full-cock position, and now you could fire." (Lategan 1971:524)

In sum then, it is naïve to presume that Bushmen were wiped out simply because colonizers had firearms. This is historically unlikely for three reasons: Reloading was slow and clumsy; there was a high rate of misfire and there was only minimal accuracy. These factors were not such a drawback when hunters were in large parties and firing into large herds of game, but when the gun was used as a weapon of warfare against Bushmen, the odds were at least even, if not with the Bushmen.[9]

The crucial factor in "pacifying" the Cape Bushmen in the seventeenth and eighteenth centuries (e.g., Marks 1972, 1981) and in the Namibian wars of the nineteenth century was not so much firearms as mobility from horsepower. The Kaukauveld, with its deep sand, limited water and endemic horse sickness, ensured that local Bushmen were able to retain their autonomy until well into the latter half of the nineteenth century. The firearms revolution occurred after 1880, when the old guns gradually gave way to the Martini-Henry rifle, and later, the German Mauser rifle, most deadly of all, finally signaled the technological change.

Dispossession of Land in the Northeastern Namibian Frontier Zone

From a Bushman perspective, the decisive moment was not the penetration of capital but the arrival of the state. Prior to this, Kaukauveld Bushmen were more than able to hold their own against antagonistic outsiders. The role of the state was critical because it encouraged settlers by providing protection and collateral for loans and by intervening in the control of labor (Bley 1971; Drechsler 1969).

The nature of Bushman social organization, coupled with the coercive nature of the authoritarian colonial state, made violence the means of choice whereby Bushmen were to be controlled. In this respect the notion of "primitive accumulation" or "booty capitalism" has merit[10] in that it directs attention to the continuous process of (violent) dispossession, which according to most dictionary definitions is the hallmark of the frontier, but which more academic definitions overlook.

If in the political economy of genocide committed against Bushmen, the means of coercion constituted the sufficient conditions, then surely the dispossession of their land constituted the necessary condition. Laws of the state authorized this settler access to Bushman land. A comparison of the maps provided by Glass (1939) in the 1930s with those of Budack (1980), although it does not convey a completely accurate picture, provides a sense of the extent of dispossession while the territory was administered by South Africa as a mandate of the erstwhile League of Nations. The point is well made by Wilbur Jacobs: "Next to outright extermination the best technique of destroying natives was dispossessing them of their land. Land for the aborigines was all important because it was a spiritual ingredient of their culture; it determined their social groupings and status; and, finally, it was the source of their livelihood" (Jacobs 1971:285).

The process of land dispossession did not occur overnight. Instead it took place in spurts, which were related to changes in the world economic system such as the Great Depression, changes in attitudes in the metropoles and submetropoles (cheap land for settlers was seen as one of the ways of solving South Africa's explosive "poor white problem"), ecological factors (droughts) and, of course, the resistance of the Bushmen.

In practice, Bushmen lost their ancestral grounds through three forms of enclosure: The area in question was declared "open" to white settlement, or more marginal areas became either "native" reserves for other blacks or a game reserve. White settlers posed by far the greatest threat. Both German and South African administrations did their best to attract white farmer-settlers, and their efforts were reflected in the increasing proportion of land placed under white farmers. In 1903, this represented 4.4 percent of the total landmass; by 1910 it was 13 percent and by 1963 it amounted to 48.7 percent (Barnard 1964).

The expansion of settler farming in general can be gauged from Table 21.1. Table 21.2 focuses on the two districts with high Bushman populations, Grootfontein and Gobabis. The number of cattle in the Grootfontein district increased from 7,600 in 1908 (Kulz 1909:116) to 13,611 in 1912 (Rafalski 1930:140) to 50,860 in 1929 and 115,222 in 1937 (LGR 3/1/7).

The farming-expansion trajectories of the Grootfontein and Gobabis districts were different. In Grootfontein, whites moved in much earlier and forcibly dislodged Bushmen from their water holes. Later, in an effort to prevent cattle smuggling and illicit cattle dealing, farmers were

Table 21.1 Expansion of Settler Farming, 1904–1970

	Number of Farm Units	Area (million hectares)
1904	458	4.8
1913	1,331	13.4
1938	3,305	25.6
1946	3,980	34.4
1960	5,216	39.0
1970–1971	4,842	36.0

Sources: Richard Moorsom, *Transforming a Wasted Land* (London: Catholic Institute of International Relations, 1982), p. 30; Jurgen Bahr, *Kulturgeographische Wandlungen in der Farmzone Südwestafrikas* (Bonn: Bonner Geographische Abhandlungen, 1968), p. 34.

Table 21.2 Number and Size of Farms, Grootfontein and Gobabis Districts (selected years)

	Grootfontein		Gobabis	
	Farms	Area (hectares)	Farms	Area (hectares)
1904	25	—	20	—
1913	173	777,077	108	773,473
1982	1,058[a]	3,548,031	829	4,039,216

[a]Combines Grootfontein and Tsumeb districts.

Sources: Oswin Köhler, *A Study of Grootfontein District* (Pretoria: Government Printer, 1959); Köhler, *A Study of Gobabis District* (Pretoria: Government Printer, 1959); South African Farm Consultants, "Report on Agriculture to the Administration for Whites," Windhoek, 1983 (mimeo); Gerhard Pool, *Die Herero-Opstand, 1904–07* (Cape Town: HAUM, 1979), p. 287.

settled along the Omuramba Ovambo, thus effectively encircling the Heikom Bushmen living to the south of this Omuramba. After 1945 the authorities were forced to expand the Police Zone and reappropriate Game Reserve No. 1 to accommodate settler expansion. Bushman residents of the Etosha Game Park also suffered when a sizable chunk of the reserve was excised for white farming purposes.

In Gobabis district white settlement occurred later, partly because the railway line did not reach Gobabis until the 1920s but also because of a general lack of surface water and the prevalence of stock diseases brought on by phosphorus-denuded grasses. Penetration of the "crown lands" was gradual. The first graziers were usually farmers with so-called grass licenses, that is, farmers who, owing to drought or other factors, were given emergency grazing in these areas. They pressured the administration to put up a stock-proof fence along the Botswana border in the 1950s and eventually opened up the area that is now known as the Rietfontein Block Farms.

State and Capitalism

The state was and is a powerful and important variable:

The essential point is that the state takes on the central role of managing and representing the myriad encounters and struggles between classes and agents of different modes. The state provides economic, social, and political services for capitalist penetration, orchestrates the destruction and restructuring of elements of the pre-capitalist mode . . . and copes, so to speak, at the level of cohesion of the whole social formation with the dislocative consequences of the expansion of the capitalist mode. (Lamb 1974:131–132)

But monolithic interpretations must be avoided, for the state was involved in a dialectic of both destruction and preservation of indigenous societies.[11] Two additional caveats must be entered: First, although surface phenomena may have similar results, the structures that generate these phenomena are different.[12] Second, one needs to differentiate between the different phases of capitalism, as, for example, the eras of merchant capital and its subsequent transformation into authoritarian capital. This point is important, if only to dispel the myth that there was a qualitative difference between German and South African colonialism. When rhetoric is separated from action, the differences between the German and South African administrations in their relations with Bushmen merge into a single nightmare. Variations in policy and action toward Bushmen did not arise because of "culture" or "race" but were a direct result of the incorporation of Bushman people into different phases of the world system. During the period of merchant capital, "ethnicity" or "culture" of the merchant-hunters was insignificant. Later, the court sentences imposed upon Bushmen for various misdemeanors show no initial difference in severity. Similarly, settlers convicted for killing Bushmen were treated just as leniently by the South Africans as they were by the Germans.[13] Law played an important role in the subjugation of Bushmen: "Because of the weakness of capitalist penetration, law and state have the job of integrating and maintaining the colonial economy or the whole colonial social formation. They have to tie the traditional and the capitalist modes together into an operative whole yet keep the two sufficiently apart to preserve the integrity of tradition" (Fitzpatrick 1982:169–170).[14]

Table 21.3 Categories of Convictions of Bushmen, Grootfontein District (in percentages)

Charge	1916	1920	1937	1956	1966	1976
Assault	1.9	3.6	6.1	7.0	8.2	30.0
Stock theft	38.9	62.7	31.7	12.8	10.2	4.0
Theft	24.0	10.8	4.9	11.5	10.2	44.0
Masters/Servant	3.7	1.2	13.4	24.4	24.5	0.0
Pass/vagrancy	27.8	1.2	31.7	28.2	12.2	4.0
Weapons	0.0	2.4	14.6	4.9	0.0	0.0
Liquor	0.0	0.0	8.5	17.9	6.1	0.0
Game violations	0.0	1.2	7.3	5.8	12.2	0.0
Number	54	83	82	156	49	50
Bushmen as a % of all cases	50.4	29.1	30.5	15.8	7.6	5.9

Note: These figures exclude white convictions, which are minimal.

Source: LGR (Magistrate Grootfontein), 1/3/1–54, "Criminal Record Book."

The major weapon in the state's arsenal for internal pacification is law that is used to tackle "problems." Such legal interventions often amount to unstated policy. In these terms, the "Bushman problem" underwent changes in emphasis over time and these changing emphases indicate, in a rudimentary way, the differing phases of incorporation into the currently dominant authoritarian capitalist mode of production. Initially most cases involved workplace-related offenses, and in the Grootfontein district most of the offenders were Bushmen, but the total number of offenses was still relatively small. In Grootfontein, this period lasted from 1896 to circa 1911, when stock-theft offenses started to increase, peaking in 1920, when 62 percent of all Bushman convictions were in this category. It then showed a steady decline, until in 1976 only 4 percent of all Bushman convictions were for stock theft.[15] Thus in 1920, over 70 percent of *all* stock-theft cases involved Bushmen, but by 1976 that had dropped to only 20 percent of all stock-theft cases. Clearly, judging from court records, the proclivity of Bushmen to engage in stock theft had been neutralized.

At the same time there was a consistent increase in the application of the Masters and Servants Proclamation before it was finally abolished in the early 1970s. This major legal mechanism for forcing Bushmen to "settle down" on white farms or move beyond the Police Zone shows a constant, if erratic, application, gradually serving its purpose and then going into decline. Table 21.3 indicates a gradual transition from relatively autonomous hunting-and-foraging groups to a situation of rural proletarianization. In this regard, it is especially significant to note that in 1976, 30 percent of all cases in the Grootfontein district involved assaults, and that these assaults were almost exclusively by Bushmen upon Bushmen, an indication of the disintegration of old social forms (Marshall 1976).[16]

These court actions suggest overlapping, and at times interwoven, phases of incorporation and changes in the definition of the "Bushman problem." Initially there was a period of relatively minor labor problems. This was followed by a definition of the problem as one of banditry and stock theft and typically associated with rapid white encroachment onto Bushman land. This phase was effectively culminated by World War II. It was thought that once Bushmen had been "tamed," they had to be made into "reliable" farm workers by virtue of the master-servant laws, and this constituted the ensuing phase of incorporation, which is still current, although on a vastly reduced scale. This was the first formal wave of incorporation into the colonial order, during which time the "Bushman problem" was tackled by changing the laws. It was obvious, for example, that the vagrancy laws were aimed not so much at blacks in general as at Bushmen in particular, and no other population group suffered the problem of having one of its key instruments of production, in this case, bows and arrows, declared illegal.

During the second wave, the emphasis shifted from the legal realm to that of policy and planning, for as Romanyshyn (1971:379) noted, "The desire to maintain the stability of existing patterns of power and privilege may motivate concern with planning to deal primarily with threats to social order." Laws are subject to international scrutiny. Policy and planning are less subject to scrutiny, and the public facade of planning legitimates the regime. The second wave of incorporation took place after World War II and coincided with the increasing international focus on the territory. It was characterized by the promulgation of a Bushman reserve and attempts to tamper with the autonomy of the last of the Bushman foragers, by extending administrative control over them. This administrative control served as a de facto insurance policy for the first wave, since one of its purposes was to discourage desertions from white farms. The closing phase of this second wave occurred in the late 1960s and early 1970s. It was superseded by a "praetorianization" phase, perhaps the ultimate material manifestation of the role that Bushmen currently play in the ideology of authoritarian capitalism of the white settlers.

Ecological Extraction on the Frontier

Bunker made the point that the labor theory of value, which is the premise of much contemporary work in "world systems theory," does not work in situations like those pertaining to northeastern Namibia because the exploitation of natural and human resources uses and destroys values that cannot be calculated in terms of labor or capital (Bunker 1984). Extractive economies are different from productive economies. Models of productive economies neglect the physical effects on the environment, distribution of population and construction of infrastructure. Mandel described the dynamics of the interaction between extractive and productive economies well when he described the world system as "an articulated system of capitalist, semi-capitalist, and pre-capitalist relations of production, linked to each other by capitalist relations of exchange and dominated by the world capitalist market" (Mandel 1976:48–49).[17]

Here only one of the more dramatic effects on the environment will be discussed, namely, the wide and frequent reports of a "crisis" in settler agriculture. Farming subsidies, bad management and inexpensive labor have resulted in severe environmental abuse. The situation has been exacerbated by the fact that the system encouraged speculators to purchase farmland, graze it extensively, make high profits during the "good years" and then move on. On the basis of a study of farming practices in the Kalahari Sandveld, Leser noted: "The continuous expansion of the farmland even in ecologically favorable areas, proved . . . to be negative, when, as a result of farm division, economically unviable units emerged. The small yield was compensated by large herds of cattle, the result of which was vegetation degradation" (Leser 1975:abstract).

On the basis of extensive archival research Schmokel (1985) concluded that settler agriculture was essentially a "cultural activity," and that without the various state subsidies, white-settler agriculture would collapse. As what goes up must also come down, it follows that if capital can penetrate, it can also retreat. It could thus be argued that the recent situation represents a retreat of capitalism in parts of the country, defeated in no small part by an environment that it has abused.

Overgrazing was the result of complex factors, including inadequate fencing and low soil nutrients, but the major social factors were undoubtedly the increasing subdivision and the short-term orientation of various farmers (speculators), the latter undoubtedly stimulated by the international situation. Even where "new" farmland was brought into play, grazing pressure increased (see Table 21.4).

An important consequence of this predatory farming practice was bush encroachment. Over eight million hectares of prime grazing land are affected by bush encroachment, and as a result, cattle-raising productivity has declined by as much as 50 percent. Some areas are covered by up to 10,000 bushes per hectare, mostly of the *swarthaak* and sicklebush variety, and another four million hectares are reported to be threatened.

Table 21.4   Grazing Pressure, Indicated by Hectare per Livestock Unit

	Grootfontein District	Gobabis District	Namibia
1945–1946	10.20	13.02	21.0
1949–1950	11.39	12.20	16.9
1954–1955	8.10	9.60	13.9
1959–1960	7.80	9.80	12.7
1982[a]	13.10	10.80	12.7

[a]The decrease in pressure in 1982 is the result of a crippling drought as well as the fact that more land was available following implementation of some of the Odendaal Commission's recommendations.

Sources: Jurgen Bahr, *Kulturgeographische Wandlungen in der Farmzone Südwestafrikas* (Bonn: Bonner Geographische Abhandlungen, 1968), p. 34; South African Farm Consultants, "Report on Agriculture to the Administration for Whites." Windhoek, 1983 (mimeo).

Nearly 25 percent of the total land area is suffering from bush encroachment (Duvel 1984), and in the primary cattle-raising areas, the percentage rose to between 40 and 50 (South African Farm Consultants 1983). However, during this period bush encroachment was viewed by South African military strategists as a form of scorched earth policy, because it was the "best possible deterrent to terrorist infiltration" (South African Farm Consultants 1983).

By 1983 the marginal status of white commercial farming had become clear. Of the 205 farms in the Tsumeb district, only 49 were occupied by full-time farmers (South West Africa Broadcasting Corporation [SWABC]-TV, 4 June 1983). Similarly, in the Otavi district there were only 62 full-time farmers, living on the 296 registered farms. This caused such severe security problems for the South African military forces that many of these border farms were made available to neophyte white and black farmers at favorable terms. Unofficially, a special effort was made to settle Herero on these farms, as they were believed to be the most vehemently anti-SWAPO people in the country. The colonizers, thus, as members and active participants in the world system, whatever their individualized syncretic motives, were mainly interested in two things on the frontier: cheap land and cheap labor, both of which could be easily abused and both of which required certain cultural constructions to facilitate their exploitation.

Chapter 22

The Culture of Terror and the Inevitability of Violence

From the anthropological point of view, both racially and culturally, the Bushmen occupy a place quite apart in the human family.

—*Gusinde*

When I see the little people I know they are dream-figures that really hunt and really provide me with food and that they really see me but also do not see me because I exist in their dream, and they feed their dream by caring for me. We meet each other and know nothing of each other.

—*Stockenstrom*

What gave the Grootfontein and Kaukauveld area its distinctly permanent "frontier" air was the weakness of the capitalist mode of production there. The constraints of environment, "development policies" and indigenous socioeconomic characteristics simply did not permit the achievement of a capitalistic social system and ensured the inevitability of violence.

States have frontiers, and the state definition of the frontier as the boundary beyond which its law does not hold concurs with local-settler usage of the term. For settlers beyond the frontier, a higher degree of violence is acceptable than would be tolerated elsewhere in the territory. The inimical violence of this area was not the product of the rugged individualism of the "pioneers," be they white or Herero, operating beyond the law of the state, but the product of a fierce competition for resources or the factors of production. As Foweraker pointed out, "This violent exploitation is itself in no way capitalist, but is achieved precisely in the absence of institutionalized capitalist social relations of production" (Foweraker 1981:174). In frontier zones, violence achieves exploitation. Violence is the basic mechanism of social control in the absence of other mechanisms. Foweraker's considered conclusion that primitive accumulation is not an historic phase in the evolution of capitalism but rather a hybrid mode of accumulation that is subordinate to capitalism and that cannot reproduce itself except by destroying the environment is valid in this case as well.

The common settler view that Bushmen "have no sense of property . . . are unable to judge the real value of their wages . . . prefer wages in kind to cash [and] when coins are given them they get lost in the sand or are given to the children for toys" (Pyper 1950:51) thus has a certain logic to it. It suggests that Bushmen decided on only minimal involvement in the wider capitalist economy, preferring to invest in trinkets and other assorted artifacts that formed an integral part of their "domestic economy" (Wiessner 1982).[1] Taussig has persuasively argued that the fundamental catalyst for the production of terror is a "lack of commoditized social relationships, in interaction with commodity forces emanating from the world . . . market" (Taussig 1984:479). Power is derived from controlling access to goods that are socially valued. Bushman ability to "drop out" of employment and engage in alternative livelihoods (that is, foraging) constantly emphasized their autonomy and made it necessary for market-oriented livestock breeders to engage in violence in order to ensure their operations. But violence required dehumanization, a cultural construction. A useful lead in this regard can be found in the missionary discourse.

Ideological Resistance: The Cultural Construction of Missionaries

For arch-racists, missionaries represent a problematic segment of settler society because, in their business of proselytizing souls, they must, almost by definition, define Bushmen as humans. But do they? What influence did *volkekunde* have on their representations? And what did the failure of their enterprise tell us about Bushman vulnerability?

There were numerous attempts to explain the failure to achieve long-lasting conversions; they all followed the synoptic explanation offered by the Synodal Missionary Commission. The commission explained the backsliding after 1973 as the result of "the clash with the old culture," the more ready availability of cash, the influence of "Western culture" and the fact that attacks by the devil were still too strong. In offering this explanation, the synod was influenced by a detailed exegesis put forth a few months earlier by Swanepoel. Swanepoel made the following points in trying to explain the failure of Bushman missionization: (1) The missionary focus on "belief alone" was too abstract. (2) Bushmen were incapable of distancing themselves from their "old" culture. Thus (3) the devil was exploiting their doubts. Church attendance was antagonizing the spirits, who manifested their displeasure by inflicting their living relatives with disease. Bushmen were, needless to say, ignorant about the germ and virus theories of disease. (4) The break from the old religion entailed a break with other old customs. "A Bushman never wants to be an individual, but always regards himself as part of a group. If you break this relationship, then he is totally rudderless and uprooted and he feels vulnerable to unavoidable dangers." Finally (5) there were external cultural influences, epitomized especially by the brewing of strong liquor. The ready availability of sugar meant that beer brewing had increased dramatically, and this was leading to sexual estrangement, adultery and fighting. In sum, Bushmen were dislocated and tossed around by numerous fears and insecurities about which whites did not have the vaguest concept (*Die Regte Mense*, 2/1976). Such a diagnosis led logically to a policy of trying "to root out the old heathen customs and sinful habits" (*Die Regte Mense*, March 1977).[2]

Weich's explanations displayed insight and a degree of philosophical acceptance of the situation. He wrote quite simply, "It appears as if a large number just looked for 'bread' and were therefore disappointed in their expectations" (*Die Regte Mense*, February 1975). Power, as Hyden pointed out, flowed not so much from the barrel of a gun as from control of access to socially valued goods (Hyden 1980). In the press statements announcing the mass conversions, the missionary secretary also announced that the Dutch Reformed Church Mission was relinquishing control over its most powerful means of coercion: "The shop is now so big that the [government-controlled] Bantu Investment Corporation has been asked to take it over" (*Die Suidwester*, 12 September 1973).

But even Weich was unable to rise above himself and question the total structure of the situation, including the basic irrelevance for Bushmen of the doctrines of the Dutch Reformed Church Mission. Nor could he break out of the deeply ingrained dogma of blaming the victim for the victimizer's lack of success. In 1982, when the social world of the Bushmen at Tsumkwe was collapsing all around them, Weich made one last effort to understand their rejection of Christianity. He felt that three factors were important. First, Bushmen had a deep-rooted fatalism—they knew no sorrow; death did not scare them. Second, there was a spirit of stupefaction about them epitomized by their weltanschauung—if the pain does not hurt, why treat it? "If everything is faint and unreal then there is no pain." Third, the evil powers, epitomized best by the revival in trance dancing that led to situations of mass hypnosis, had to be combatted (*Die Regte Mense*, February 1982).

Anthropologists, however, have persuasively argued that the trance dance reaffirms and strengthens kinship relations, which for their part serve to shape the relationship between people and available resources.

They have also argued that trance dances are one of the most important mechanisms that Bushmen have for coping with the vortex of change that is sweeping them off their feet (Guenther 1976, 1979a; Katz 1982; Lewis-Williams 1981).

Indeed it is clear that the strength of Bushman ideological autonomy and the failure of missionization are key factors in understanding the vulnerability of Bushmen. Missionaries, the Comaroffs argued, laid the ground for the integration of indigenes into the industrial capitalist world because domination involves "the incorporation of human subjects into the 'natural' taken-for-granted forms of economy and society." Although indigenes might have debated and rejected clerical dogmas and doctrines, by participating in this dialogue they were subtly internalizing its categories and values, especially those with regard to time, money and literacy. Such exercises generate a novel perception of the world and the role of human agency. The world becomes one of rational individuals (Comaroff and Comaroff 1986).[3]

The Changing Image of Bushmen and the Culture of Terror

One can start in this regard with the cultural values expressed in the talk of the settlers, namely that of "taming" "wild" Bushmen. Implicit in such rhetoric is the notion, not of development or peaceful coexistence, but of subjugation.[4] Taming suggests a fundamental difference between those defined as tame and wild; between "civilized" and "barbarian"; between those who live by the law and those who are outside the law; between humans and animals. This fragile and at times highly flexible, but important, mental line, is also a cerebral frontier. And indeed settlers see themselves as living in a frontier situation.

But we need to move from the general sociocultural milieu to the specific case. In particular, we should address the question, Why did the Germans always distinguish between the *Eingeborene* and the *Buschleute*, a distinction that the South Africans followed? The first point to make in this regard is that these distinctions are arbitrary cultural constructs. Even the academic classification by which Bushmen were subdivided is arbitrary. The elastic nature of these categorizations is most clearly seen in settler distinctions between tame, semitame and wild Bushmen. Bushmen moved freely between these categories. The distinction between "wild" and "tame" was not so much a descriptive distinction as a principle of colonization.[5]

In another sense the Bushman image in frontier areas was a flexible one. One day they might be seen as vermin of the veld, but the following day a woman might be regarded as human enough to be taken to bed or set up as a concubine. This suggests that the image was not meant to provide an ideological justification for intended behavior as much as a rationalization for past actions. The discursive power of the settlers and their kindred is dramatically demonstrated in their ability to switch their stereotypes of the Bushmen almost at will. That phenomenon is perhaps the most mundane indicator of Bushman underclass status. It is the underclass status of Bushmen that exaggerates their cultural ambiguity and makes them susceptible to genocide when they are enveloped by the state. This ambiguity has also led the Western imagination to develop a long cultural "tradition" about them, resplendent with metamorphosing images of evil (Taussig 1984:468). And it is this cultural construction of evil, coupled with market pressure, that leads to terror in northeastern Namibia.

The frontier is a "zone of death," an area of unpredictability. Nothing can be taken for granted. People and even symbols find their ambiguity amplified with attributions of animalesque powers and drug enhancements. Such a milieu provides a surface explanation and makes credible allegations of atrocities committed by the terrorizers. Analytically, the theoretical assemblage that immediately suggests itself is Victor Turner's notion of liminality and antistructure. "Liminality" is a concept developed from van Gennep's classic analysis of rites of passage. Undergoing this rite the subject "becomes ambiguous, neither here nor there, betwixt and between all fixed points of classification; he passes through a symbolic domain that has few or none of the attributes of his past or coming state" (Turner 1974:232). In a similar analysis Leach (1976, 1977) has illustrated the situation with a Euler diagram in terms of "Situation A" and "Situation Not A." In the center is a gray area of ambiguity. People placed in this area are *in* but not *of* the world. They are different but alike, despised yet held in awe. They have both animal and human qualities and possess both secular and mystical power. It is not only the whites and, more recently, the young troopers in the South African army who have attributed mystical qualities to both their opponents and their own supporting cast of Bushmen. On the contrary, such a discourse is intrinsic to the imperial process.

The attributed ambiguity of Bushmen served at once to shield them and to lay them open to acts of destruction, epitomized by the almost random stereotyping. It was not only Europeans and settlers and troopers who imprint mysticism onto Bushmen. Other colonized groups have also engaged in such exercises of the cultural imagination. Herero and Tswana often employed Bushman healers and trancers in times of illness (Shostak 1983:219; Lee 1979). Botswana Bushmen attached to the settlement of Kgalagadi patrons not only did the menial labor of watering cattle, cleaning the kraal and fetching firewood but were also called upon

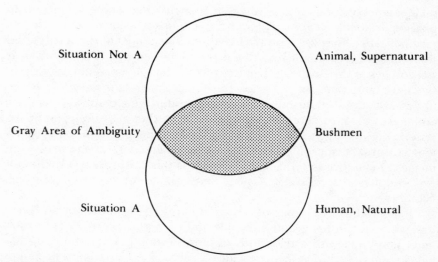

Euler diagram: Bushmen as "betwixt and between." *Source:* Derived from Edmund R. Leach, *Culture and Communication* (New York: Cambridge University Press).

to act as ritual functionaries, dance for rain and treat the sick (Kuper 1970:45). Similarly, on the settler farms of Botswana's Ghanzi district, Bushmen served as ritual experts for the African farmers and farm workers (Guenther 1985). A survey of Ovambo attitudes toward Bushmen conducted in 1984 found the most strongly held belief concerned the magical powers Bushmen were said to possess (Marshall forthcoming).

Similarly, in southern Angola around 1944 women of the pastoral Nyaneka-Nkumbi people started being possessed by *ovindenda* spirits. In this state of possession the women spoke in Bushman ("the most despised people . . . with whom all crossings and alliances are avoided"). Diviners were ineffective in removing these spirits, and the possessed had to be given eggs and sugar and sometimes chickens (Estermann 1979:200–202). Similarly Angolan Herero were sometimes possessed by foreign spirits called *ovindende* (spirits of the Bushmen) or *ovikwankala* (Kwanyama term for Bushmen) (Estermann 1981:161). Estermann, an authority on the people of southern Angola, does not mention any Ovambo speakers' being possessed by such spirits. Likewise my own search of the Ovambo literature does not disclose any such cases. Of their various neighbors, the Bushmen got on best with Ovambo speakers. Whereas other groups took Bushmen women as concubines, Ovambo would often marry them and Bushman males would take Ovambo wives.[6] But these groups were relatively tolerant of Bushmen and lacked the destructive mobility of pastoralists or the settler state.

In many ways the marginal status of Bushmen resembles that of peripatetic minorities found in other parts of the world (Rao 1987). A key difference, however, is that the peripatetic niche of Bushmen occurred in a frontier zone. Frontiers, in the words of some of the foremost southern Africanist historians, are "zones of interaction between people either subject to different political authorities or engaged in different modes of production, or indeed recognizing no formal authority at all" (Marks and Atmore 1980:8).[7] In short, it is a spatial representation of Leach's Euler Diagram that I have used in discussing the cultural construction of terror. Could it be that the invention of the Bushmen is a product of our own frontiers?

The parallels between these events and those that happened in Nazi Germany are striking,[8] and indeed Hannah Arendt has argued (see Gann and Duignan 1977 for a critique of her thesis) for lodging the origins of totalitarianism in the colonial experience. Certainly events in Namibia *anticipated* those in Nazi Germany to an extraordinary degree. Indeed a number of criticisms of Arendt's thesis are voided when it is noted that, like anthropologists, colonial administrators differentiated between *Buschleute* and *Eingeborene* in their discourses.

The Bushman discourse was premised on the alleged fundamental *unassimilability* of Bushmen, in which genital distinctiveness played a central, if at times submerged, role. This debate was especially dominant from 1906 to 1914, a period when it was explicit German colonial policy to wipe out Bushmen. As a largely male-dominated discourse, Bushman studies demonstrated in a Foucaultian mode the discourse and display of the power of *man*. Surely there can be no better display of the deployment of power in nineteenth- and twentieth-century Europe than making people strip to have their genitals measured? George Mosse argued that this male fixation was intimately connected to the nature of bourgeois respectability and German nationalism (Mosse 1985). Interestingly, most of the participants in the great Bushman debate rapidly established radical conservative credentials. Franz Seiner, Rudolph Pöch and Siegfried Passarge were well-known activists for restoring greater Germany, and many of the most prominent Nazi racial hygienists cut their academic teeth on the Bushman debate (Proctor 1988; Muller-Hill 1989). Indeed, the last scientific article that the most renowned Nazi racial hygienist, Eugen Fischer, wrote concerned Bushman genitalia.[9]

Portrayals and policies toward Bushmen and Jews are frighteningly similar, and there are striking parallels of Bushman and Jewish imagery in this scientific discourse.[10] Muller-Hill (1988) has noted that the sexuality of mental patients and Gypsies alarmed and frightened German scientists for a long time and argued that hating and exterminating Jews had its origins in ill-comprehended aspects of sexuality, which is why the extermination of Jews and Gypsies took on an almost ritual-like quality, while the Slavs were worked to death (Muller-Hill 1988).[11]

On Forgetting and Anthropological Arrogance

Science, especially anthropology, has contributed toward the shaping of this image. Indeed, science has a vested interest in the Bushmen, for, as Trefor Jenkins said, from the vantage point of science, the Bushmen are "southern Africa's model people" (Jenkins 1979:280). Whereas film-makers and journalists were the Bushman image makers par excellence, it was scientific research that lent credibility to their enterprise. Indeed in a sense they were simply the popularizers and amplifiers of the scientific colloquy. Their discourse on Bushmen exemplifies our fascination with strange customs, the search for laws of development and the enchantment of misunderstanding. Anthropological publications were readily misused by popularizers and politicians alike. As Alexander Leighton said, "Their findings are used like a drunk uses a lamppost, for support not illumination." Among contemporary anthropologists, few have suffered more from such misreadings than Richard Lee, who as an active opponent to the apartheid regime had to bear the indignity of having his work misused by the SADF in a totally different context to justify their Bushman "recruitment policy." Lee's dilemma is not only a personal one but a central one to the practice of anthropology. Undoubtedly there are many reasons why the Bushmen became an attractive field for study. Richard Lee, one of the most prominent Bushman scholars, explained the special appeal of the Kung thus:

> For one, they are among the few remaining representatives of a way of life—foraging—which was, until 12,000 years ago, the universal mode of human existence. For another, observers are attracted by their extraordinary culture, their narrative skills, their dry wit and earthy humor, and the rich social life they have created out of the unpromising raw materials of their simple technology and semi-desert surroundings. (Foreword in Katz 1982:ix)

It is of course erroneous to assume that most of this literature was written by English-speaking anthropologists. On the contrary, certainly in Namibia most of the influential literature is German and Afrikaans. Other factors also contributed toward Bushmen becoming one of the most heavily scientifically commoditized human groups in the annals of science. Apart from their paedomorphic features, which might have tugged at the Boy Scout in some of the more romantic scientists, there was also the assumption that "virginity was valuable" (Clarke and Ogan 1973). Periodically one finds reports that yet another last group of "wild Bushmen" has been rediscovered. This tradition is especially strong in the filmographic treatment of Bushmen (most recently demonstrated in Paul Myburgh's *People of the Sandface* [see Gordon 1990b for a critique]). It is also found among administrators and especially those ego boosters of scientists, the press.[12] Scholars also engaged in such claims. Dunn is typical. One of his articles started with this ringing revelation: "As I am perhaps the only survivor of those who came in contact with the true Bushman, and saw him in his own country, living in his natural way" (Dunn 1937:1050). Dunn was not the first nor will he be the last to claim to have had contact with the last of the "wild Bushmen" (see, e.g., Peringuey 1911; Wilmsen and Denbow 1990). Such claims engender a sense of importance in scientific documents of this type.[13]

Despite the extensive research on Bushmen in recent years (Tobias 1978), covering many aspects of their biology, psychology, language and culture, their image has not changed much; in fact, at the risk of oversimplification, I would suggest that there is little difference between the current scientific and the popular image of the Bushmen. For whether we portray them as living in "primitive affluence" or "struggling to survive," the overwhelming textbook image is that they are *different* from us in terms of physiognomy, social organization, values and personality. When we were lounging with a smug sense of ethnocentric superiority in the Victorian era, we saw the Bushmen as the epitome of savagery. But later, in the turmoil of the 1960s, when students were asking serious questions about the nature of Western society, social scientists reified the Bushmen's egalitarianism and generosity, virtues seen to be seriously lacking in Western society. If Bushmen did not exist, we would surely have invented them.[14]

Many studies of "Bushmen," while paying lip service to the wider historical context, have treated them "as if" they are an isolate, which was accepted academic practice during an era when positivism reigned supreme in science, including anthropology. Researchers, especially the more sensitive, were aware that Bushmen did not really live in isolation. Instead they felt that the task of describing the complex interaction between Bushmen and the wider society should be left to other researchers. "Do you have an image of God?" Lorna Marshall, the doyenne of Bushmen ethnography, asked an elderly Ju-/wasi of Nyae Nyae. "Yes, God is a White-man on a horse with a gun," he replied (Lorna Marshall, personal comment).[15] This image of God as a white man on a horse with a gun captures the past of the Bushmen as no other metaphor can. Other observers have commented on how Bushman comportment changes when there is a black present to witness the proceedings.[16] Indeed, Ju-/wasi language, according to the Reverend Weich, has built into it symbolizations of inferiority—such was the degree of their harassment by pastoralists (Weich in *Die Regte Mense,* February 1982).

But perhaps the numerous Bushman researchers[17] are not deliberately ignoring the past history of Bushman-settler relationships. The submergence of this discourse might be a product of their fieldwork strategies. One of the problems with the isolationist stance is that it places too much uncritical reliance on oral history, as indeed in a sense it had to do, as few researchers managed to use the Namibian archival material or Afrikaans-language publications. But another part of the problem lies in the fact that oral history was the vogue in the early 1960s, whereas since the 1970s more and more researchers were starting to ask critical questions about the validity of oral history as a resource (see, e.g., Clarence-Smith 1977). Oral testimony is important in any study, but it must be used with caution because, in the final analysis, it tells us more about the self-perceptions of the people studied than about the actual events.

The social structure of these forager bands also accounts for the paradox that whereas Bushmen tend to present the past history of indigene-settler relationships in a relatively conflict-free light, recorded history offers a rather brutal picture of several documented cases of aborigines' being murdered or massacred. The paradox is not new: Several anthropologists, and most notably Bill Stanner, have tried to understand this apparent denial of history by Australian Aborigines. Explanation has been sought in culture: in the Aborigines' allegedly cyclical concept of time (Morphy and Morphy 1984:461). However, the Morphys pointed out that "forgetting" is an active process and related to political factors. The image of the "wild" Aborigine or Bushman is not so much an image *from* the past as an image *of* the past: It provides a justification for the present relationship between blacks and whites. Many Aborigines, and no doubt Bushmen, would accept this version of history because most of the atrocities committed upon them were done with the active collaboration of fellow indigenes. The role of Bushmen in killing other Bushmen is largely overlooked in official archives because it is part of the unrecorded history of the area (Morphy and Morphy 1984:475; Lee 1983:93–97). But if one looks, one finds clues to it. Thus in his 1947 annual report, the magistrate of Grootfontein conceded that "without the services of an expert Bushman tracker, and some inside information, it is usually impossible to discover the slaughter places of these thieves," let alone the thieves (LGR 3/1/7). In acknowledging this, he was joining a long line of predecessors who had reached the same conclusion (see, for example, von Zastrow 1914; ADM 3360, Lieutenant Beckley, Letter 16 August 1919; Marshall 1976:283). The use of "tame" Bushmen to serve as spies and guides was regarded as usual (Kavango Monthly Report, September 1927; Marshall 1976).

The relationship between the dehumanization of the other and genocide is well established, but what has intrigued recent commentators on Bushmen is how dramatically their image has changed over the past few decades from that of "Brutal Savages" to that of "Harmless People" (Guenther 1980; Schrire 1984; Marks 1981; Wright 1977), or in the case of the Namibian Bushmen, within the space of sixty years from "Vermin" to "Beautiful People." This change is generally attributed to two factors: First, as Bushmen no longer constituted a "threat," colonizers could afford to beautify them. Second, perhaps in a rather too self-congratulatory tone, this change is attributed to the work of anthropologists. There are, however, a number of problems related to this simplistic approach.[18] The social position of the expounder of the stereotype within the social hierarchy is more important than the notion of the given stereotype changing because of the cumulative impact of knowledge about Bushmen. Most of the works cited to support the thesis of the progression from brutality to beauty are aimed not so much at the general public as at a specific European audience. As such the changing image appears to be more the product of the increased alienation/ urbanization of the writer than a portrayal of the actual situation. Indeed, it is clear to one working through archival material that the stereotypes held by farmers on the frontier zone have not changed that much. If anything, the divide between those who think that the Bushmen are good workers and those who think the opposite appears to have widened. During the German era these contradictory tendencies were already readily apparent.

These differences are also reflected in academic work on Bushmen. Elizabeth Marshall Thomas did not invent the phrase the "Harmless People." At the turn of the century German academics like Felix von Luschan and Gustav Fritsch were already referring to the Bushmen as the "unfortunate children of the moment." And in 1912 Hauptmann Mueller referred to them as the "Harmless People." The point is that the image of the Bushmen, whether they are portrayed as Vermin or Beautiful People, has *always been ambiguously different.* In my estimation this is especially marked in the more Germanic scientific literature.[19] To be sure there is an important counterpoint to this in the more literary-humanistic tradition epitomized by the work of the Marshalls, where the stress is not on difference but on commonality and empathy (Gordon 1987a), but this genre is not treated by academics or the media as being as definitive as the more turgid scientific prose.

Because the proof of the theory lies in its praxis, where do we go from this analysis? Malinowski, for all his faults, had a clear sense of direction:

> It has always appeared to me remarkable how little the trained anthropologist . . . has so far worked and fought side by side with those who are usually described as pro-Native. Was it because science makes people too cautious, and pedantry too timid? Or was it because the anthropologist, enamored of the unspoiled primitive, lost all interest in the Native enslaved, oppressed, or detribalized? . . . I for one believe in the anthropologist's being not only the interpreter of the native but also his champion. (Malinowski 1937:viii)

But is that enough? In the 1930s in South Africa a major intellectual debate raged as to whether the task of anthropology was basically to "translate between different cultures." Most social anthropologists, and especially Schapera, argued that to do so would be to play into the hands of the segregationists and perpetuate *difference*, whether it be invidious or not. Instead they tried to analyze South Africa as a single social system, thus giving equal weight to both black and white. Such a theoretical framework obviously stressed not *difference* but similarity and had strong integrationist overtones. This is what much of the post-1980s Kalahari scholarship is emphasizing. It is also a necessary first step to ensuring that our own research does not get used as a justification for genocide. In the 1960s and 1970s it was commonplace to shellac anthropologists as colonialist lackeys and of course there was much truth in those charges, although they did present a monolithic image of the anthropological community and ignored the dialectical nature of anthropology. Now, most excitingly, the dominant theme has changed. Recent efforts at moral and political engagement with and on behalf of those labeled "Bushmen," as epitomized by the Ju/wa Development Foundation (see, e.g., Biesele 1990) and its forerunners, the short-lived Bere Scheme (1972 to circa 1976) and the Kalahari People's Fund, founded in 1973 (Lee 1979:25), are doing much to restore anthropology to its rightful place as the most humanistic of the social sciences. As an anthropologist, I will be able to look my fellow Namibians straight in the eye. As a Namibian celebrating recently hard-won independence with one of the most liberal constitutions in the world, I am obligated to raise troubling questions and contentious issues with my anthropological colleagues. In a stumbling way this book has attempted to do both.

Appendix

Letter from Magistrate Gage, Grootfontein,
to Gorges, Secretary of the Protectorate*

Grootfontein, 21st Decr. 1918

My dear Mr. Gorges,

I am taking the very great liberty of addressing you direct and privately instead of officially on a matter which, I cannot help feeling, is one requiring the personal consideration of this Protectorate. I trust when you have read what I have to say, you will exonerate me for any breach of etiquette I may be committing in adopting this course.

I assume[d] duty here on a Monday and on Tuesday I went to inspect the Gaol, and I found there, amongst others, three Bushmen awaiting trial on a charge of murder (as regards the charge I gather there is little chance of proving it but a charge of robbery might be substantiated). These Bushmen when paraded with the other prisoners, were trembling so much that I remarked on it to the Gaoler. A couple of days later they were brought before me under escort with a fixed bayonet (the charge being murder) for remand, and their terror was pitiful to behold.

At the risk, Sir, of incurring your displeasure, I say that it is nothing short of cruelty to keep these wild creatures confined in Gaol. It is like catching a bird in your hand when you can see its heart throbbing against its breast and you know that unless it is soon released it will die of sheer terror. These wild things have no idea what is going to be done to them, they see themselves surrounded and quite helpless, and what can they know about our humane and just treatment—to them it appears that any moment may be their last, and they live for days and weeks in this terrible suspense. Naturally they do not know that I have not the power, if I saw fit, to order the guard there and then to plunge the bayonet into them. They have been living this life of torture now for some weeks, and it will be weeks perhaps months, before it is possible to conclude even the preparatory examination. Meanwhile they have to live on food to which they are totally unaccustomed, and they will have to be kept in confinement. This alone

---

*This letter is found in file ADM 13/26, Bushman Raiders, Grootfontein.

must mean misery to a wild creature, but added thereto is their terror of what may possibly to their way of thinking be done to them.

Please excuse me if I have sketched a somewhat lurid picture and let the circumstances be my excuse.

And the remedy? I must leave that to you, Sir. With my limited knowledge of natives, I might even say absolute ignorance of Bushmen, I am not justified in even making a suggestion. But it almost seems to me that to flog these poor Bushmen, even most unmercifully and let them go free, would be more humane than the present treatment of them. Naturally I appreciate the difficulties of adopting a policy of summary trial and corporal punishment for Bushmen in particular, and I am completely at a loss to know what else could be done. But is it not recognized that Bushmen are a race apart, untamed and untameable, when every other native in South Africa, including even the rawest Ovambos only recently coming into contact for the first time to their existence with white men, become amenable to some degree of civilisation however small. Would this not justify some special policy being adopted in regard to Bushmen only and not applicable to other natives?

I greatly fear I may have gone too far in my remarks and perhaps even deserve your displeasure, yet I feel I must risk it and trust you will receive what I have said as it is intended, namely by no means a criticism, but inviting your consideration of a question which perhaps has not yet received as much thought as it requires.

I am charmed with this place and cannot be sufficiently grateful to you for sending me here. I only hope I may prove worthy of your confidence.

I wish you and Mrs. Gorges all the compliments of the season.

Yours Sincerely,
R. H. Gage

Petition from Farmers of Nurugas*

November 1929

The farmers of Grootfontein district, whose farms are situated in the Bushman area, are continually involved in a struggle for existence with these natives. The Bushman is a wholly untamed individual, who has no conception of mine and thine and who regards the life of man as little as that of an animal. His chief business is cattle-theft and highway robbery. He attacks Ovambos and Okavango natives, who are homeward bound, kills them and robs them of their property. Even the native laborers on the farms and several of the farmers themselves have fallen victims to their poisoned arrows. There is constant warfare with these people who are at advantage over the others as long as energetic measures are not taken. They appear in bands of varying numbers, and having threatened the

---

*This petition is found in file SWAA A50/26, Bushman Depredations, Grootfontein, 1925–1946.

herds (very frequently carrying out their threats too) they take possession of the stock and disappear to their hiding places in the bush. Straying cattle constantly fall into their hands. It can be easily proved that several farmers have never been able to note any increase in their herd books; some of them have fewer cattle than they started with. Many of them are verging on despair. But the effect is not only noticeable in the case of the individual farmer; it concerns the whole district.

Many a prospective settler, who would like to settle in this district, has been frightened away by the prevailing state of affairs. The development of the district is hampered and this affects every business undertaking.

Many of the farmers are dependent for their running costs on their herds. But how are they to do this, while the Bushman exacts tribute and constantly lays hands on the breeding stock or the marketable oxen? It is quite plain that their victims are being ruined.

It is true that the Police take some note of the complaints of the farmers and there are several of the miscreants in the gaol at Grootfontein. But to deprive the Bushman of his liberty is not sufficient punishment, especially while the sentences are so lenient. They receive fine clothes, such as they have never before possessed, the food which hitherto they had to steal or seek in the bush, is placed before them beautifully prepared and they are certainly not overworked. They leave gaol in the best of health and it is no wonder that some of them immediately take to robbery again in order to return to enjoy the munificence of the State. Many of them have confessed this. Severer measures should be adopted.

We have had many years of experience in the treatment of natives, particularly Bushmen, and we therefore take the liberty of making the following proposals to Your Excellency:

1. The cattle thief must never be allowed a moment's peace; he must be kept aware of the fact that the limb of the law is constantly threatening him. It is essential that there should be a constant patrol of the threatened area. The strength of the various stations should be increased or police should be brought into these parts from time to time from other districts and police raids should be organized. Patrols consisting of a few individuals have the greatest difficulty in finding the tracks of the miscreants and are, moreover, exposed to great danger.

2. A proclamation should be issued and brought to the knowledge of the Bushmen, that they are to retire beyond the Police Zone, i.e., to the other side of the Omuramba u. Ovambo and the Omuramba Omatako. Those found outside these reserves should be brought to trial. Cattle theft should be made a capital offence.

3. Thieves found *in flagranti* or those who attempt to escape arrest by flight should be fired upon. This is merely an act of defense, for the Bushman himself does not hesitate to use his fearful poisoned arrows, where the slightest wound can be fatal.

4. In circumstances, such as described in section 3, the farmer should have the same right—it should be assured to him in writing.

5. *Deportation:* Cattle thieves who confess their crime or who are convicted, but not sentenced to death, should be transported for life to one of the islands off the southern coast. It is no use deporting him to any place from which escape is not impossible as the Bushman escapes when the least opportunity offers and does not fear a tramp of hundreds of kilometers to his tribal area.

We are convinced that these are the only means of assuring peace to the farmers who fear for life and property by day and night. Only then will they be able to reap the fruits of their arduous toil.

Every delay means further loss, for the Bushmen are very active at present. More than 30 animals were driven away from the farms Bushfeld, Dornhugel, and Nuisib last week and natives were killed.

We hope to receive Your Excellency's sympathy and assistance in this matter, and sign:

Notes

Notes to Chapter 1

1. Made at a cost of R 3 million, it has been the largest money-spinner ever to have been produced in South Africa. "After eight months in the USA it already grossed over R.22 million and is now the second most popular foreign film ever, just behind 'La Cage aux Folles.' Worldwide the film has earned nearly R.200 million since 1981, R.80 million in Japan alone. It has set box-office records in France, Canada, West Germany, South Africa, India and New Zealand" (*Pretoria News,* 16 May 1985). By 1987 it had grossed over U.S. $200 million. Its white male star, Marius Weyers, reportedly received less than $20,000 in salary (*Valley News,* 15 December 1987, p. 24). One can only surmise what Xao, the Bushman star got. And so successful was it in Japan and France that Xao was specially flown over for interviews.

2. The film's producer, Jamie Uys, denies this: "I don't make social statements. . . . I make films merely for entertainment. . . . I would like to show the Kalahari to people because very few people venture there. . . . And the Bushmen are worth knowing. They have no pretensions about life. For them it is a simple task of surviving" (*To the Point,* 17 October 1980). The plot is simple. It concerns the deleterious consequences when an empty Coca Cola bottle is thrown out of an airplane flying over the Kalahari Desert and is picked up by a Bushman. The bottle causes endless disruption in the supposedly idyllic harmony of the Bushman community. Lest this harmony escape the viewer, it is juxtaposed with scenes of life amid the hassle and rush of a complex urban environment. Xao, the hero, then takes the bottle and determines to journey to the end of the world in order to return the bottle to the gods. The film documents this pilgrimage. It reaches a climax when Xao rescues a number of schoolchildren, who together with their beautiful white female teacher have been abducted by a band of "terrorists," led by a scruffy-looking Cuban called Sam Bogia, who carried out the abduction after having bungled a coup d'état. Anyone knowledgeable about the situation in northern Namibia would know that the South Africans were fond of claiming that SWAPO, the movement that had been battling South Africa for independence for Namibia, engaged in such abductory activities and, moreover, its members were thought of as "Cuban pawns."

3. As I document later, the SADF was inspired by the success of its earlier-recruited Angolan Bushmen units and decided to extend recruitment in the late 1970s to Bushmanland proper and to Bushmen living on settler ranches. It

should, in fairness, be pointed out that in addition to Bushmen that joined two South African battalions, a number of Bushmen were members of SWAPO (see further details in Chapter 20).

4. The crass use of names and icons to sustain the symbolic dominance of Bushmen is a phenomenon worthy of further analysis. The original base used to train Bushman trackers was called Alpha (the first). Omega (the last) base was later built to house Angolan Bushman refugees who were mercenaries in the Pied Crow Battalion, of which the emblem, the white chest of the crow, it was said, "symbolized the white leadership element."

5. It is a widespread idée fixe. According to another *Soldier of Fortune* article: "Troops of the Bushman Battalion are perhaps the best indigenous trackers in southern Africa today. Much of their skill comes from the Bushman's inherent tie with the land, their nomadic hunter-gatherer heritage which ensured that only those with the sharpest eyes, best hearing and most empathetic feel of the bush survived" (Mill 1987:34).

6. Details on the Bushman situation are to be found in a monograph (Gordon 1984b).

7. This is not to deny that scholars were unaware of change. On the contrary, most of the rightly acclaimed ethnographies on the Bushmen acknowledge the fringe status of the people they describe and the Bushmen's being part of a wider society but, having recognized this unpleasant fact, focus on them as if they were hunter-gatherers living some relatively uncontaminated existence. Recently, as anthropologists have rediscovered history, this emphasis has begun to change. This has generated a large and at times acrimonious debate about the status of those labeled "Bushmen." Particularly pertinent salvos in this debate include Schrire 1980, 1984; Wilmsen 1983, 1989a; Solway and Lee 1990; Wilmsen and Denbow 1990; Volkman 1986.

8. In addition there are some so-called Cape Bushmen and the extinct Namib-San.

9. The estimate of 30,000 was made by Oswin Köhler, reported in the *Frankfurter Allgemeine Zeitung*, 23 April 1979. Bob Hitchcock provided (in a discussion) the 87,250 estimate distributed as follows: Angola: 8,000; Botswana: 41,750; Namibia: 33,000; South Africa: 2,500; Zambia: 1,500; Zimbabwe: 500. For an argument that makes the case that these government-based estimates are probably too high see Gordon 1987b.

10. The region skirts what was known as the Police Zone, or Red Line, a boundary established by the German colonial regime and continued by the South Africans. That boundary signified the point beyond which settlers could enter only with a permit and in which there was ostensibly no police protection. It also functioned as a veterinary blockade cordon: Livestock were and still are not allowed to pass from beyond the zone to settler farms.

11. The coverage provided by this book is necessarily limited historically and geographically. Temporally, it is confined to the past 150 years: the period for which we have reasonable written records. Spatially, I have the luxury of not having to deal with the situation of Bushmen in Botswana because of the first-class work done there recently by Wilmsen 1989a, 1989b; Hitchcock 1982,

1987b; Lee 1979, 1983; Guenther 1985. Unfortunately, largely because of the unsettled situation in Angola, I was not able to obtain information on that country.

12. An important contemporary source for a "Bushman Voice" is the recent films of John Marshall (e.g., *Pull Ourselves Up or Die*) and the Nyae Nyae Development Cooperative (Biesele 1990). Since the 1980s the situation has improved remarkably.

13. One consequence of taking a regional perspective is that in dealing with the question of Bushman identity, we can take a situational approach rather than the older ascriptive approach, which is/was so characteristic of the isolationist stance in Bushman studies. In essence, the ascriptive approach defines Bushmen in terms of a package of fixed, objectively verifiable cultural attributes and genealogical kinship charts, while the situational approach emphasizes that identity is open to changing collective definitions and fluctuating emotional intensities (Enloe 1980).

In this study, the point of departure is situational criteria of the type first developed by Frederick Barth (1969). Precedents for such a stance are not hard to find. In short, even allowing for the definition of people as Bushmen, one should also allow for changing identities. Hunting and gathering are only part of a wide range of economic pursuits that are open to anyone. People like Bushman may switch from agricultural pastoralism to hunting and foraging and then back again. This process works both ways: People usually defined as blacks can engage in foraging for periods of time, and "Bushmen" have been known to take up agriculture and pastoralism only to switch back later to a hunting/foraging mode of subsistence (Hitchcock 1982). But by opting solely for a situational mode of explanation of Bushman identity, we run the risk of throwing the proverbial baby out with the bathwater because, as van Zwanenberg (1976:14) pointed out, "As hunting and gathering was usually considered the least desirable form of subsistence, it was hunter-gatherers who tended to take on the social clothing of the people around them."

A situational approach, however, by directing attention to individual strategies, tends to downplay the reality of systemic exploitation: It often looks so closely at the flowers that it ignores the spectacle of the fields. Thus if we examine the district censuses for the northeastern districts, we see that the Nama also show a decrease in numbers, despite the fact that they are the physiological group, par excellence, to which the "Bushmen" could be expected to switch. However, the numbers of "negroid" Damara, with whom the Bushmen are said to intermarry, have remained more or less constant. In short, identity switching might have taken place, but only on a small-scale, individual basis. In my experience, even if a Bushman does switch to wage work, he or she still retains the stigma of being labeled a Bushman by both blacks and whites.

14. Of course the range of variation of adaptations has been stressed by a number of researchers and some useful, albeit secondary, work has been done on the impact of development work and change, but this is largely a post-1970s phenomenon and, more important, has had almost no impact on the crucial high school and college textbook market both in the United States and in Southern Africa.

15. Russett quoted Cooter to the effect that *ideology* is simply "a worldview, or the partial view of nature and human nature expressed by a group or class which informs perception and conceptualization" and comments that "so construed, science and ideology, far from being polar opposites, are part and parcel of one another" (Russett 1989:188). The role of scientists as popularizers of the Bushmen stereotype is complex and controversial. An interesting illustrative example is the poem "The Fat-buttocked Bushmen," written by the eminent Harvard anthropologist Ernest Hooton (1946). I am indebted to Greg Finnegan for pointing out this piece of arcana.

16. A few scientists, however, addressed the question of what could be done to avoid such a devastating future (for example, Heinz 1975; Hitchcock 1980). Since the 1970s and especially the 1980s the situation has commendably changed.

17. Richards, for example, noted that many prominent Africanists believe that "it is a remarkable comment on the unchanging character of late Stone Age life that a twentieth century San was able to recognize a range of vegetable remains and tools excavated from a 4,000 year old camp site. . . . It seems especially important not to confuse technical and social categories in this respect. The ability to call a spade a spade even after several millennia must not be taken to imply continuities of social and political life" (Richards 1983:38–39). What I am interested in is not so much what anthropologists and associated scholars have said but what the public-at-large *believe* they have said.

18. Anthony Giddens has defined the underclass as a category of "lower-class" workers "heavily concentrated among the lowest-paid occupations . . . chronically unemployed or semi-employed" and often further distinguished by their ethnic origin. Such an underclass is assimilated neither culturally nor, more important, into the prevailing structure of market rewards. It is not a lumpen-proletariat in the conventional sense of the term because it is not located outside the dominant structure of capitalist production relations and is generally too dispersed to sustain a broadly based "class" movement (Giddens 1973:112).

19. A typical example is Karl Frey, appointed to the South African Senate on account of his expert knowledge of the "natives," with the specific warrant to represent the interests of the Namibian indigenes, who explained the circumstances of the Bushmen in the 1950s as follows: "They live in the game reserves which white men may not enter. In this way the Administration, has, so to speak, created Bushman reserves where they may live undisturbed according to their old Bushman customs. . . . In spite of all that the Administration is doing to prevent the Bushmen from being crowded out by the ever expanding civilization, there is no certainty that its efforts will be successful. The reason is that the Bushmen themselves remain unapproachable and do nothing to help the white man to assist them . . . he shows no sign of ever submitting himself to the customs of other races in the country" (Frey n.d.).

The imagery and mythology implicit in this statement is widely perpetuated by popular writers in both Afrikaans and English. For example, the perennially popular author, Lawrence Green, wrote: "In German times, the little Bushmen were classed . . . as vermin. *One cannot say that they did not deserve it* for many a German soldier died with a poisoned arrow in him and many a herd of cattle was driven off by Bushman raiders" (Green 1980:27; italics added). Bushmen then retreated from flocks, firearms, houses and money (Green 1945:162) into the "inhospitable" Kalahari Desert where the South West African administration "treats them wisely." "As long as they remain beyond the limits of white settlement, they may use their bows and arrows, even in game reserves, to provide themselves with food" (Green 1945:139).

20. Best epitomized by John Marshall's classic film *N!ai: The Story of a !Kung Woman*, the plot of which parallels *The Gods Must Be Crazy* to a remarkable extent. The imagery presented in *N!ai* is of a happy egalitarian world only recently contacted; with contact has come inequality, which in turn created widespread conflict. Since then John Marshall has changed his position substantially and launched a major audio-visual attack on the "myth of the wild Bushman" (see Marshall forthcoming). Tomaselli (1986:77–101) contains a good discussion of the media impact of Bushmen.

Notes to Chapter 2

1. The famed Lake Ngami was already quite a popular place. In that same year, 1849, a party of Griquas had moved up to settle at the lake and some had even settled at Taogo and Libebe (Nienaber 1989:xxix).

2. For critical assessments of Galton's ethnographic attempts, see Stocking 1987 and Fabian 1987.

3. Prichard, it should be remembered, was a prominent member of the Aborigines' Protection Society. Indeed so much did this philanthropical body esteem him that when he died they commemorated his work with a five-part serial obituary.

4. The standard references on South Africa are Szalay 1983; Schott 1955; Strydom 1929. In 1862 a special commissioner was appointed in the Cape to try to protect the last Bushmen in the northwestern Cape. It was in that decade that Wilhelm Bleek did the first direct scholarly research on Bushmen remnants from this area when he interviewed twenty-eight Bushmen who had been caught by the authorities and sent to work on the breakwater in Cape Town. The fate of the last handful of South African Bushmen is discussed in Gordon 1985.

5. Galton was probably following his missionary hosts too closely and thus exaggerating. More generally the situation approximated that which the Dutch trader van Oordt described for the Bondelzwarts among whom he lived in the early 1880s: "The Damaras, Bushmen and others have equal rights, and enjoy the same protection of Bondelzwart law as the actual Namaquas themselves. Naturally this does not prevent a Namaqua from considering himself much higher than a Kafir or Bushman" (van Oordt 1980:106). The dominant characteristic was one of symbiosis: Honey, hides and *veldkos* (field food) were traded for clothing tobacco iron and an occasional sheep or goat. As Tindall (1856:27) pointed out, the Nama saw Bushmen as rogues, but "they do not, however, generally follow out an exterminating policy towards the wanderers of the desert, but are rather more disposed to avail themselves of every advantage." He also

witnessed a case where a Bushmen had been accidentally wounded by a Nama and the Bushman was able to extract a sizable compensation.

In reality it was not simply a question of serve or die. Relationships between precapitalist pastoralists and foragers were highly flexible and ranged over a wide array of possible relationships. The archaeologist Graham Clarke has listed some of them: tolerative (no immediate change); symbiotic (a mutually beneficial relationship); parasitic (advantage to one side only); competitive (change in one or more competitors); and disoperative (disadvantageous to one or more systems) (cited in Wadley 1979:6–7).

6. This observation of Tindall's would seem to corroborate Elphick's (1985) hypothesis of the origin of the Khoi, or Hottentots, as lying in the north-central Kalahari. In the unsorted "Cocky Hahn" papers at the Windhoek State Archives there is a remarkable note offering an explanation for the term *!Kung:* "Deurtrek namenlyk die gebreide vel wat hulle gebruik voor Broek" (The tanned hide that they use as pants), providing further corroboration to Tindall's and Elphick's observations. I am indebted to C. Stern for this reference. The issue of the relationship between those labeled Bushmen and those labeled Hottentot or Khoi is an issue central to Southern African ethnology and goes back at least to Andrew Smith. Whether the Bushmen were simply impoverished Khoi or a type sui generis is a debate that was featured in the pages of the *South African Commercial Advertiser* as early as 16 September 1829 and 10 October 1829.

7. Later linguistic research done by Dorothea Bleek, Ernst Westphal and Oswin Köhler indicated that the Nama speakers belong to a language group classified as either Central Bush or Tshu-Khwe, whereas the Kung belong to the Northern Bush language group. Thus from a linguistic perspective, the statement by Hahn is not quite correct.

8. As he put it in his book: "There is no difference whatever between the Hottentot and Bushman, who lives wild about the hills in this part of Africa, whatever may be said or written on the subject. The Namaqua Hottentot is simply the reclaimed and somewhat civilized Bushman, just as the Oerlams represent the same raw material under a slightly higher degree of polish. Not only are they identical in degree in features and language, but the Hottentot tribes have been, and continue to be, recruited from the Bushmen. The largest tribe of these Namaqua Hottentots, those under Cornelius, and who now muster 1,000 guns, have almost all of them lived the life of Bushmen. In fact, a savage loses his name, 'Saen,' which is the Hottentot word, as soon as he leaves his Bushman's life and joins one of the larger tribes, as those at Walfish Bay have done" (Galton 1889:42).

9. The history of Bushmanology provides many illustrations of this. Here a brief example must suffice: In his underrated classic, *The Savage Hits Back* (1937), Julius Lips mentioned the case of a 1913 report in *Anthropos* entitled "Newly Discovered Bushman Paintings . . ." in which the author remarked about the paintings: "They all bear traces of extreme antiquity. Though they have been continually exposed to rain and storm, the colours are still quite fresh and vivid." Had the writer been less enigmatic, Lips noted, he might easily have recognized the figure to be the recently deceased mistress of the British Empire, Queen Victoria! (Lips 1937:232).

10. Archaeological material suggests the possibility of the presence of cattle in this area, but such presence I suspect was of a temporary nature and came from the Botswana side (see Denbow 1984; Hitchcock 1987b; Wilmsen 1989a, 1989b). Denbow (1986) pointed out evidence in the northeastern part of Botswana that indicates the presence of livestock (cattle) and small stock (sheep and goats) around A.D. 500–600. Archaeological evidence of livestock has been found in the Gautscha area of Namibia as well, and there is some evidence of domestic animals on the Kavango River to the north that dates to around A.D. 200 (Bob Hitchcock, personal comment).

11. Underpinning the settler myth that the various "ethnic" groups were living in bellicose isolation from each other was the notion that their forms of subsistence were mutually incompatible. This myth was most clearly stated by Vedder when he wrote, "Where the cattle of the Herero trod, there was Hereroland and where the Nama hunter cast his eye, there was Namaland" (Vedder 1938:177). This explanatory model has been followed by many colonial anthropologists (e.g., Bruwer 1966b) and assumes economic competition between different groups. Contemporary ecological research suggests that this conflict has been much exaggerated (Western 1982). Ecologically, for example, the standard myth that Herero cattle drove away the Bushman's game, thus forcing Bushmen to kill Herero cattle, which led to Herero trying to exterminate Bushmen, simply does not hold because cattle and game usually have different feeding regimes. Game went into a marked decline with the introduction of firearms, which signaled the penetration of the capitalist world system.

12. McKiernan, a Yankee who traded in Hereroland from 1874 to 1879, reported that Ovambo blacksmiths were, at that time, to be found all over Hereroland: "They bring with them a small stock of iron and copper and travel about from village to village, making knives, arrow-heads, spear-heads, beads and rings, for which they receive sheep and goats which they are required to give to their king" (McKiernan 1954:74).

13. Contrary to the settler myth that contact between Ovamboland and the rest of the country was almost nonexistent, there existed widespread trade and contact; nowhere is this better affirmed than in the fact that in 1887 many Herero and Nama refugees fled the German colonial depredations and obtained succor in Ovamboland. This was repeated more dramatically during the German-Herero war. One of the very real fears of the German colonizers was that the Ovambo kings might decide to intervene substantially on the side of the Herero (see generally Stals 1968). Indeed they might have, as already in 1867 Maherero, the Herero chief, was busy negotiating an alliance with Ovambo kings in an effort to bring about a general peace (Vedder 1937:485). In addition Tlou (1985:71) reported a treaty of friendship, sealed with an exchange of cattle between Maherero and Letsholathebe, the Tawana king, providing their respective people asylum in times of need.

14. Lorna Marshall described the dynamics of this process as it occurred in the 1950s: "The odds are with the Bantu in the trading. Big, aggressive, and determined to have what they want, they easily intimidate the Kung. Several . . . said that they tried hard not to trade with Herero if it was possible to avoid

it because, although the Tawana were hard bargainers, the Herero were worse. /Qui . . . said he had been forced by a Herero . . . to trade [his] shirt and pants . . . for a small enamel pan and a little cup. /Tikay had more gumption. A Herero at the beginning of a negotiation with him brought out a good sized pile of tobacco but took from it only a pinch when it was time to pay. /Tikay picked up the object he was trading and ran off. . . . The Tawana values are a little better. A well-tanned gemsbok hide brings a pile of tobacco about 14 inches in diameter and about 4 inches high. The values vary. Some reported to us were three duiker or steenbuck skins for a good-sized knife, five strings of ostrich-eggshell beads for an assegai" (Marshall 1976:306).

15. "Coloreds," in the interminable South African terminology, refers to people of "mixed-race" ancestry.

Notes to Chapter 3

1. De Almeida 1965 pointed out that Kwankhala and Sekele are properly categorized as Kung and that all the men could speak a Bantu language.

2. In Ovamboland itself it is possible that Bushmen were involved both in iron mining and the working of it. In southern Angola, Bushmen were apparently connected with the mining of iron. The major diggings were at Omupa, near Kuanyama, which was regarded as Kung Bushman territory. Loeb wrote, "According to one native account [the Kuanyama] conducted the journey as if it were a military expedition, although they always obtained the consent of the Bushmen before they set out" (Loeb 1962:192). Moreover, "the [Bushmen] owners of the bellows receive a share of the iron in payment for the use of their equipment" (Sckar, cited in Loeb 1962:191).

3. The evidence as to who these Bushmen were, whether they were Heikom or Kung, is confusing but in all likelihood they were Heikom. The literature does not refer to which subgroup they belonged. Because this study is about the role of "Bushmen" within the larger social formation and because it is the colonizer's categorizations that I am ultimately interested in, I simply use the colonizer's blanket term.

4. In this they learned the old political lesson, that strangers make ideal servants of power because they have no basis for challenging the ruler's hegemony.

5. Obviously this does not mean that there was *no stigma* attached to marriages with Bushman women. Another useful material indicator of intergroup relations are the terms of trade in exchanges. Certainly by this count, exchanges were the most equitable in South West Africa because six ostrich eggs apparently fetched one Ovambo cow (Lebzelter 1934a). This is also indicative, of course, of the relatively low value that Ovambo attached to cattle, which was a major cause of friction with the pastoralists.

6. Brigitte Lau (1981) showed some of the major defects in Vedder's historiography. This does not mean that we should ignore Vedder, only read him with extreme caution.

7. Hahn was concerned that the original term *ovakuruha* would be replaced by the new "Ozumbusumana." His fears were groundless (Hahn 1985, 28 June 1857, 1009–1010). *Ovakuruha*, however, refers not only to those labeled "San" but also to some of the Namaqua like the /Aonin (Brincker 1886:225, as cited in Nienaber 1989:152–153). The gloss of 'original people', as I pointed out, fitted in well with the colonial ideology of trying to justify dispossession of the Herero and Namaqua.

8. Similarly Luttig (n.d.:53) wrote: "The Ovatjimba may at present be considered as a group of outcasts, as they do not possess the requisite number of cattle necessary for social significance. This explains the fact that they do not live in villages as do the rest of the tribe. They lived a scattered existence in the veld."

Iliffe has summarized the extensive literature on Bushman-pastoralist relations in neighboring Botswana, showing that the Basarwa (as Bushmen are known in Botswana) were incorporated by the Tswana-speaking pastoralists and subjugated as unpaid domestics, hunters or herdsmen (Iliffe 1987:74–76). Relations were generally friendly between the Bushmen and the agricultural Ovambo and reasonable with the Kavango people, who engaged in cattle raising and subsistence horticulture. However, relations were generally of a negative nature with people who practised pastoralism, be they either Herero or Afrikaans speakers. Such a statement would appear to be applicable globally (see, for example, Schott 1955; Leacock and Lee 1982).

9. Obviously in evaluating such historical evidence, one should be mindful of the fact that such outrages were often exaggerated by those parties desiring to legitimize colonization. However, a careful examination of the colonial literature and rhetoric of this period shows that although the internecine warfare between Nama and Herero might have been used for such purposes, atrocities committed against Bushmen and Bergdamara were never an issue, as most whites believed that Bushmen were on the path to extinction anyway. This negative assessment of Bushman-Herero relationships does not of course deny that there were cases of amicable relations between them. Indeed the ethnographic literature is almost exclusively concerned with such amicable examples. My task here is simply to provide evidence that questions this rather fortuitous image.

10. Writing about Ghanzi Afrikaner farmers, Margo Russell reported that the local Bushmen welcomed them because they offered protection against local blacks who took their women, children and hides (Russell 1976).

Notes to Chapter 4

1. In addition, Tlou mentioned that the discovery that ivory could be made malleable by heating and thus shaped into various forms and that hippo teeth did not discolor with age meant that the demand for ivory increased in the 1860s (Tlou 1985:68).

2. For example, in 1846 a missionary reported about 350 ships anchored off Ichaboe Island collecting guano (Kienetz 1977). Cooper 1982 also supplied details.

3. The value of this trade appeared to have peaked in 1878 when the governor of the Cape Colony, Sir Bartle Frere, valued the trade at some 200,000 English pounds (1881). A single trader, Erikssen, claimed to have over 60,000 English pounds worth of goods in the country. In his heyday he employed more than forty Europeans. In 1877 he exported through Walvis Bay over 600 gallons of brandy; 1,000 gun barrels; 20,000 pounds of gunpowder; 3,900 pounds of coffee and 51,000 pounds of sugar. For general details see de Kock 1948.

Palgrave estimated the white population in Namibia, including missionaries and traders, at 150. In 1876, the value of the ivory and ostrich feathers was put at 45,000 English pounds (Vedder 1938:446). The trading firm of Erikssen was said to have had a turnover of 200,000 English pounds per year (von Moltke n.d.[b]; Frere 1881).

4. So large and significant was this extracolonial trade that the Cape Colony tried to limit the export of firearms to indigenes, most notably by the Sand River Convention in 1852. Such legislation made these routes even more attractive, as they were more amenable to a highly lucrative informal trade. Smuggling in liquor and firearms from Port Nolloth and other points east was also rampant. Often traders would ship loads of firearms direct from St. Helena or even the United States in order to avoid paying duty and hence increase the already considerable scale of profits (Kienetz 1977:567).

5. The cattle route fell into disuse within a few years (Volkmann 1901; Clarence-Smith 1979), and the ivory market shifted away from Walvis Bay to Mossamedes, in Angola. But the route was not forgotten. In 1903 Rohrbach visited Grootfontein and noted that the farm Guntsas was owned by a livestock syndicate that intended to export cattle through Bechuanaland to Mafeking, in South Africa (von Weber 1983:95).

6. J. Herbst described the following situation in the southern Kalahari, which was certainly applicable to the northeast as well: "When the Bushmen had learnt the use of the rifle from the Bastards [so-called Coloreds] and Whites [in 1863], they were armed and had to do most of the hunting, while the Bastards remained at home. The skins and feathers were brought to them while the meat was eaten by the Bushmen. The rifle therefore played an important part in the taming of the Bushman for realizing the impotency of his own weapon as compared with that possessed by the Bastard, he naturally allied himself to the latter, at first, and when these became subject to the colonial laws, he went over to the Hottentots further north" (Cape Colony 1908:7).

It was customary for the traders and hunters, be they European, Cape Coloreds, Bastards or Griquas, to arm the local populace in order to have them hunt on a commission basis. Hugo Hahn gave evidence in 1882 that he had seen nearly 500 rifles south of Gobabis at trader Robert Duncan's outpost, which were "loaned out" to local people to use in hunting (Cape of Good Hope 1882:40). Other firms sent out wagons with up to sixty "natives" armed with rifles, under the supervision of one or two Europeans. The wagons returned when they were loaded with about four tons of ivory, feathers, horns and skins. One such firm alone had sixty wagons equipped in this manner (Frere 1881).

7. So famous—or notorious—was Gordon Cumming that *Punch* responded to the publication of his book, *The Lion Hunter: Five Years' Hunting and Sporting Adventures in South Africa*, with a poem entitled "The Gordon Is Cumming."

8. Griqua Bastards were "colored" people from the Cape Colony, usually of a European father and a Griqua mother (see also chap. 6, n. 2). Kruger was to establish quite a reputation in Namibia and will reappear later in this book as a Bushman chief. Some of his white companions included John Hickey and Charles Sabatta (Tabler 1973).

9. Undoubtedly, this strategy was modeled on the pocket republic of Stella-land, which was established in 1882 and incorporated into British Bechuanaland in 1884. There was also a perhaps unintended symbolic dimension to naming the pocket republic after Benjamin Upington, the Cape prime minister, because in 1879 he had been involved in the notorious "Koegas Atrocities" case as attorney general. This case arose out of the cold-blooded shooting by some northwestern Cape farmers of a number of captured Bushman males and females. Despite a strong summing up against the accused farmers, the jury found the farmers not guilty, to much spectator applause. The *Cape Argus* attacked Upington for failing to have the trial transferred to a more neutral area for jury selection. Upington sued the newspaper for libel, and the judge found that indeed most gruesome atrocities had been committed against the defenseless Bushmen and that the attorney general had behaved "reprehensibly, but that nevertheless criticism of him had gone too far and he should be awarded nominal damages" (cited in Sachs 1973:61).

10. That the mineral wealth of the area was of prime interest to Jordan and other whites becomes clear in the dispute that arose over the concession. Robert Lewis, a confidant of the Herero chief Maherero, also claimed the mineral rights over the area on the basis of a concession given to him by the chief. Lewis did his utmost to have Jordan and his band of trekkers removed from the vicinity, and some authors have suggested that he might have played a role in the killing of Jordan. After Jordan's death, his concession was acquired by an Anglo-German consortium, the South West Africa Company, which immediately set about organizing operations. They sent out the mining engineer Matthew Rogers, together with a large party of miners, who arrived in the area in December 1892 (Sohnge 1967). Shortly after that, a German police and military station was established, which prepared the way for the great land rush by white settlers after 1903. The connections between this early multinational cooperation and state formation in this regard are unclear but suggestive.

Notes to Chapter 5

1. Bushman was distinguished from Hottentot on the basis of the latter's gendered noun-class structure.

2. Observed Wilmot (1895:4): "The language of these people [Hottentots and Bushmen] was essentially the same, and was a pure form of the ancient Coptic tongue of Egypt. At least, this is the confident opinion of Dr. Bleek. . . . According to his theory, the Bosjemans of South Africa are identical with the

pigmies of Herodotus, and these people together, together with the Hottentots, to whom they are allied, have by degrees, through many centuries, been driven southward by more powerful tribes."

3. More significant, Hahn demonstrated that in the colonization process of Namibia, the role of science, even the fledgling discipline of anthropology, played a key, if neglected, role in the establishment of the German settler state. Returning to precolonial Namaland after his studies, Hahn set up shop as a trader and soon found that the practice of anthropology had many advantages: "As far as I have to do with the natives, I can say that they don't give me much trouble but the reason is this: They all believe, in this country, that because I take observations, and make collections, and held a *Raad* [council meeting] with the Captain of the Veldskoendragers, that the Government sent me in as an official person; of course I leave them in their belief" (cited in Palgrave 1877:xxii).

Hahn was forced to leave Rehoboth in central Namibia, after a Herero chief intercepted a letter that he wrote to the big-game hunter and adventurer, van Zyl, who was headquartered in Ghanzi (present-day Botswana), inviting him to move to Rehoboth with from fifty to a hundred Dutch Boers. Within a few years, Hahn assured van Zyl, he would control the whole region (Goldblatt 1971:65; Esterhuyse 1968; de Kock 1948).

Later, while in enforced residence at the Cape, he was visited by Vogelsang, the agent of Adolf Luderitz, who persuaded him to draw up a detailed memorandum on the economic prospects of the Transgariep (Namibia). Hahn also provided a list of people whom Vogelsang should contact and advice on how to negotiate with the "natives." Armed with this advice Vogelsang left Cape Town for Angra Pequena (later Luderitzbucht) and thence to Bethanien where, after plying the local Nama chieftain, Josef Fredericks, liberally with alcohol, he concluded two treaties and thus formally launched the German colonial effort on South West Africa. Later Hahn returned to Namibia as an agent for the Kharas Khoma Land Syndicate, where applying his expert knowledge he managed to extract such outrageous concessions that the Bondelzwarts threatened to rebel against their chief. As a result, Theodor Leutwein, the governor, refused to certify all Hahn's concessions (Goldblatt 1971:124). A contemporary, Georg Hartmann, the agent of the South West Africa Company, found Hahn a thoroughly fascinating person, but a "ruffian" who held an unbearably high opinion of himself and his methods of dealing with local chiefs. Goring, the first imperial commissioner, and his successor, von François, both had a similarly high regard for him (Voeltz 1988:34). Luderitz and his colleagues had a clear sense of appreciation for science. It was Luderitz, after all, who sponsored Schinz's 1884–1887 scientific travels.

Notes to Chapter 6

1. An astute product of his time, Leutwein was swept up in the importance of inventing neotraditions, a fashion that had its heyday in the late nineteenth century. Ceremonial government, as Herbert Spencer realized, is the most elementary form of rule. Neotraditions were a critical ingredient in successfully

engaging in the "white man's bluff." As Hendrik Witbooi, famed guerrilla leader, once remarked on being subjected to one such ritual, "I know the German Emperor is more powerful than I am, but you don't have to keep reminding me" (cited in Bley 1971:64). Hobsbawm and Ranger (1983) are the standard reference to the invention of such colonial neotraditions.

2. The term *baster* is multivocal. It can refer to (1) progeny born out of wedlock; (2) mulattoes or "half-castes," the products of black-white liaison; or (3) an "ethnic group" known as the Rehoboth Basters.

3. Brigitte Lau (in Hahn 1985:1256) defined Griquas in the following way: "a new group emerging around the turn of the last century, socially/economically similar to the Oerlams [Nama-speaking 'acculturated' people], rising in considerable wealth and independence. The name was adopted in 1813 by the two main clans, the Barends and Koks." Griquas were settled in South Africa in Griqualand East and West and lost their autonomy to the Cape government in the 1870s.

4. In contrast to the current anthropological viewpoint, which points out that Aribib is a Nama name, Viktor Lebzelter said that "Aribeb" (his spelling) was not a Heikom but a Kung (Lebzelter 1934b:20). Indeed it is quite feasible that "Aribeb" is a Namaized Kung (Zhu) word.

5. The treaty's four brief paragraphs deserve to be quoted in full: "The Bushmen cede to the German government the entire territory to which they believed up to now to have claimed. It extends from the area of Outjo to the area of Grootfontein. The northern limit is the Etosha Pan. The southern limit is formed by the northernmost werfts of the Hereros.

"In return, the German government promises to provide the Bushmen with security and protection against everyone.

"The Bushmen may not be driven away from the water-hole Naidaus, where they are presently. They are also entitled at all times and everywhere on their former territory to collect veldkos. In return, they promise not to oppose the settlement of German farmers but to be of assistance to them and to remain on good terms with them. In particular, they promise not to set grass fires.

"Captain Aribib vows to remain always loyal to the German government and to meet its requirements with good will. He receives, as long as he fulfills this obligation, an annual salary of 500 marks. For every grass fire noted in the areas described in para.1, 20–50 marks will be deducted."

Leutwein, on receiving a copy of the treaty from von Estorff, pointed out that he had himself concluded a similar treaty with Aribib at the end of 1895. He considered that any changes should be made by agreement with Aribib and not through the conclusion of a new treaty. The provision under which the Bushmen ceded all their land was particularly problematical because, according to the official view, Bushmen did not own land. Von Estorff was to arrange matters accordingly (ZBU 2043, draft reply initialed by Leutwein, 7 December 1898).

6. As Bley put it: "He constantly attempted to put their political and social functions on to a personal level. Their plans for their tribes could thus be glossed over as personal traits of character of the chiefs: ambition, the desire for prestige

and power, good living and luxury. The constitutional position of the chiefs in their tribes could be ignored by turning them into important private citizens of the state. . . . Leutwein avoided admitting the clash of interest between German and African claims. He hoped that by the cautious application of the 'right treatment' one could cover up the chief's decisive loss of function" (Bley 1971:39).

7. The South Africans, when they took over the country in 1915, also initially respected these treaties. Bushmen were allowed to stay and, indeed, were encouraged to settle in the Etosha Game Park, while the farms of Guigab, Hiebus Nord, Chudib and Chudib West were reserved for Johannes Kruger and his followers for the duration of his lifetime (Gordon 1989).

8. After Jordan was murdered and the Republic of Upingtonia failed, Jordan's concessions were taken over by the South West Africa Company, which, apart from settling twenty-five Boer families in 1895 as a security measure against the Bushmen, preferred to hold on to its extensive land holdings in the hope that increased settlement would raise their value (Schenk 1974).

9. Official mythology portrays these German colonizers as "farsighted officials" who persisted in their noble efforts of game conservation "in spite of the confusion and destruction caused by the Native Risings" (Schoeman 1982). They were not the heroes they were made out to be. Far from being pioneers, Namibian officials actually lagged behind their compatriots in other parts of Germany's African empire.

Notes to Chapter 7

1. This was one of the few occasions when the farming and mining settler factions made common cause. Of course one needs a sense of proportion here: The total settler population in 1911 was 8,026 according to Gann (1987:13), consisting of the following categories: 881 civil servants; 2,072 soldiers and police; 2,578 artisans and industrial workers; 1,390 farmers; 1,035 merchants and storekeepers and some 70 missionaries and clergy. This small body supported a vibrant press consisting of at least four newspapers, each representing distinct regional and economic interests.

2. Although little about them can be found in the official records, the Court Returns for 1913 indicate that a number of Bushmen were caught and convicted of highway robbery and murder of "Barotses," or Northern Rhodesian indigenes. The archives are rather scanty on these Bushman attacks, yet even the settler press conceded that they were probably more important than attacks on settlers. For example, the *Südwest Zeitung* (17 October 1911), after reporting Sergeant Alefelder's death, seems to express more concern at the potential disruption of the labor supply than the woes of the farmers. "According to reliable sources, the problem of the Bushmen in the Outjo area is just as noticeable as in Grootfontein. The farmers of the area had to put up with cattle theft by the devious population for some time; especially endangered, however, were the nomadic Ovambos. They have been overtaken by such fear of the Bushmen that a group of 30 strong people will throw away its belongings and flee, even if only two Bushmen show themselves with bow and arrow.

"For this reason the District Office is taking serious action. Mobile police stations have been set up, which pursue the marauding mobs. The station Okakeujo is to be strengthened only because of the Bushmen problem."

3. Seitz's major source was Theal's *History of South Africa*. For a thorough dissection of Theal's procolonialist biases see Saunders 1988.

4. Most of Passarge's observations were made immediately after the rinderpest epidemic. One of his companions in 1897 was Lord Lugard, who felt that Passarge was unduly brutal in his treatment of indigenes (Thomson and Middleton 1959:142).

5. Indeed Schultze was in many ways representative of the dominant paradigm within German *volkerkunde* (ethnology). In 1914 in the authoritative *Das Kolonialreich,* he provided the following cant of empire: "The ethnologist may lament the fact that a portion of humanity with such strongly developed characteristics as displayed by the tribes of German South West Africa, especially the Hereros and Hottentots, in their physical, intellectual, and political peculiarities, will one day become wholly melted down in order to be put into circulation again as common day labor coin, stamped with the imperial eagle and the Christian cross, with the inscription 'colored laborer,' to constitute an economic value. But the struggle for our own existence allows no other solution. At the same time work is the only solution for them: He who doesn't want to work perishes here with us as well; we have no reason to be more sentimental in Africa than in Europe. We who build our houses on the graves of those races must, however, take twice as seriously our obligation to avoid no sacrifices for the purposes of civilization, i.e. for the greater development of all means of existence in this new land" (Schultze 1914:295).

6. Thus, contrary to popular myth (see, for example, Grimm 1928; Unterkötter 1955), Vedder, the dominant figure in the Rhenish Missionary Society, did not convert the first Bushmen in 1911.

7. Illustrative of this relationship is the letter written on 19 December 1913 by the Präses (chief executive officer) of the Rhenish Mission to the governor: "In reply to your Excellency's letter regarding the question of making Bushmen sedentary, I am able to reply that the Rhenish Mission is prepared to put up captured Bushman families on its farm Gaub and gradually to make them sedentary by habituation to agricultural labor. The Mission hopes that the principle of not breaking up families, which the Government too has recognized, will be taken into account as far as possible in transferring Bushmen to Gaub. Desertion presumably will be feared less—even if it will never be entirely preventable—if the men can remain with their women and children.

"If there should be people speaking the Nama language among the Bushmen that have been brought in, it would greatly facilitate the work of the Mission as well as the study of the as yet relatively little-known Bushman language, if such individuals could be sent to the Mission along with the others.

"For the maintenance of the women and children as well as male Bushmen who may be wholly or partially incapable of work, the Mission requests a reimbursement of 50 Pfennig per adult person and a boarding allowance of 24 Pfennig per child. The Mission would be grateful if, in case a large-scale settlement should require the employment of a special white employee, the annual salary of such a person, to the amount of 2400 marks could also be paid. It furthermore requests that Bushman families, once accepted in its care, should not be taken away from it in short order, to be assigned to some farmer or other as laborers. Such a proceeding would run counter to the purpose of sedentari- zation. Should the Mission, as may easily happen, run into serious difficulties with the farming community as a result of cattle thieving, or other robberies committed by deserting Bushmen, the Mission hopes that the Imperial Govern- ment will afford effective protection against unjust accusations or possible claims for damages.

"For its part, the Mission will do everything in its power to prevent unpleas- ant incidents" (ZBU 2043, Olpp, Prases).

Notes to Chapter 8

1. The view from the periphery was rosier. A Dr. Zachlehner of Grootfon- tein claimed that from the beginning of 1913 there had been no further depor- tations (because of high mortality rates? because of von Zastrow's interventions?) to the coastal areas, and of the approximately 250 Bushmen who had been detained at Grootfontein the previous year, only 8 had died, mostly from pul- monary causes brought about by poor nutrition, change of diet, and the fact that they were unused to hard work (ZBU 2043, letter dated 1 May 1913).

2. Gann and Duignan noted: "For reasons of economy the Germans were reluctant to grant tenure to the majority of their officials, and non-tenured civil servants were liable to be dismissed upon the expiration of their contracts. The service therefore contained a considerable proportion of men who could not afford to criticize their superiors or report abuses, lest they be punished by the loss of their livelihood" (Gann and Duignan 1977:88).

3. Indeed his classification of where Bushmen lived is strikingly accurate by contemporary knowledge. He classified the Kung into four groups: first, the Kumgau, or northern group, whose area extended from Tsintsabis in the west and snaked eastward to Guntsas farm whence it turned northeast and stretched up to the Kavango River. Their chief was the (in)famous Namagurub. (In a later comment on von Zastrow, Köhler said that the Kum'gau might be the people Vedder called Xom-Khoin and as the name Nama-gorub is Nama in its linguistic form, this group might in fact be Heikom rather than Kung [Köhler 1959]. Köhler, of course, assumed that Bushman groups should somehow be "pure.") The second and third groups were both called Nog'au (still people). The north- ern group lived around Karakuwisa, while the southern group inhabited an area stretching from the Omuramba Omatako to the Bechuana border and beyond. They were the worst stock thieves, according to von Zastrow. The fact that he was able to meet over 400 Nog'au at Otjituo on one day is suggestive of a high population density (von Zastrow and Vedder 1930). The fourth group were the Ae'au, who were to be found further east of Karakuwisa and lived in the Kaukauveld. While von Zastrow's assignment of the names might be somewhat wrong and his geography a bit off beam (or is this a consequence of large-scale

European settlement?), he appears to be remarkably accurate if we connect Kum'gau with the northern Kung, and the Nog'au with those known presently as the central Kung, or Ju-/wasi (also Zu/asi; Zhu/twasi; Ssu-gnassi). The Ae'au reveal themselves to be the southern Kung (Makaukau; Auen; //Kau-//en) who live not so much east of Karakuwisa as southeast, near Ghanzi and in the Gobabis district (Marshall 1976; Lee 1979; Westphal 1971).

But even this system of classification was "untidy" as there was what was later to be labeled another official ethnic group, the Damara or Berg-Damara, living in the same broad area. The Berg-Damara were Nama-speaking "negroid" ironworkers and foragers, similar in terms of underclass status. Very little is known about the Damara in the northeast, except that there are numerous references in the state archives to the fact that Bushmen and Damara farm workers would often intermarry, thereby betraying their lack of "racial pride." That there were Damara in the Omaheke is obvious. An old map that is a summary of the state of accumulated knowledge in 1914 (Schultze 1914) has a Damara group, the Sandamab, living in the vicinity of Nyae Nyae. In their stirring reminiscences of the Thirstland Trek, Prinsloo and Gauche (1933) mention that a number of Bushmen near Tebra (just north of Nyae Nyae) killed a trekker and that these Bushmen stood under a Berg Damara chief who was "more cunning and dangerous than a snake" (Prinsloo and Gauche 1933:30).

4. Von Zastrow's opinion later found widespread support. "It appears," wrote Sergeant Coetzee from Steinhausen, "that farmers who consistently chase the Bushmen from their farms are the only people who have trouble with them" (LGO 3/1/60, Gobabis Annual Report 1930). And in this he was supported by the venerable Vedder in the South African Senate (South Africa 1951:5620). Revenge had been recognized as a strong motive earlier by Lieutenant Hull in Grootfontein (ADM 273, Hull to Mil. Mag. 24 December 1915) and later as well (LGR 3/1/7, Meintjes memorandum 1939), and especially in cases where the meat or farm produce was left to rot in the sun. The sergeant, investigating the stock theft complaints of farmer Pleitz of Hayas Farm, reported that Pleitz did not pay his workers and that it was "strange" that he was the only farmer in the area to have suffered losses from stock theft by Bushmen.

5. On settler dependency and state intervention in Grootfontein district, see von Weber 1983:174.

6. Except for some indirect support from the ethnologists in Berlin, most academic Bushman experts were not forthcoming in their support of von Zastrow. This is not surprising since most of them were employed by large companies when they did their fieldwork. Passarge, perhaps the most prominent, for example, had been employed by the British West Charter Land Company to work in Botswana and was directly involved in arranging for Cecil Rhodes to dispossess the Bushmen of the Ghanzi Block and replace them with white settlers. Schinz, as we saw, went out to Namibia under the aegis of Luderitz.

7. Link provided some statistics in his memorandum: Between June 1911 and August 1913, two whites were killed, while four farmers had killed an unspecified number of Bushmen and the military had officially accounted for fourteen Bushmen deaths.

Notes to Chapter 9

1. Since most farmers were inexperienced and farms were not fenced in, stock losses were understandably high. Bushman theft formed a convenient scapegoat in such matters.

2. The very fact that Becker thought that it was appropriate to brag about such deeds to the police is a powerful statement on how officials saw their relationship to Bushmen. Becker eventually got ten years for this crime. For other reports of farmers killing Bushmen and not being punished for it, see Sangiro 1954; Mattenklodt 1931:185. In another murder case, *Rex v. Thomas* 1917 SCC, it was reported that the small stock was periodically stolen from the farm Bushfeld. Thomas knew by rumor who was responsible, but although he chased the alleged miscreants, he was unable to capture them. Normally he took an interpreter with him on his rounds but on that day apparently did not. His rifle had a cartridge in it and the safety catch did not work, supposedly because it was rusty (but he later removed the rust). He surprised a Bushman party and then fell, and the rifle went off and killed a Bushman. Thomas was acquitted. Superficially, it appears that the South Africans were more severe because they used the death sentence more often on whites than did the Germans, but this is deceptive, as becomes apparent when one examines the court correspondence. Death sentences were invariably commuted. Indeed, I do not recall finding any cases of whites going to the gallows for murdering indigenes.

3. In Nama, the Heikom Bushman language, the suffix -*ib* indicates male gender, and the suffix -*es* indicates female. There clearly was a small error in translation here.

4. For other cases involving torture by farmers, see *Rex v. Nauhas and Jakubowski* 1919 SCC; *Rex v. Schilg* 1919 SCC; *Rex v. Kremer* 1915 SCC; *Rex v. Tinschmann* 1917 SCC.

5. Revenge worked the other way round as well. The fear of Bushman revenge was recognized by farmers and served as a check on the more outrageous abuses. This was the reason why, for example, farmer Bohme of Kakuse West appealed to the governor for assistance in 1915.

6. Voswinkel was a farmer in the area who was also found guilty of murdering Bushmen by the new South African regime. Their escape is chronicled in Raif 1935 and Mattenklodt 1931 and rapidly gained heroic proportions in German settler folklore (see, e.g., Grimm 1928).

Notes to Chapter 10

1. Indeed, it comes as no surprise to learn that the first anthropological research that the South West African Administration sponsored was on Bushmen. Not only were they in danger of extinction, but they were a "problem" as well. And when the State Museum appointed its first ethnologist, he felt that his first priority was to research the Bushmen.

2. Brownlee was from a famous Transkeian "Native Administration" family. He later authored a number of semiacademic papers on the Bushmen. See, e.g., Brownlee 1932.

3. Early in 1917, the magistrate of neighboring Otjiwarongo reported that various Bushmen had been arrested for hunting and vagrancy on very little evidence. He then got to the root of what he felt was the "problem": "It is very difficult to get this class of natives to do any work and when any of them are sentenced to imprisonment, their families, which are large, become a charge of the Government. I shall be glad therefore to receive instructions as to the disposal of such families" (ADM 105, 27 January 1917). In response, he was told not to arrest Bushmen for hunting or vagrancy but that Bushmen should be removed from the "inhabited" portions of the district and warned not to return, since they are "classed amongst the protected wild animals."

4. The "regrettable reprisals" refer to a number of cases in which established German farmers were charged and convicted of murdering and otherwise abusing Bushmen, some of which have been discussed in Chapter 9.

5. Thus Doke reported that Grootfontein farmers differentiate between wild and tame Bushman: "The wild Bushmen whom they only see when starvation drives them out of the Kalahari and the tame Bushmen, who come and work in the lands and with the cattle for periods" (Doke 1925:41).

6. In 1928, the Gobabis magistrate wrote that "the 'wild' Bushman keeps to himself and it is seldom that he is convicted for an offence. The crimes, mostly stock-theft, are committed by the 'semi' tame Bushmen and this usually when he deserts service. The average Bushman is underfed" (SWAA, A50/25, Magistrate, 20 April 1928). Twelve years later, with his characteristic bluntness, "Cocky" Hahn, the Ovamboland native commissioner, wrote that "thieving was caused by hunger pure and simple" and it was impossible for the Bushmen to exist on the food issued to them by farmers. Moreover, they were constantly being pushed off their own land. He was surprised that there was not more stock theft (SWAA, A50/67, NC to CNC, 5 September 1940).

7. Yet two weeks later he had Hull transferred from Native Affairs for incompetence!

8. Indeed, the whole policy of segregation whereby other blacks, principally Herero, Damara and Nama, were allocated inadequate reserves was also part of this policy. As settlers were in the process of establishing themselves on land that was historically Herero, most of the new land allocated to Herero belonged historically to Bushmen. Some of the implications of this are discussed in Chapters 13, 18, and 21.

9. This claim was based on the testimony heard in a single court case. However, my own reading of the court records shows that only by the most fertile stretching of the circumstantial evidence could one even suggest that cannibalism might have occurred.

10. Some of the versions of this event are at such variance with one another that the unsuspecting reader might be forgiven for believing that Bushmen regularly killed off magistrates (not to mention farmers) in a most perfidious manner. Cf., for example, *Cape Argus,* 10 July 1961; Sangiro 1954; Oldevig 1944; Green 1945; Legendre 1939; Farson 1941; Voigt 1943.

11. The Gobabis Farmerverein (German farmer association) later commented that the administrator was forced to be wary of the "nigger-loving Union press." The administrator denied, however, that the caution displayed in this case had led to disrespect for the police (SWAA, A396/7, 3 August 1922). The question remains, nevertheless: Was it in fact the threat of the "nigger-loving Union press" that led the administrator to order the magistrate to try a nonviolent approach? A survey of the Gobabis court records shows that Magistrate van Ryneveld had been found guilty of assaulting his black servant girl shortly before these events. Unfortunately, van Ryneveld's personal file in the State Archives has vanished, but it seems highly likely that this conviction had caused the administrators to issue such an instruction. In addition, the administrator had just gone through a period of intensive press criticism for excessive use of force in suppressing the Bondelzwarts Rebellion in the Warmbad district (Goldblatt 1971).

Notes to Chapter 11

1. For example, Grayson, the magistrate at Gobabis, wrote: "I think that in every case where the man is convicted, the children above the apparent age of 8 years should be apprenticed. This could be done without any fuss and any publicity" (SWAA, A50/25, September 1922). No record of reply to these suggestions could be located in the archives, but it certainly appears to have been adopted (see, e.g., Wendt 1981).

2. As the Grootfontein magistrate did in 1923: "The other main source of farm labor is the Bushman. For heavy farm work, he is useless and it is difficult to instill any knowledge of agriculture into him. There are two difficulties in regard to Bushmen—one is that they cannot work for more than a few weeks at a time and the other is their propensity to steal mielies [corn] and grain generally. The race get very little more civilized as the years go and it is difficult to think that there will not be trouble in the future between it and the European settler" (South Africa 1923).

3. Thus, for a first conviction the following sentences could be given: (1) imprisonment of up to eighteen months; (2) spare diet and/or solitary confinement for up to three months; (3) a maximum of ten strokes; (4) a combination of any of the above; (5) a fine of up to 200 English pounds; (6) a combination of fine and imprisonment. On second conviction, penalties were increased to two years' imprisonment and fifteen strokes in any combination.

4. The Vagrancy Proclamation allowed for "any person found wandering abroad and having no visible lawful means, or insufficient lawful means of support . . . who [cannot] give a good and satisfactory account of himself, . . . shall be liable to be imprisoned, with or without hard labour, and with or without spare diet, and with or without solitary confinement or either of them, for any period not exceeding three months." Furthermore, "every person found without the permission of the owner . . . wandering over any farm . . . shall be deemed and taken to be an idle and disorderly person." Moreover, "no person shall visit the servants or employees of any owner or occupier of land without his permission

[which must be obtained beforehand]." The proclamation also gave the local magistrate the power to remove "all squatters trespassing upon waste crown land."

5. For an illustrative case concerning the Herero in Basterland, see Pearson 1981:40. The barrage of laws that the Bushmen and other indigenes had to face parallels to a remarkable extent the Statutes of Kilkenny, which the precapitalist English invaders imposed upon the Irish in 1376 (Hallinan 1977).

6. Finally, according to Schoeman, the administration showed its muscle in 1920 by resettling nineteen Bushman families among the Nama south of Gibeon. This "experiment" was apparently unsuccessful, as no further mention is made of it or similar schemes (Schoeman 1975). Unfortunately, I was unable to trace this material in the archives.

7. Undoubtedly lack of language proficiency contributes to high conviction rates. Bushmen have been tried and convicted without having understood a word of what was said in the court proceedings.

8. This pattern of fear of the police was so well enshrined that even in the 1950s P. J. Schoeman in his interim report on the preservation of Bushmen recommended that uniformed police not be allowed to patrol in the Kaukauveld.

9. One suspects that the awesome reputation of such policemen was deliberately encouraged, because when people were as difficult to apprehend as Bushmen were reported to have been, such a reputation can be a very effective device of social control. This is brought out most clearly in the use during the late 1970s and throughout the 1980s of Bushmen by the South African Defence Force.

10. This belief was of long duration. As the station commander of Steinhausen put it in his annual report for 1939: "The Bushman very easily resorts to stealing, and once he starts stock-thieving it is not an easy matter to take him into custody, as he is in his element as a *hunted creature*" (italics added).

11. Thus Magistrate Grayson of Gobabis complained: "Some years ago the Administrator ordered that Bushmen should not be prosecuted for game law contravention in outlying portions but with personnel changes this has started again. Bushmen argue that they cannot live without meat and since they are prosecuted for killing game and cattle, it is easier to kill cattle" (SWAA, A50/25, 22 September 1922). Fourteen years later, the Gobabis magistrate was again moved to complain and issued clear instructions that "police are not to prosecute a Bushman for shooting game, and if the Bushman knows that [!] it is possible that it will reduce stock theft" (SWAA, A50/25, 3 November 1936).

12. At the police stations like Tsintsabis, prisoners were leg-ironed and tied to an iron ring in the cement floor of the corrugated iron cell to prevent them from escaping (SWAA, A82/21). Not a pleasant way to spend a hot summer's day or a cold winter's night!

Notes to Chapter 12

1. "Native policy was basically the attempt to overcome the shortage of labor," as the economist Rädel (1947:74) put it, or to paraphrase Malinowski, in Namibia the White Man's Burden was carried by Blacks!

2. See also *Rex v. Thuantha et al.* 1920 SCC, where it was claimed by a Bushman that "the Bushmen of Gasamas kill Ovambos every year."

3. See also, for example, *Rex v. Xaie et al.* 1927 SCW.

4. As the magistrate noted, echoing Gage, "It is essential to take steps without delay to restore confidence amongst the laborers who propose to come south."

5. Sometimes such expeditions went to white-occupied farms, where horns and hides were traded for tobacco, items of clothing and knives. A typical expedition brought in twenty antlers and twelve hides. Farmers felt compelled to offer decent terms of exchange in such cases, for they feared that if they did not, they would lose livestock. Needless to say, the government took a dim view of this type of trade, as it was felt that it encouraged Bushmen to decimate the game and, furthermore, provided the farmers with an excuse to poach.

6. In 1926 in order to organize the flow of migrant workers from the north to the Police Zone, employers banded together to form two labor-recruiting organizations. The Southern Labor Organization was responsible for recruitment in Ovamboland, and the Northern Labor Organization recruited in the Kavango region. In the 1940s these two organizations were merged to create the South West Africa Native Labor Association (SWANLA). SWANLA was in turn replaced in the 1970s by various "ethnic" Homeland Labor Bureaus.

7. Bushmen apparently had a limited choice in this matter, as it was government policy to prevent them from engaging in contract labor in the Police Zone. "I have consistently refused their applications," wrote the commissioner, "on the grounds that I do not consider the Bushmen as sufficiently advanced to understand the obligations of an ordinary contract" (SWAA, A50/67, NC Runtu, March 1948). Instead Bushmen functioned to subsidize de facto the costs of reproducing Kavango contract labor migration by working as cheap labor for the Kavango migrants. For a similar situation in Botswana see Wilmsen 1989b:281ff.

8. Some black deserters were, like the white settlers, quick to use the myth of Bushman bandits to their own advantage. Deserters would, on occasion, remove their clothes and dirty themselves up and then go to the police claiming that they were legal workers who had been attacked and robbed of all their possessions including, regrettably, their "passes."

Notes to Chapter 13

1. In 1962, for example, there were only sixty-three registered boreholes in the Waterberg East Reserve and forty-nine in Epukiro (Wellington 1967:387).

2. Much of this information was derived from extensive interviews with F. R. Balt, who was a welfare officer at Aminuis and Epukiro for many years after World War II. See also the various district ethnographies compiled by the government ethnologist, O. Köhler. Nowadays, cans and bottles of beer have also made their appearance as remuneration for services.

3. Bushmen also used kinship terms to refer to those people for whom they worked. Bushmen sometimes had different kinship terms for people who worked

as pastoralists (sometimes referred to as "uncles") as opposed to those who continued to forage in the bush (who were called "nephews"). Some researchers go as far as to argue that kinship terminology is indicative of implicit socioeconomic stratification in Bushman societies (e.g., Wilmsen 1989a:166–176).

4. The superintendent refused to take action against the Bushmen because they were allegedly "too uncivilized to properly understand what they had done." He also argued against the Herero request for the following reasons: (1) Such an order would be impossible to implement; (2) Bushmen who were periodically in white employ might run away permanently as a result of such action; (3) Bushmen prefer to work for natives, and the Herero take as many as "offer themselves," and thus there might be a grass-roots Herero reaction to such an act (SWAA, A50/25, Mag. to NC Whk., 15 June 1927).

5. Later, in 1948, when the police did offer to patrol the reserves, the various Herero reserves turned down this offer, claiming that the headmen and board members were doing a satisfactory policing job (SWAA, A3/111).

6. Nevertheless, a perusal of the incomplete annual reports for the magisterial districts covering the major Herero reserves indicates that conflict between Herero and Bushman was more common than usually alleged. Typically, officials would discover Herero abuses of Bushmen by accident. The following two cases, which were discovered incidentally when one of the Bushman participants was arrested for some other offense, provide some useful insights into Herero-Bushman relationships.

In *Rex v. Wetondowando and Kanomotwa* 1932 SCW, two Herero were charged with killing a young Bushman female, Chokai. The accused had gone hunting and killed a kudu, which they had placed in the branches of a tree, intending to return the next day to collect the meat. However, before they could do this, another Herero observed blood on his dogs and thus suspected meat nearby, so he got some of his "tame" Bushmen to go and investigate. The Bushmen located the meat and, after having given a share to their "master," proceeded to eat the remainder, at which stage the two accused arrived and proceeded to club the eight unarmed Bushmen with knobkerries. The woman Chokai tried to protect her young infant with a small sapling, but this gesture of resistance so angered the accused that they drew their axes and hacked Chokai to death. When the distraught husband wanted to report the murder to the police, the Herero, including the local subheadman, dissuaded him from doing so. "You say you are going to the police, can you tell them anything? You don't know the law . . . the law does not pay." The husband accepted the three oxen and one heifer that were given to him as compensation. "Herero Fritz told me to eat the meat quickly and leave nothing over." The oxen were killed shortly thereafter and the meat shared with the Herero. The hides were traded to the local Herero. One fetched some beads, the others were exchanged for a goat and a dog. In passing sentence, the judge noted numerous inconsistencies in the Herero evidence. He also commented on the state of abject subservience in which the Bushmen were living under the Herero, even having to refer to them as "Baas." These comments are in line with observations made in other court cases. In *Rex v. Namseb and Toetab* 1927 SCW, for example, two Bushman males were arraigned for killing another

Bushman in a matter involving a young maiden. The accused had wanted the maiden as a wife for a relative living beyond the Police Zone. The deceased had refused this request on the grounds, inter alia, that the girl was "working" for a Herero and they would have to get his permission, which was unlikely to be granted.

7. As Neser, the assistant secretary, wrote, with a touch of unintended irony, in 1941 after the South African Bushman imbroglio: "If the Bushmen are to be preserved in their natural state, it follows that they must be in the vicinity of game . . . it may be possible later to establish a Bushman reserve which would overlap the game reserve so that Bushmen would have access to the game. It is not considered that a small number of Bushmen would seriously deplete the herds of game in the reserve, and all suggestions in the past for the establishment of a Bushman reserve which . . . have been advocated from influential quarters, have had to be abandoned owing to the improbability of the Bushmen being got to settle down. If they are allowed to roam and hunt over portions of the [Etosha] game reserve this may provide a solution to the problem" (SWAA, A511/1–4, Neser memo, n.d.; A50/67/2).

8. The history of South West Africa is littered with various Hahns. The most pertinent for our purposes are the Reverend C. H. Hahn, the pioneer and longtime missionary among the Herero and traveler to Ovamboland in 1858. Other Hahns of importance include Dr. Theophilus Hahn, the librarian of the Grey Collection in Cape Town, who wrote learned papers on the Bushmen; and last, "Cocky" Hahn, or *Shongola* (Sjambok), an ex-national rugby team player, who was native affairs commissioner in Ovamboland from the end of World War I to the beginning of World War II as well as part-time warden of the Etosha Park after 1928. He was a man of near-legendary reputation (see, e.g., Green 1952; Farson 1941).

9. Compare also Crosby's contradictory statement: "The Bushmen do not intermarry with the Ovakwanyama, but poor Aukwe men and poor Ovakwanyama men sometimes use women of other tribes according to the testimony of one Bushman" (Crosby 1931:353). Another useful material indicator of intergroup relations is the terms of trade in exchanges. Certainly by this count, Ovambo exchanges were the most equitable in South West Africa because six ostrich eggs apparently fetched one Ovambo cow (Lebzelter 1934a).

10. Although archaeologically the Iron Age record goes back at least to A.D. 200.

11. The term *slavery*, uncritically used by administrators, obscured a very complex social phenomenon that might better be seen in a variety of relationships like voluntary servitude, bondsmanship and symbiosis. For a discussion of "slavery," or clientship, and *bothlanka* (a form of serfdom) in the nearby and influential Tawana state, see the definitive oral history–based research of Tlou (1985). Tlou suggested that slavery per se was unlikely because intensive labor was not required. The relationship was more akin to fosterage and was often voluntary. The major legal difference was that *wapika* and *bothlanka* were denied access to the courts.

Notes to Chapter 14

1. As far as I could ascertain, the Bushman bow and arrow legislation is still applicable.

2. Further supportive inferences can also be made from statements cited in Chapters 8 and 9 dealing with Bushman hunts during German colonialism.

3. Interned during World War II, Metzger put his time to good use by producing a popular book on the Bushmen, eventually translated into English as *Narro and His Clan* (1950).

Notes to Chapter 15

1. For example, the Okahandja magistrate optimistically reported that in the Steinhausen area: "The farmers . . . assure me that they are excellent sheep and cattle herds [for] seldom or ever do they sustain any losses through straying [due to their excellent eyesight and tracking capabilities]. It is also certain that he will never steal stock belonging to his master. The greatest complaint . . . appears to be that of . . . deserting at any time and leaving his master in the lurch. This . . . only happens when nature calls him to the wilds. . . . In view of their physical structure it is doubtful whether they could be put to hard manual work immediately. This will have to be taught to them step by step . . . they are very willing when taken in and in the correct manner. An attempt to thrash him or even a harsh word will do more harm than good. Neither have they the foggiest idea of getting something together in their own welfare" (SWAA, A50/67, Mag. Okahandja to Sec. Whk. 14 June 1935). By 1939, undoubtedly influenced by remarks made by the secretary for South West Africa, the Okahandja magistrate had changed his mind: Far from making useful herders, "he is unsuitable for manual labor by instinct as well as by upbringing and even should he conquer his feelings of revulsion for work and seek employment, he commands such a low wage that he finds the sacrifice not worthwhile" (South Africa 1939). Sometimes within the same district, contrary evaluations on the worth of Bushmen were made. Thus in Grootfontein district the police of Otavi found that the majority of Bushmen made good servants although they still suffered from the "incurable habit of carrying bows and arrows which they consider indispensable." In contrast, their colleagues at Nurugas found Bushmen to be untrustworthy laborers, deserting "without any provocation or reason" and squatting about the water holes on the unoccupied farms. "We have no end of trouble with Bushmen," they continued, "and are often shot at with poisoned arrows . . . however we keep a sharp lookout and prosecute all vagrants and deserters" (LGR 3/1/7, Annual Report, 1937). The one common feature of all these situations in which favorable evaluations of Bushmen are contained is that Bushmen are found in comparatively small numbers in these areas of jurisdiction.

2. Other officials agreed: "Farmers find the Bushmen the cheapest kind to engage as it is a known fact that most of these Bushmen are only working for their food and tobacco, and now and then they get a blanket or a shovel,"

reported the station commander at Tsintsabis rural police station (LGR 3/1/7, Annual Report, 1936).

3. In Botswana Bob Hitchcock reported that farmers also hired Bushmen "because they were used to life in the Bush" and "would not want to move to town" (personal comment). Latter-day Namibian farmers also use the same type of rationale.

4. For example, in 1946, 161 contract worker desertions were reported to the police; yet a year later, 139, or 86.3 percent, were still "at large."

5. This was essentially the same point that Vedder had made to the South West Africa Constitutional Commission the year before and again in 1951 in the South African Senate. It was advice well taken (as befits a man of Vedder's stature among whites; see, for example, Voigt 1943; Ahrens 1948). Vedder was quite free with his advice to farmers on how to "tame" their local Bushmen: Be flexible, he advised, let them work half days if need be. All they want is a bit of friendship and then they will stay, he told the SWA Commission in 1936 (South Africa 1936:1249 of verbatim evidence).

6. The minutes of the Permanent Mandates Commission (League of Nations 1930: 140, 15th Meeting) reported the following exchange of views on this case: "Mr. Courtney-Clarke (SWA Administration). They had been immediately arrested and a very serious view had been taken by the Administration—so much so, that they had been tried by the High Court and sentenced. Mr. Ruppel (Mandates Commission) pointed out that the sentence had amounted only to a fine of 5 pounds. Mr. Courtney-Clarke said that this might seem lenient, but the judge had probably taken into account that their actions had been due mainly to youthful exuberance. Mr. Sakanabe was curious that nearly one year had elapsed before the trial." The court's reasoning that manstealing had not occurred because Bushmen could have escaped is found in current arguments by apologists to assert that Bushmen are not exploited and terrorized by their black neighbors.

7. Consider also the case of Mrs. Commandant Meyer of Omaruru, who wrote to the Secretary for South West Africa requesting permission to obtain a Bushman girl of between ten and twelve: "I would very much like to have a little girl to train and therefore to keep for good," she wrote, adding that the police sergeant at Namutoni had said that she could have one (SWAA, A50/67, Meyer to Sec., 9 June 1940). This system has a close similarity to the notorious system of *inboekselings* practiced in the South African Republic (see Delius and Trapido 1983 for details).

8. This precedent was established during the German era: "I am assured by many farmers that the *Dienstbuche* were frequently not written up after the noting of the first year's contract, which was held to renew itself automatically from year to year," wrote Lieutenant Hull from Grootfontein in 1915 (ADM 13/35, 6 December 1915).

9. See, e.g., *Rex v. Feuerstein* 1918 SCC. For popular accounts of farmers killing Bushmen and never being punished for such deeds, see Sangiro 1954; Mattenklodt 1931:185.

10. See also *Rex v. Kahoekabond and two others* 1923 SCW, where the farmer hid some murder evidence and then said to his Bushmen, "You have told lies to

the police and now you and your family will go to Windhoek to get hanged."
Intimidated, the Bushmen deserted.

11. Of course there were exceptions. Some farmers did attempt to look after
the interests of the Bushmen, but they were usually a small, wealthy minority.
An example is A. Courtney-Clarke of Keibib farm, the brother of the secretary
of the territory, who wrote numerous letters of protest and even provided his
Bushmen with legal representation on occasion when he felt that the police were
unjustly persecuting them. When he leased his farm, he had it written into the
agreement that the lessee was not to interfere with Bushmen living there.
Another farmer who wrote letters on behalf of "his" Bushmen (I use the
possessive here, not in a proprietary sense, but rather in a moral one) was Fritz
Metzger of Hochfeld. But documented reports about the altruistic behavior of
farmers are rare, although Bob Hitchcock pointed out that in Botswana poor
farmers were said to be helpful to Bushmen in part because they were so heavily
dependent upon them for assistance (personal comment).

12. The poor health and nutritional condition of Bushmen on farms in both
Namibia and Botswana can be illustrated by comparing the reports of Metz,
Hart and Harpending (1971) with those of Jenkins et al. (1987), Jenkins (1988),
Fernandes-Costa et al. (1984), van der Westhuizen et al. (1987) and O'Keefe and
Lavender (1989). Thanks to Bob Hitchcock for these references.

13. Even in the 1950s, Lutheran missionaries reported that farmers were
forcing their Catholic laborers to attend Lutheran services (Weineke 1956).

Notes to Chapter 16

1. In addition Lebzelter suggested that a reserve for the Nogau and Naron
be created in the Gobabis district where they could live with the /Gowanin (Sand
Damaras) and gradually transform themselves into goatherds and tillers of small
gardens.

2. Cf., for example, Chief Police Inspector Naude's circular cited in Chapter
14.

3. Yet Vedder had pointed out in his evidence that Bushmen were no more
nomadic than other indigenes and that, indeed, Bushmen were probably less
prone to trek than others.

4. Administrators have always been ambivalent toward academics; this is
well expressed in the Wembley Exhibition pamphlet the administration published
in 1925: "The Bushmen live mostly in a wild state, but in the districts in which
they have come into contact with civilization they have been found to make good
and faithful herd-boys. . . . To the student of anthropology it is one of the most
interesting portions of South Africa, and offers an unrivalled field for research"
(South West Africa 1925).

5. Thus A. Meyer, one of the leaders of the resettled Angola Boers, who
were notorious for their harsh treatment of indigenes, wrote a remarkable letter
to the administrator, pleading for a Bushman reserve. "As is well-known, the
Bushmen are dying out, but while they are still here, and while they are still

regarded as people, they deserve human treatment" (SWAA, A50/67, 10 September 1936).

6. The committee was to (1) investigate the distribution, number and mode of life of the Bushmen; (2) examine the physical condition and nutrition of the Bushmen; and (3) assess what anthropological and linguistic research was needed to supplement existing data in order "to settle outstanding problems of primary interest to the scientist" (Schapera 1938). Clearly the committee saw its task as conducting a salvage operation for science. Humanitarian concerns seemed to have disappeared. On the instructions of the committee Schapera drew up a detailed questionnaire, which local field officers were supposed to complete. Judging from the archival files, this was not a task officials did with any enthusiasm.

7. In neighboring Botswana Charles Rey, the resident commissioner, opined in 1936: "I [see] no reason whatever for preserving Bushmen. I can conceive no useful object to the world in spending money and energy in preserving a decadent and dying race, which is perfectly useless from any point of view, merely to enable a few theorists to carry out anthropological investigations and make money by writing books which lead nowhere" (cited in Wilmsen 1989b:272).

Wilmsen believed that "by no stretch of the imagination was Rey's reaction . . . representative of majority opinion among British administrators" (Wilmsen 1989b:272). This might indeed be stretching the imagination, given the Namibian experience. Moreover, Rey went on to become a resident expert and senior official, and a grateful government even knighted him for his colonial services. Hardly the career of someone who espoused "unrepresentative" positions!

8. And note that this was in the rainy season when Bushmen would have been dispersed. Bushmen constantly "surprised" Europeans. Thus a newspaper article describing a journey "Overland to Lobito Bay" (*Cape Times,* 1 January 1926) describes a visit to a Bushman village in southern Angola where there was an iron forge: "When one realizes that this, as far as we know, is the only record of metal work by Bushmen . . . it came as a great surprise to find him working iron. The knives they forge, though of rough metal work, have a good cutting edge and are fitted with very well-worked wooden sheaths."

9. The influence that Watts had on colonial stereotyping cannot be ignored. He wrote numerous textbooks for use in white Namibian schools, and many history and geography textbooks currently in use in primary schools are still based on his original text (see, for example, Lemmer n.d.; Malan and Malan 1982).

10. Andrew Musingeh (personal comment) pointed out that there was endemic nonvenereal syphilis among Bushmen; thus the disease was not necessarily the product of sexual contact with other groups.

Notes to Chapter 17

1. For additional data on this situation, see Chapter 21.

2. Smuts and Edwin Loeb had met during the founding of the United Nations in San Francisco, and Loeb's diffusionist hypothesis postulating a Medi-

terranean origin for the Ovambo would have sat well with white settlers intent on justifying their territorial claims. In American anthropology Loeb was a conservative diffusionist.

3. As indeed they had, for the paterfamilias, Laurence Marshall, was the founding president of the Raytheon Corporation.

4. Significantly, shortly after this event John Marshall was denied a visa to reenter Namibia for around twenty years. He thought it was because his family had intervened to prevent Herero encroachment on Bushman land. Later he was told by an official that it was because he had allegedly slept with a Kung girl.

5. He was followed by at least six *volkekundiges* (ethnologists) who have done research on Bushmen.

6. Its extraordinary influence derives from the fact that in its various editions it was prescribed at all Afrikaans universities. It is still reflected in official thinking, as for example in the Marais Report of 1984. This mythology was also, of course, very much part of the liberal definition. Thus Wellington: "The little folk seemed unable to alter their ways even when given cattle and sheep and encouraged by the Cape settlers to use them for breeding. The kindness seems to have been misplaced; the Bushman appears to have been unable or unwilling to adapt himself to the pastoral life and his near extermination followed" (Wellington 1967:135).

7. In addition, the distinguished African colonial administration expert, Lord Hailey, had recently visited the territory and argued, in his suppressed report, that there was an urgent need for an expert study to be made of the "Bushman problem" (Hailey n.d.).

8. Changes in the legal status of Bushmen also helped to shape the public discourse. In 1948 the attorney general ruled that because Bushmen in the Kavango Native Reserve could not be dealt with according to customary law, special arrangements would apply, namely, the Native Commissioner could summarily dispose of any Bushman cases without even the necessity of informing the police! Exceptions to this ruling were limited to cases of "revolting cruelty" and rape of "European women" (Olivier 1961:241–242). From this date the courts start taking a more lenient approach in sentencing Bushmen. The very "primitiveness" of Bushmen now constituted extenuating circumstance. In the landmark case, *Rex v. Kgau* 1958 SCW, his lordship adduced "primitiveness" from the following observations: "The accused did not apparently realize the seriousness of the case. In a completely childish manner he would laugh at the evidence being led. His attitude was completely childlike and childish. It appears as if this visit to Windhoek was the first contact this group of people had with civilization."

9. Of this thousand pounds, six hundred went to the Kavango Guard Scheme and the rest was used by the police. Typically a police station like Namutoni would receive 100 pounds of mielie-meal, 10 pounds of salt and 10 pounds of tobacco per month for 200 "wild" and 180 "tame" Bushmen. Not overly generous.

Newton, a traveler who visited Karakuwisa in the early 1950s, presented the following vignette: "Four Okavango guards were in charge at Karakuwisa and also cared for a large clan of Bushmen who were living in the neighborhood.

These 'tame' Bushmen were supplied with tobacco and salt, which with meat . . . and blankets, means heaven to a Bushman. Through them, contact was maintained with the 'wild' ones, mainly to recruit them for road work. It is simple work they do; the tyre tracks of the lorries are scooped out to the depth of about a foot and these are filled up with cut grass, then the sand is thrown over it for a couple of inches in depth. . . . Weekly trucks . . . [carrying labourers] can now travel with ease" (Newton n.d.).

10. Initially it was to have been chaired by Dr. L. Fourie, the retired territorial medical officer and author of various papers on Bushmen; however, Fourie was terminally ill and Schoeman was appointed to chair it instead.

11. Afrikaner nationalists had a great respect for academics and, if it came to increasing their authority, even anthropologists. At the World Court Hearings on South West Africa in the 1960s South Africa decided to mount a frontal counterattack to justify Apartheid. Of the twelve expert witnesses they called no fewer than four were *volkekundiges*. Others, like P. J. Coertze and B. van As, served as consultants to the South African team.

12. Like Bain before him, he engaged in a bit of showmanship by arranging for the public exhibition of some Bushmen in Cape Town at the van Riebeeck Festival, which commemorated 300 years of white settlement (for a description see Schoeman 1952). About the only positive reaction to this piece of showmanship was that Schoeman managed to persuade Professor Brock of the University of Cape Town to bring in a team of medical experts to undertake a comprehensive medical survey of the Bushmen (Bronte-Stewart et al. 1960).

13. These ideas are still fashionable as, for example, in the Marais Report (1984), which sees Bushmen as set on a path of self-destruction because of their supposed inherent fatalism.

14. In 1947, the Kaukauveld portion of Game Reserve No. 2 (Etosha) was set aside "for the sole use and occupation by natives" and a further 3,406 square kilometers of the park was apportioned to white farmers (de la Bat 1982:14). It was thus not surprising that Nature Conservation decided not to de-proclaim Game Reserve No. 1, as the Game Preservation Commission had recommended (and upon which assumption the Schoeman Interim Report had recommended that Karakuwisa be the headquarters of the proposed Bushman reserve). Rather it kept this area as a bargaining chip, so that in 1958 when this area was finally de-proclaimed, Nature Conservation was able to exchange it for a vast tract of land in the west between the Hoanib and Ugab rivers. In 1964 as a result of recommendations by the Odendaal Commission, large segments of the Etosha Park were transferred to Ovamboland (ironically, precisely that section that the Schoeman Interim Report had suggested be set aside for the Heikom Bushmen).

15. But even this was not new: Already in the 1930s some tourists were complaining that the price of a shilling a photograph, which some "perfect" Bushmen were asking, was outrageous (Ahrens 1948; also Goldblatt 1978). There are close informal and formal connections between the South African Parks Board and the South West Africa Department of Nature Conservation. Indeed conservationists' arguments are remarkably similar. Compare, for example, those made by the South African National Parks Board in 1936 concern-

ing Bushmen in the Kalahari Gemsbok National Park (see Gordon 1985). Johannes Kloppers, who worked in the Kalahari Gemsbok Park and later wrote a laudatory book about the chief warden of the park, Joep le Riche, provided an accurate reflection of official opinion when he largely ignored the Bushmen until he came to list the major developments in the history of the park. "I wish I was in a position to add another to this impressive list of protestations, and that is the removal of the Bushmen out of the Gemsbokpark," he concluded (Kloppers 1970:189). He listed what he perceived to be the problems created by Bushmen resident in the park: First, their numbers had increased because the park had attracted many outsiders; second, their ideas about "nature conservation" differed from that of their patrons; third, apart from their guaranteed lifelong ex gratia rations, they had started to make more and more demands: (1) They wanted to keep dogs; (2) they wanted to hunt freely; (3) they wanted freedom of movement; (4) they wanted to be free to receive visitors; (5) they wanted better housing [utterly "untraditional"!]; (6) worst of all, they did not want to be humbled by working. (Not surprisingly, le Riche would apparently have to go and catch "deserters" and bring them back).

Finally, "in the course of the years they have racially gradually disqualified themselves from protection in a national park. The original idea, which one should always keep in mind, was to give a pure group of 'full-blood' Bushmen special protection in order to prevent their possible complete disappearance from the face of the Kalahari. Exactly here they had no bigger enemy than themselves. They bastardized with Namas and Bantu and only an expert could determine with any precision as to exactly which ethnological group they belonged. Most still look quite like Bushmen and partially maintain their traditional lifestyle (insofar as it means not having to work), but otherwise there is little to note of pure Bushmen. Only a few can still speak Bushman language! Their clothing is also not traditional anymore except when one of the young women notices some-one with a camera and realizes that a quick return to the traditional will provide them with a useful fee. This is the naked truth. The rest, insofar as it is possible for them, are westernized or bantuized. Their desirability as a tourist attraction is under serious doubt, as is the desirability of letting them stay for an indefinite period in the Park. They have disqualified themselves" (Kloppers 1970:190–191).

16. The progress of the administration toward achieving this goal was charted by newspaper reports: In July 1958, the administrator said that he hoped to proclaim a Bushman reserve in the near future "and to gather the majority of Bushmen into that area to improve conditions for them. His visit had impressed on him more than ever the need for *game preservation*" (*Cape Argus*, 12 July 1958). The delay was officially attributed to the takeover of the administration's Native Affairs Department by the South African Bantu Affairs Department (*Cape Argus*, 29 July 1959).

Notes to Chapter 18

1. The figures on Table 18.1 are substantially underenumerated, as *unpaid* workers were not recorded. In 1975, 87.8 percent of all Bushmen were involved

in white agriculture, and this constituted 11.7 percent of the total agricultural work force (Cruywagen 1975). According to the 1981 census, only 3.9 percent of Bushmen were "urbanized" and 50.2 percent were to be found residing on settler farms.

2. This description shows remarkable similarities to "traditional" residential patterns. Mathias Guenther showed how farm Bushmen in neighboring Botswana maintain some important continuities with their "traditional" life-style, especially with regard to their "band" organization, their continued reliance on the "sharing" ethos, their nomadism and their maintenance of ties with freer-roaming relatives (Guenther 1976; 1979b).

3. On the contrary. Consider the case of *State v. Britz and Gougorob*. The accused were respectively sergeant and constable stationed at Tsintsabis. On patrol beyond the Police Zone they assaulted two Bushmen males, and when this did not produce the required information as to the whereabouts of one, Kassie, the torture became more crude. The two Bushmen were forced to have sexual congress with a Bushman woman. The one male was then charged with bestiality and the other with incest (*State v. Britz and Gougorob* 1962 Grootfontein Mag. Court).

4. He continued: "Apparently what happens is that the Europeans arrive in the area and spend a few days talking to the Bushmen and persuading them to come to work on the farms. The Bushmen steadfastly refuse and then the Europeans choose a time when a few men are present and hustle them onto their cars and drive off. It is a matter of amazement to me that the Bushmen did not disappear in the early stages and I can only suggest as a reason that the curiosity factor and the attraction of the bright lights of civilization are working potently amongst them to overcome their natural timidity" (SWAA, A659, McIntyre to CNC, 11 November 1955). The phenomenon of blackbirding alas cannot be relegated to that of historical curiosity. In 1987 the *Namibian* (16 October 1987) reported on a Gobabis "kidnap" case involving the abduction and assault of a Bushman family.

5. Köhler, the government ethnologist at that time, provided a contrary description: "The regular diet and way of life may account for the large Bushman families on farms. To these Bushmen, it would hardly occur to run away. Even single Bushmen who have gone back to the veld now seem to come back after a time. But life on the farms lowers the Bushman's physical powers of resistance. Farm diet generally differs a good deal from that of the veld and this may be a factor" (Köhler 1959a:25). This ignores the obvious point that Bushmen might not have anywhere else to go to and thus were forced to start "stabilizing."

6. Indeed, it was symptomatic of the expanding alliance between the aspirant Herero petite bourgeoisie and the ruling settlers that a top priority of the Department of Water Affairs in the early 1980s was to provide Hereroland with water, either by canal from the Kavango River or by drilling.

7. The three men who escaped were later apparently murdered, but the state did not have enough evidence to charge anybody for these crimes.

8. Of the 19 cases of perjury I came across in an examination of over 600 court cases, most of them, 15, involved Hereros. Of course this reflects the bias

of the courts, but at the same time, it might also suggest a flexible definition of reality (see Poewe 1986), which has implications for assessing the validity of testimonies gathered by naïve social scientists from any informants, be they Herero, Afrikaner or Kung, on a brief fieldwork trip.

9. It is probable that similar events are still occurring. In 1981, the Botswana government applied for the extradition of two Tswanas, Messrs. Ditsabue and Mothebi, sometime residents of Aminuis Reserve, on the charge of having murdered two Bushmen in Botswana. The Gobabis magistrate granted the extradition request, but their lawyer appealed and was successful on a technicality, which meant that the Botswana government had to reapply. While all this wrangling was taking place, they were released on bail and nearly a year later jumped bail. They wrote a letter to the Gobabis police explaining their reasons for doing so: They were tired of waiting, that there were others involved, including a prominent Tswana councillor. Three rifles had been used, including one belonging to the Tswana chief, Kgoswang. The court declared the bail forfeit in March 1983.

The information that I gathered during field enquiries in the Gobabis district provides further background. The Tswana in Aminuis had apparently become upset at the number of cattle alleged stolen by Bushman marauders from across the Botswana border, so they worked out a plan, with Herero connivance, to solve the problem. Their solution involved chasing the Bushmen on horseback, armed with firearms. At least five Bushmen were said to have been killed, both in the area between Aminuis and the border and in Botswana. When the culprits realized that the law was after them, they arranged for Ditsabue and Mothebi to take the blame and thus exculpate the others. At the same time, they arranged for bail and the services of one of the most expensive lawyers in Windhoek. It was suggested that this cover-up was made possible with the aid of government money because the Tswana and Herero were prominent supporters of the government and known to be benefiting from the largesse of fashionable Namibian pork-barrel politics. Officials in the attorney general's office in Windhoek agreed that events as sketched above were probably valid but pointed out that there was nothing they could do as the two main parties had vanished and, besides, the events were said to have taken place in Botswana.

That tensions between Herero and Bushmen still exist is evidenced by the statement of a Heikom leader, Mr. Soroseb, who complained that white farms were being taken over by Herero in the north of the country, and that Heikom refused to work for Herero (*Die Republikein*, 3 December 1980).

Notes to Chapter 19

1. An important question in this regard is what influence the Marshall family had on government policy. In my estimation they had no direct influence. Although McIntyre knew and used the Marshall vehicle on occasion, he had, like most of his colleagues, contempt for anthropologists, especially foreigners (see, e.g., Budack 1980). I suspect that he chose Tsumkwe and not Gautscha as

his headquarters precisely because it was a small settlement and away from where the Marshalls did most of their work.

2. The government welfare officer's report echoed this and spelt out policy with dreadful irony: "A home had to be found for the uprooted [!] Kung, but the natural carrying capacity of the area which is going to become Bushmanland is such that it cannot accommodate any new arrivals. Accordingly, the plan at Tsumkwe is to try to lessen the Bushman's dependence upon nature by teaching him how through work he can get his own foodstuffs by himself. Also to break down the century old institutions like the band and band territory so that the !Kung can finally all live together in a Bushman Homeland" (South Africa 1962:13).

3. The almost contemporaneous Marais Report puts the total Bushman population of Tsumkwe at 552, with 1,776 living in military bases in Bushmanland (Marais 1984:33).

4. The impact of Tsumkwe on the near contemporary socioeconomic, health and nutritional status of Ju-/wasi has been superbly (and powerfully) analyzed by Marshall and Ritchie 1984; Marshall forthcoming; Biesele 1990; Hitchcock 1987a, 1988a. I could not even hope to offer a pale imitation of their powerful data; thus, rather than repeat their findings, I prefer to focus on a factor that has not received attention, namely, the impact of missionaries.

5. Already in 1963, the South African minister of Bantu administration recognized the positive publicity value of showing off its Bushman projects (*Cape Argus,* 14 June 1963).

6. Despite this comparative neglect the number of Bushman adherents grew substantially in the farming districts. By 1965, for example, there were over 2,695 Bushmen members of the Northern Synod. In 1967 the Lutherans again started to undertake missionary work, specifically among the Ovamboland and Botswana Bushmen. In Botswana, however, it was seen as a "general" mission because to have focused on one ethnic group would have upset that government (Kritzinger 1972:305). During this period the Catholics kept a rather low profile. They did manage to obtain some concessions from the government, probably because the newly appointed Bushman affairs commissioner, McIntyre, was a Catholic and had invited the Catholics to work in Bushmanland, but they had been unable to accept because of a lack of funds. Shortly thereafter, the Dutch Reformed church commenced operations in Bushmanland, and when some Catholic workers from the order of Les Petits Frères de Jésus were available, they were stationed in one of the Catholic church's "traditional" spheres of influence, the Kavango. The basic premise of this order is to live with and like the people they are serving, which predictably did not sit well with a regime bent on implementing a policy of Apartheid. It also apparently worried some conservative senior members of the church hierarchy in Windhoek, who felt that their efforts were bound to fail, because they believed that the Bushmen wanted to become like whites and did not want whites to live like them. Needless to say, the order soon found conditions in Angola more amenable and moved their operations across the Kavango. When Angolan Bushmen fled to Botswana to escape the civil war in Angola that raged in 1975, some of these brothers accompanied them and helped them to adjust to life in Botswana (Lee 1979).

7. He apparently did not get on with McIntyre, who was Catholic, and so set out to be as independent of the commissioner as possible.

8. In addition to the Dutch Reformed church, the Gereformeerde, or Dopper, church also has a missionary action among the southern Kung in the Gobabis district. That church also started in 1961 and by 1971 could claim 200 baptized and 39 confirmed members. Its relative success can be ascribed to the fact that it works almost exclusively with proletarianized farm workers. Its missionary, the Reverend van der Westhuizen, like the Reverend Weich, is a longtime student of Kung linguistics and is also involved in Bible translation. His mission serves a similar folk-hero function for students from Potchefstroom University.

9. Swanepoel was offered a missionary position in Grootfontein, where he would focus on the Bushman farm laborers ("Dutch Reformed Church Rescues the Bible for the Bushmen" was how *Die Suidwester,* 29 January 1973, interpreted this change).

10. By 1980 Weich reported that no Bushman had attended church services for the past several months (John Marshall, personal comment, and my own observations).

11. A black evangelist was stationed at Tsumkwe, and Weich was to visit every month for a week. The mission property was sold off to the administration. The price obtained was indicative of the comfortable relationship between the Dutch Reformed Church Mission and the administration: Whereas the buildings had a book value of R 18,300, the Bushman affairs commissioner valued them at R 55,000 and eventually bought them for R 43,000.

12. Information for this section is derived largely from missionary newsletters, especially *Die Regte Mense* (The right people), which are on file at the secretariat for the Dutch Reformed Church Mission church in Windhoek. In 1982 Swanepoel was appointed Bushman affairs commissioner with responsibility for all the Bushmen in Namibia.

13. Bushmen membership of the Dutch Reformed Mission church at that stage looked something like this: There were 126 Caprivi members, none baptized; 100 Tsumkwe members, all baptized; 52 Tsumeb/Grootfontein members, 50 baptized; and an unknown number of members from Gobabis.

In the so-called operational area in the northern areas of Ovambo and Kavango, the DRC Mission was also favored by the army. When called up for military service, clergymen of most other religious denominations, or at least those of the dominant churches in South Africa, but not the budding DRC clergymen, refused to work as clergy in the operational area. Full-time proselytizing while on military service was seen as part of the army's Civic Action Program. When a U.S. journalist visited the Caprivi, where an army battalion composed mostly of Bushman refugees from Angola was stationed, he reported: "At Omega Base, a young Army chaplain, Lt. Gert van Rooyen of the Dutch Reformed Church, is busily converting them. The base now has 159 'baptized and confessed' Christians, he says proudly" (*Christian Science Monitor,* 19 May 1981); and Dominee van der Merwe, who did his commando service at the base in 1978, discovered 120 "declared" Christians. "I stand really dumbfounded at their knowledge of the bible," he said (*Paratus,* May 1978). What is interesting about this report is that in Angola, most of the mission work among the Bushmen had been done by the Catholic church and traditionally, the western Caprivi was always regarded as a Catholic "sphere of influence," emanating from its station at Andara.

Notes to Chapter 20

1. The ensuing controversy generated a substantial literature; see, e.g., Marshall and Ritchie 1984; Gordon 1984b, 1985.

2. By 1983 Nature Conservation had a budget of R 12 million and employed over 300 whites: 100 as field officers, 200 as tourist officers and 15 as researchers. This was a far cry from 1955, when it had a modest budget of R 61,000, 3 white and 28 black employees. It also controlled 56,546 square kilometers of the total landmass of 824,290 square kilometers that constitutes Namibia. Thus Namibia already has one of the highest percentages of its territory devoted to parkland (Wilkinson 1978:603–624).

3. "Vasekele" is the local name given to the Angolan Kung Bushmen (Estermann 1976).

4. In reality, they were employed as bounty hunters, being paid by the number of ears brought in: not a particularly endearing practice.

5. What is interesting about these statements is that, until recently, the army consistently denied that SWAPO was very effective in Angola, let alone in Namibia, and that SWAPO's activities amounted mostly to planting a few isolated land mines. The military appear to have been caught in their own web of doublespeak. Certainly, it is highly improbable that SWAPO was militarily active in Bushmanland or its environs.

6. Press reports, however, downplayed the suggestion by some of the white soldiers that the Bushman's tracking ability was overrated. Most Bushmen born after 1960 have lost the ability to track, as well as most of their other veldcraft skills, according to anthropologists (J. Marshall, personal comment; Lee 1983).

7. Reflecting on his experiences, Commandant Hall of Omega opined: "I have been accused that I am interfering with noble tribal members, but there is nothing noble about people who are riddled with sickness. The Bushman in his natural state had no noticeable [*behoorlike*] tribal system—only a reasonably desperate day-to-day existence. We are busy changing their lives drastically and we are reacting thereto by attempting to give them skills and values. It is a responsibility which we must accept and do something about. If the Bushman must eat our food, have good money in their pockets, and buy our products, we must give them new values. It will be disastrous if we do not do it. These values are those of health, hygiene, education, and the use of land. I like to believe that we are succeeding. I came to the Caprivi as an ordinary soldier. Now I am a sort of headman and father-confessor to them. They come to me for advice and to solve domestic problems. I have already divorced couples, but usually I just listen to their stories and say that they must come back next week. In nine out of ten cases they become reconciled. This undertaking has become my whole life. When the Defence Force withdraws, I would not like to see these wonderful people

sinking back into their aimlessness, but it could easily happen" (*Die Volksblad*, 6 September 1980).

8. The officer-in-command of Bushmanland, Commandant Buitendag, summarized his approach: "What we are doing is to offer the Bushman survival possibilities . . . we can help create something where vacuums in the development still exist. After prolonged contact with the activities of the Battalion the resident Bushmen will become aware of the advantages of permanent housing, the value of money which has to be earned, the necessity of general health and welfare. To a large extent, the Bushmen have yet to realize that there is not much time in hand to grasp at these survival possibilities" (*Paratus*, February 1983:31).

9. Instead, ironically, it was left to Dominee Weich to raise questions about the army: "Dominee Weich said a civil action campaign spearheaded by the army had cut Bushmen away from their roots without placing them firmly in the 20th century. If all went well the army effort would bear fruit in three generations but if the political future of SWA turned sour the Bushmen would be lost forever. He said he thought the dream of Bushmanland's army commander, Major Pinkie Coetzee, of turning Bushmen into cattle farmers was possibly a bit idealistic. . . . Major Coetzee . . . believes Bushmanland could carry 200,000 head of cattle" (*Sunday Times*, 27 July 1980).

Notes to Chapter 21

1. He was of course only following the precedent of a long tradition of scholarship. As Reenen van Reenen, probably the most plagiarized Afrikaner writer on Bushmen, put it: "We do not like to talk about Bushman-Settler relations" (van Reenen 1920:22).

2. "Misunderstanding" is a common explanation. See, for example, Coetzee 1972:131 and, of course, Vedder 1937 and South Africa 1951.

3. Leo Kuper (1981) is one of the few scholars to have tried to deal analytically with this issue. He suggests that certain common conditions give rise to all types of genocide and these certainly seem to be applicable in the case of Bushmen: First, there is a dehumanizing of the target group: Bushman were clearly seen as animals and treated as "vermin." Second, there is vulnerability. The very nature of Bushman social organization, with its strong egalitarianism, its lack of loyalty to a larger group (except in a few notable cases) and its highly touted "flexibility" (Leacock and Lee 1982), made it vulnerable to the better-organized retributive forays of the colonizers. Third, there is a definite material advantage to the victimizers, epitomized best, perhaps, by the ethnocentric argument that the Bushmen stand in the way of "progress." The list of factors contributing to the demise of the Bushmen could be extended to include superior technology (horses and muskets) and brutality (Worsley 1984:4); unauthorized changes in the rules of warfare (Leach 1977) and knowledge and exploitation of indigenous social systems (Todorov 1985). But a mere listing of variables does not lead to much understanding of the process of genocide. My concern is with trying to understand how, on an abstract level, genocide could be considered a policy, while at the same time, with trying to grasp the dialectics by which local-

level officials, policemen and members of the judiciary could so easily send Bushmen to prison even when the former believed that they were sending the Bushmen off to a sure death.

This is not to deny that anthropologists and other scientists were not concerned about cases of mistreatment. In Namibia the intervention of the Marshalls was probably an aggravating factor that resulted in John Marshall's being denied a visa for twenty years. In Botswana anthropologists took cases of mistreatment of Bushmen to court and even reported senior government officials for assaulting their workers, but the government turned a blind eye to these charges and warned the researchers that they could be forced to leave the country.

4. Thus Wilmsen (1989b) in a well-received, if controversial, book used maps extensively to make the case for extensive interaction in the Kalahari but overlooked the fact that mapmaking was "the servant of colonial plunder, for the vision and knowledge constituted by the map preceded and legitimized the appropriation of territory" (McClintock 1988:151).

5. If this were so, one would expect near contemporary Afrikaner anthropologists who played a critical role in the ideological formulation of Apartheid to emphasize this. In fact they, like Solway and Lee (1990), tend to downplay the oppression of those labeled "Bushmen" and present an image of pristine primitive affluence (see, e.g., Steyn 1985; Bruwer 1965; Booyens 1980).

6. He has since modified his stance to a position similar to mine (Wilmsen and Denbow 1990).

7. One of the major problems bedeviling the study of social banditry in Africa has been a lack of adequate material (see, for example, Isaacman 1977; Crummey 1985). The early optimism of Isaacman (1977) has been eroded by a rather dour denial of the worth of resistance studies. O'Malley complained that banditry studies in general seem to have "generated a pseudo-liberationist rhetoric which barely conceals theoretical dogmatism and a cavalier disregard for the variability of capitalist relations of power" (O'Malley 1981). The data used in this study are also fragmentary and based largely on court cases. Court cases can provide a useful, if somewhat neglected, introduction into social history. But of the various sectors of the Namibian populace, Bushmen have a reputation among whites for their straightforward honesty, demonstrated by their general tendency to plead guilty to the offense as charged, with a minimal statement from the dock. Of course what administrators saw as candid honesty, and anthropologists and missionaries took to be yet another manifestation of fatalism, from a Bushman perspective were perfunctory performances of admissions of guilt and the product of fear and white brutality (for a similar phenomenon in Papua New Guinea, see Bulmer 1972).

8. Contrary to Palgrave, who is cited earlier in this study. Palgrave was a commissioner of the Cape government who had a clear mission to draft a report that would convince reluctant politicians to annex Damaraland.

9. Moreover, arguing by analogy from Australian material, the "hang fire" or time delay between the first charge, which gave off a flash, and the second, which propelled the cartridge, not only gave Bushmen time to duck out of the way but also made it very difficult to hit moving targets (Broome 1982:39–40).

10. According to Worsley: "What Weber termed 'booty capitalism' and
ordinary people called piracy or pillage: the use of force either to seize goods
produced by others in quite non-capitalist ways or to compel them to collect
what nature provided, not so much mercantile activity as a kind of indirect
hunting-and-collecting under duress. Based on the use of the means of violence
and often backed up by the power of the State, these were supremely *political*
forms of economic activity, a phrase Marx called 'primitive accumulation'"
(Worsley 1984:7 [author's emphasis]).

11. As Clastres observed: "A socio-historical analysis makes it possible to
bring into perspective two phenomena: ethnocidal culture and the State form of
society. The refusal of multiplicity, the dread of difference—ethnocidal violence—are the very essence of the State. As this is true for barbarian empires as
well as for civilized Western societies, what is it then that differentiates the
Occident? The ethnocidal capacity of the Western world is unlimited because of
the nature of its regime of economic production: capitalism, whether private or
state, which cannot possibly remain confined within bounds. Concomitant with
the amazing productive force of industrial society is its terrifying destructive
power" (Clastres 1974:110).

12. I would argue that the Namibian Bushman situation is not even comparable to that of the Cape Bushmen in South Africa in the eighteenth century,
because not only was the political economic structure different, but there were
also major ideological differences (see, for example, Szalay 1983). The treatment
the Cape Bushmen received at the hands of the Dutch and British was similar to
that meted out to vagrants in the metropole of that time. The "Bushman
troubles" of 1911–1920 occurred in a significantly different ideological climate.

13. Superficially they might appear different, but these differences are
minimized when paroles and remissions are taken into account.

14. Such a formulation, while correct, does not do justice to the Bushman
situation as it can confuse cause with effect. Ironically an indirect (and sometimes
deliberate) consequence of the administration's policy against Bushmen was to
make for the more efficient exploitation of the densely populated, black migrant
labor reservoirs of Ovamboland and Kavango.

15. The one extenuating circumstance that South African courts accept is
"meat lust," especially in cases where black employees are convicted of killing
and consuming their employers' livestock. I am indebted to Justice Bethune of
the Windhoek Supreme Court for this observation. This rationale is probably—
or possibly—derived from von Luschan's (1906) argument that such a meat lust
was biological in the case of Bushmen.

16. Lee 1983:93–97 argued that homicide and assault were far more prevalent than Marshall suggested. However, most of Lee's cases are derived from
memory. One aspect of "Sanography" that has consistently been overlooked is
the role of the white middle-class field-worker as "pacifier."

17. Or as Bunker put it: "Not only the world system but also local modes of
production and extraction constitute discrete units of analysis whose mutual
effects can be seen in the ways in which local actors—including those deriving
power from organizations that operate beyond the local area—reorganize local

modes of production and extraction in order to take advantage of exchange opportunities in the world system" (Bunker 1984:1021).

Notes to Chapter 22

1. The lack of externalized commoditized social relationships is also probably a factor in the excessive alcohol consumption at Tsumkwe. One could argue that given traditional Bushman values of mobility and egalitarianism, alcohol was easily shared and relatively inexpensive. The decision to spend money on alcohol in such circumstances was a rational one, given the limited opportunities for capital investment in Bushmanland and, moreover, accorded with traditional values and mobility. In short, what else could they spend their cash on? Large sums of money would lead to theft (Peterson 1984:68).

2. This analysis by Swanepoel tells us more about anthropology as practiced by Afrikaans-language universities than it does about what is happening to the Bushmen. In essence, it is a regurgitation of the racist theories of P. J. Coertze, the doyen of Afrikaans anthropology. Coertze argued that the critical difference between black and white "cultures" lay in the fact that the former were more bonded; that is, the more "primitive" the culture, the less individuality there was. The emphasis on "culture" also allows for a convenient way of "blaming the victim" (see Gordon 1988).

3. This religious resistance by Bushmen had unintended consequences. According to a press report, titled "Bushmen, a Source of Great Damage," a farmer, Karel Meyer of Tsumeb, asked: "Who and what is a Bushman? He is not a believer. I refuse to be told that he believes in God like I believe in Him. He has a religion. It is called theft. He is born into and socialized into this religion. The parent believes that he must teach the child to steal. The man who cannot steal means nothing, because he can bring nothing for his family or his friends" (*Die Suidwester,* 3 May 1969).

4. As defined by the popular Afrikaans author Sangiro (who also put in a spell as chief game warden at Etosha): "[By] tame ones, I mean that small section who learned to appreciate the advantages of a regular life and who stay constantly with a farmer or another employer while the 'half-tame' ones work for a while and then vanish as soon as it has rained and veldkos is plentiful. Wild Bushmen, of course, do not work for farmers" (Sangiro 1954:116).

5. I follow Morphy and Morphy (1984) here. In terms strikingly reminiscent of the Namibian situation, they argue that in Australia "the function of the tame station black was to mediate between the colonizers and the Aboriginal population—to ensure a harmonious relationship. . . . It was clearly economically necessary that many of the blacks should remain 'wild' as the stations could only support a small population of Aborigines. The basis of recruitment to the category 'station' black was not what the whites assumed. While the whites thought it reflected differential attitudes to the civilizing forces of European culture, in reality it appears to have reflected differential relationships to the land on which the stations were built. The station blacks appear to be drawn from those clans owning land in the immediate vicinity of the station as well as

of course, Aborigines brought in from outside" (Morphy and Morphy 1984:471). Their conclusion that "the concept of the 'wild blackfellow' was not so much a myth as an integral part of the process of invasion: a justification for the seizure of land and [as a means of dividing Aborigines among themselves] an instrument of colonization" (Morphy and Morphy 1984:476) appears to hold in the Bushman case as well.

6. Similarly, some Bushmen believe that a spirit, significantly named "Damara" (Herero), kills them and takes their daughters (SWAA, A198/3, undated). According to another reference, "There is a singular belief, which is universal among the Namaquas, that some individuals possess the power of curing pains in any part of the body, and that this power is in the possession of some of the servile races, Hill Damaras or Bushmen" (Ku'eep 1857:368).

7. The frontier concept has had a checkered history ever since Turner propounded his famous, albeit ethnocentric, frontier thesis in the United States. In Southern Africa the frontier notion has also played an important analytical and ideological role. Contemporary liberal historiographers typically see the frontier as a "territory or zone of interpenetration between two previously distinct societies. . . . The frontier 'opens' in a given zone when the first representatives of the intrusive society arrive; it closes when a single political authority has established hegemony over the zone" (Lamar and Thompson 1979:8). This definition too, suggests that Bushmen are the cultural representation of the frontier experience.

8. The resemblance to the way Hitler saw the Jews is uncanny. Shortly before his death, Hitler, in his dictated political testament, had this to say: "The Jew is the quintessential outsider. The Jewish race is, more than anything else, a community of the spirit. In addition, they have a sort of relationship with destiny, as a result of the persecutions they have endured for centuries. . . . And it is precisely this trait of not being able to assimilate, which defines the race and must reluctantly be accepted as a proof of the superiority of the 'spirit' over the flesh" (cited in Muller-Hill 1989:86).

9. In it he directly pointed out the simian similarities (and even assured his audience that during periods of sexual arousal the genitals of young Bushman women became a deep red!) (Fischer 1955:63). He concluded that the distinguishing characteristic of the Bushmen was the natural *tablier,* a female Bushman genital feature. Other indigenes might have it but among them it was a question of artificial manipulation! Fischer of course was studying the Rehoboth Basters at the time that mixed marriages were banned in Namibia.

10. Compare Muller-Hill's observation: "The image which the anti-Semite has of the Jew (sensual, cowardly, deceitfully clever, greedy for power, in one word 'inferior') corresponds to the image which many European men had of women, an image which can first be found in the works of Aristotle, and continues in those of Albertus Magnus. The way in which anti-Semites view the Jew is as a substitute for the image of woman. Sons who submitted to their tyrannical fathers and who learned to despise their mothers, along with everything else which is weak and feminine, but who had to conceal this hate and scorn from the world, could take the Jews as a substitute hate-object" (Muller-

Hill 1988:90–1). As Jews were believed responsible for anti-Semitism, Bushmen were believed to be themselves responsible for provoking anti-Bushman behavior.

11. Of course, these parallels might be coincidental; however, the stream of consciousness novelist Thomas Pynchon in his acclaimed *Gravity's Rainbow* and *V* "intuitively" links Nazi policy to the German colonial massacres of the Herero. Perhaps he has an issue that merits further examination? For a more complete discussion of this issue, see my paper "Making Bushmen," presented at the 1990 American Anthropological Association meeting in New Orleans (Gordon 1990a).

12. Some random samples from a wide array: In 1944 the native commissioner on the Kavango could claim that "during all this time, nothing was ever done by the Germans or Union Government to improve the Bushman's lot" (SWAA, A50/67, NC Runtu to CNC, 27 April 1944). The press, of course, was full of stories about the "First Bushman Reserve in the World"; see, e.g., *Cape Argus,* 7 June 1960. Laurens van der Post's illustrated *Lost World of the Kalahari* (1988:259) has a photograph of a sign saying: "Welcome to Botswana's *First* Bushman Settlement Scheme." Recently I received an appeal from a Kuruman tour operator soliciting funds to "Help Save the Last Pure Bushmen in South Africa."

13. Ironically, it appears as if some scientists, like Gusinde (1957) and the ethnologists of the South African Defence Force, developed a vested interest in Bushmen becoming extinct. Rosaldo's remarks on the Philippine "Headhunters" are germane: "Their human worth was deflated at the same time that their value for human knowledge was inflated. They almost seem to have been granted scientific significance in compensation for the unilateral declaration that their conduct had no conceivable political meaning" (Rosaldo 1982:18–19).

14. This is not to deny *difference;* it would be foolhardy to act like Idi Amin did and claim that unemployment did not exist simply because he had proclaimed it illegal! On the contrary, a concern with *difference* has enriched our critique of Western society. My objection is toward its reification, and my concern is for a sensitivity of the context in which it is used. In the relatively open bourgeoise democracies, *difference* can enrich the lives of many, but in the context of totalitarian colonialism, as in Southern Africa, it can and did have deadly consequences. This is a dialectic that anthropologists have to consider and one for which there is probably no answer.

15. There is historical precedent; thus, according to Lord Lubbock: "Livingstone mentions that on one occasion, after talking to a Bushman for some time, as he supposed, about the Deity, he found that the savage thought he was speaking about Sekoni, the principle chief of the district" (Lubbock 1913:571).

16. Sander Gilman has documented a similar phenomenon in his insightful analysis, *Jewish Self-Hatred* (Gilman 1986).

17. And again I would like to emphasize that here I am referring largely to earlier work. In the 1980s this situation has changed dramatically for the better.

18. For example, in Namibia the first white commercial hunters had a generally favorable image of the Bushmen, whereas at the Cape at the same time they were regarded as "obnoxious weeds." It was only with the arrival of white settlers in Namibia that a distinctive negative stereotype started emerging.

19. But why this upsurge, this contemporary dominance of the romantic Bushman image, especially in South Africa? Perhaps a major reason lies in the realm of international politics and the recently ended low-intensity guerilla war in northern South West Africa, coupled with black unrest in South Africa, because such romanticization exonerates the beleaguered whites, in their own eyes, from accusations of racism. As David Maughan-Brown pointed out in his excellent discussion on this topic, the "Noble Savage" thrives in times of colonial war because there is a need for a statement that all is not spoiled in situations of destruction. Apart from catering to the nostalgia for the good old days, the image of the "Noble Savage" serves as an ideological compensatory mechanism when the previously pacified colonized revolt and put into disorder the stereotypes of the colonizers (Maughan Brown 1983).

References and Bibliography

Books and Articles

African World. 1919/20. "South-West Africa's Future." 17:204–207.

Ahrens, F. W. 1948. *From Bench to Bench*. Pietermaritzburg: Shuter and Shuter.

Andersson, Charles J.A. 1855. "Explorations in South Africa, with Route from Walfisch Bay to Lake Ngami, and Ascent of the Tioge River." *Royal Geographical Society, Proceedings* 25:79–107.

———. 1856. *Lake Ngami*. London: Hurst.

———. 1858. "Travel and Adventures in Ovamboland." *Cape Monthly Magazine* 4(21):156–159.

———. 1875. *Notes of Travel in South Africa*. London: Hurst.

Armed Forces. 1980. "36 (Bushman) Battalion." June: 13–16.

Bahr, Jurgen. 1968. *Kulturgeographische Wandlungen in der Farmzone Südwestafrikas*. Bonn: Bonner Geographische Abhandlungen.

Baines, Thomas. 1864, 1973. *Explorations in South West Africa*. Salisbury: Pioneer Head.

Bantu. 1961. "Administrator's Message to the Bushmen." November: 627–628.

Barnard, Willem D. 1964. "Die Streekpatrone van Suidwest-Afrika." Ph.D. dissertation, Stellenbosch University.

Barth, Frederick, ed. 1969. *Ethnic Groups and Their Boundaries*. Boston: Little, Brown.

Barth, Paul. 1926. *Südwest-Afrika*. Windhoek: J. Meinert.

Baumann, Julius. 1967. *Van Sending tot Kerk*. Karibib: Evangeliese Lutherse Kerk.

Beckett, Jeremy. 1985. "Colonialism in a Welfare State: The Case of Australian Aborigines." In C. Schrire and R. Gordon, eds. *The Future of Former Foragers in Australia and Southern Africa*. Cambridge: Cultural Survival.

Beiderbecke, Rev. H. 1922. *Among the Hereros in Africa*. St. Louis: Concordia.

Biesele, Megan. 1990. *Shaken Roots: The Bushmen of Namibia*. Johannesburg: EDA.

Billy. 1928. "A Brush with Bushmen." *Nongqai*, January: 17–18.

Bleek, Dorothea. 1922, 1928. "Report on Anthropological Research Among the Bushmen in the South West Africa Protectorate." Mimeo. 50 pp. In State Archives, Windhoek. Later published (1928) as *The Naron*.

Bleek, W. H. 1875. "Bushman Researches." *Cape Monthly Magazine* 11(62):104–115; 11(63):150–155.

Bley, Helmut. 1971. *South West Africa Under German Rule*. Evanston: Northwestern University Press.

Booyens, J. H. 1980. *Die San en Khoesan Vandag*. Potchefstroom: Pro Rege.

Boydell, Thomas. 1948. *My Luck's Still In*. Cape Town: Stewart.

Die Brandwag. 1920. "Die Mens-eters van Suidwes." 25 March: 294–296.

Brincker, P. H. 1899. "Die Eingeborenen Deutsch-Suedwest-Afrikas nach Geschichte, Charakter, Sitten, Gebrauchen, und Sprachen." *Berlin Universität für Orientalischen Sprachen Mitteilungen* 2:125–139.

Bronte-Stewart, B., et al. 1960. "The Health and Nutritional Status of the Kung Bushmen of South West Africa." *South African Journal of Laboratory and Clinical Medicine* 6:187–216.

Broome, Richard. 1982. *Aboriginal Australians*. Sydney: George Allen & Unwin.

Brownlee, Frank. 1932. "Kayische of the Kalahari." *Chambers Journal*, May: 337–347.

Bruwer, Johannes P. 1965. "Die Khoisan-en Bantoebevolking van Suidwes-Afrika." In *Ethnische Gruppen in Südwestafrika*. Windhoek: South West Africa Scientific Society.

——— . 1966a. "Die Matrilinere Orde van die Kavango." Mimeo.

——— . 1966b. *South West Africa: The Disputed Land*. Cape Town: Nasionale Boekhandel.

Budack, Kuno. 1980. "Die Volker Südwestafrikas." Series in *Die Allgemeine Zeitung* (Windhoek). Clippings on file at the SWA Scientific Society.

Bulmer, Ralph. 1972. "Victims of Progress." In M. Ward, ed. *Change and Development in Rural Melanesia*. Port Moresby: New Guinea Research Unit.

Bunker, Stephen. 1984. "Modes of Extraction, Unequal Exchange, and the Progressive Underdevelopment of an Extreme Periphery: The Brazilian Amazon, 1600–1980." *American Journal of Sociology* 89(5):1017–63.

Burger, N. A. 1978. "Die Dorslandtrek. 'n Histories-geografiese Studie." Ph.D. dissertation, University of the Orange Free State, Bloemfontein.

Cape Colony. 1879. *Cape Colony Blue Book on Native Affairs*. Cape Town: Government Printer.

——— . 1908. *Report on Rietfontein Area by J. Herbst*. Cape Town: Government Printer.

Cape of Good Hope. 1882. *Report of Select Committee on Gunpowder Trade*. Cape Town: Government Printer. A31/1882.

Chambers, Robert. 1984. *Rural Development*. New York: Longman.

Chapman, James. 1868, 1971. *Travels in the Interior of South Africa*. 2 vols. London: Bell and Daldy (Reprinted as *Travels in the Interior of Africa*, ed. Edward C. Tabler [Cape Town: Balkema, 1971]).

Chapman, William J.B. n.d. "Reminiscences of William J.B. Chapman, South West Africa and Angola." Handscript in State Archives. A.233.

Chilvers, Hedley. 1928. *The Seven Wonders of Southern Africa*. Johannesburg: S.A. Railways.

Clarke, William, and Eugene Ogan. 1973. "Social Scientists: Assumptions and Alternatives." *New Guinea*, January: 41–60.

Clarence-Smith, Gervase. 1977. "For Braudel: A Note on the 'Ecole des Annales' and the Historiography of Africa." *History in Africa* 4:275–282.

——— . 1979. *Slaves, Peasants and Capitalists in Southern Angola, 1840–1926*. New York: Cambridge University Press.

Clastres, Pierre. 1974. "De l'Ethnocide." *L'Homme* 14(3–4):101–110.

Coertze, Pieter J. 1963. *Inleiding tot die Algemene Volkekunde.* Johannesburg: Afrikaanse Pers.

Coetzee, J. A. 1942. *Dorsland-Avontuur.* Johannesburg: Voortrekkerpers.

Coetzee, J. Hennie. 1972. "The Bantu Homelands and Cultural Heterogeneity." In N. Rhoodie, ed. *South African Dialogue.* Philadelphia: Westminster.

Comaroff, John and Jean. 1986. "Christianity and Colonialism in South Africa." *American Ethnologist* 13(1):1–22.

Conniff, Richard. 1987. "When Music in Our Parlors Brought Death to Darkest Africa." *Audubon* 89(4) July: 76–93.

Cook, Edward. 1849. "The Modern Missionary." Typescript in Cory Library, Rhodes University.

Cooper, Allan D. 1982. *U.S. Economic Power and Political Influence in Namibia, 1700–1982.* Boulder: Westview.

Crosby, O. 1931. "Notes on Bushmen and Ovambo in South West Africa." *Journal of the African Society* 30:344–60.

Crummey, Donald, ed. 1985. *Banditry, Rebellion, and Social Protest in Africa.* London. J. Currey/Portsmouth, N.H.: Heinemann.

Cruywagen, Willem A. 1975. "Die Arbeidpotensiaal van Suidwes-Afrika." *Journal of Racial Affairs* 26(4):135–141.

Davies, Joan. 1943. "Palgrave and Damaraland." *Archives Yearbook for South African History* 5(2).

de Almeida, Antonio. 1965. *Bushmen and Other Non-Bantu Peoples of Angola.* Johannesburg: Institute for the Study of Man in Africa.

de Klerk, Willem A. 1977. *The Thirstland.* Harmondsworth: Penguin.

de Kock, W. J. 1948. "Ekstra-Territoriale Vraagstukke van die Kaapse Regering, 1872–1885." *Archives Yearbook for South African History* 11(1).

de la Bat, Bernabe. 1981. "Natuurbewaring in Suidwes-Africa." *Journal of the South West African Scientific Society* 35:51–61.

––––––. 1982. "Etosha 75 Years." *South West Africa Annual:* 11–22.

Delius, Peter, and Stanley Trapido. 1983. "Inboekselings and Oorlams. The Creation and Transformation of a Servile Class." In B. Bozzoli, ed. *Town and Countryside in the Transvaal.* Johannesburg: Ravan.

Denbow, James. 1984. "Prehistoric Herders and Foragers of the Kalahari: The Evidence for 1500 years of interaction." In Schrire. *Past and Present in Hunter Gatherer Studies.*

––––––. 1986. "A New Look at the Later Prehistory of the Kalahari." *Journal of African History* 27:3–28.

Denoon, Donald. 1983. *Settler Capitalism.* Oxford: Oxford University Press.

Doke, Clement M. 1925. "The Qhung Bushmen of the Kalahari." *South African Geographical Journal* 8:39–44.

Dowd, Michael. 1954. "Non-White Land and Labor Politics in South West Africa." Ph.D. dissertation, Tufts University, Boston.

Drechsler, Horst. 1969. *Südwestafrika unter Deutscher Kolonialherrschaft.* Berlin: Akademie-Verlag.

––––––. 1980. *Let Us Die Fighting.* London: Zed.

Driessler, H. 1932. *Die Rheinische Mission in Südwestafrika.* Gutersloh: Bertelsmann.

Dungan, M. V. 1927. "Southwest Africa. A Study of the International Problem Resulting from the European Colonization and the Subsequent Conquest and Mandatory Administration of the Union of South Africa." M.A. thesis. Stanford University.

Dunn, Edward J. 1937. "The Bushman." *South African Journal of Science* 33:1050–1054.

Duvel, U. V. 1984. "Plaasverbossing en invloed daarvan op ekonomies streeksontwikkeling." *SWAPLAN* 27 (November): 1–2.

Elphick, Richard. 1985. *Khoikhoi and the Founding of White South Africa.* Johannesburg: Ravan.

Engelbrecht, L. 1922. "Wagposte aan die Oekavango." *Die Brandwag* 13(9):263–8.

Enloe, Cynthia H. 1980. *Ethnic Soldiers.* Harmondsworth: Penguin.

Esterhuyse, J. H. 1968. *South West Africa, 1880–1894.* Cape Town: Struik.

Estermann, Carlos. 1976. *The Ethnography of Southwestern Angola,* vol. 1. Ed. and trans. G. Gibson. New York: Holmes and Meier.

———. 1979. *The Ethnography of Southwestern Angola,* vol. 2. Ed. and trans. G. Gibson. New York: Holmes and Meier.

———. 1981. *The Ethnography of Southwestern Angola,* vol. 3. Ed. and trans. G. Gibson. New York: Holmes and Meier.

Fabian, Johannes. 1987. "Thoughts on Anthropology upon Reading Francis Galton's Narrative of an Explorer in Tropical Africa (1853)." *Critique of Anthropology* 7(2):37–49.

Farson, Negley. 1941. *Behind God's Back.* New York: Harcourt Brace.

Fernandes-Costa, Francisco, et al. 1984. "Transition from a Hunter-Gatherer to a Settled Lifestyle in the !Kung San: Effect on Iron, Folat, and Vitamin B12 Nutrition." *American Journal of Clinical Nutrition* 40:1295–1303.

First, Ruth. 1963. *South West Africa.* Harmondsworth: Penguin.

Fischer, Eugen. 1955. "Über die sogenannte Hottentotschurze." *Zeitschrift für Morphologie und Anthropologie* 47(1):58–66.

Fitzpatrick, Peter. 1982. "The Political Economy of Dispute Settlement in Papua New Guinea." In Colin Sumner, ed. *Crime, Justice and Underdevelopment.* London: Heinemann.

Fourie, L. 1928. "The Bushmen of South West Africa." In C. Hahn, H. Vedder and L. Fourie. *The Native Tribes of South West Africa.* Cape Town: South West Africa Administration.

Foweraker, Joe. 1981. *The Struggle For Land: A Political Economy of the Pioneer Frontier in Brazil.* New York: Cambridge University Press.

Frere, Bartle. 1881. "On Temperate South Africa." *Proceedings of the Royal Geographical Society* 111:1–19.

Frey, Karl. n.d. "The Natives of South West Africa." In *South African Trades Alphabet.*

Fritsch, Gustav. 1872. *Die Eingeborenen Südafrikas.* Breslau: Hirt.

———. 1880. "Die afrikanischen Buschmänner als Urrasse." *Zeitschrift für Ethnologie* 12(3):289–300.

_____. 1906. "Die Buschmänner der Kalahari von S. Passarge." *Zeitschrift für Ethnologie* 38:71–79.

Gad, L. 1914. "Besiedlungsfortschrifte und Besitzstand der Farmwirtschaft." *Mitteilungen aus den deutschen Schutzgebieten* 27(1):36–48.

Galton, Francis. 1852. "Original Correspondence." *St. Helena Gazette*, 31 January: 2–6.

_____. 1889. *Narrative of an Explorer in Tropical South Africa*. London: Ward, Lock.

Gann, Lewis, and Peter Duignan. 1977. *The Rulers of German Africa*. Stanford: Stanford University Press.

Gann, Lewis. 1987. "Marginal Colonialism. The German Case." In A. Knoll and L. Gann, eds. *Germans in the Tropics*. Westport: Greenwood Press.

Gentz, P. 1909. "Die Buschmänner. Ein aussterbendes Volk in Deutsch-Südwestafrika." *Deutsche Kolonial Zeitung* 26:450–52.

Gibson, Gordon, ed. 1981. *The Kavango Peoples*. Wiesbaden: Franz Steiner.

Giddens, Anthony. 1973. *The Class Structure of the Advanced Capitalist Societies*. London: Hutchinson.

Gilman, Sander. 1986. *Jewish Self-Hatred*. Baltimore: Johns Hopkins University Press.

Gilsenan, Michael. 1986. "Domination as Social Practice. Patrimonialism in North Lebanon: Arbitrary Power, Desecration and the Aesthetics of Violence." *Critique of Anthropology* 6(1):17–37.

Glass, Paul. 1939. "Die Buschmänner in Deutsch-Südwestafrika." Ph.D. dissertation, Königsberg University.

Goffman, Erving. 1961. *Asylums*. New York: Doubleday.

Goldblatt, Israel. 1971. *History of South West Africa*. Cape Town: Juta.

_____. 1978. "Early South West Africa—Bench and Bar." *South African Law Journal* 95:120–129, 260–266.

Goldschmidt, Walter. 1981. "The Failure of Pastoral Economic Development Programs in Africa." In J. Galaty, et al., eds. *The Future of Pastoral Peoples*. Ottawa: IDRC.

Goodwin, A.J.H. 1936. "The Bushmen." *African Observer* 5(5):41–46.

Gordon, Robert J. 1977. *Mines, Migrants and Masters*. Johannesburg: Ravan.

_____. 1978a. "The Celebration of Ethnicity. A 'Tribal Fight' in a Namibian Mining Compound." In Brian du Toit, ed. *Ethnicity in Modern Africa*. Boulder: Westview.

_____. 1978b. "Variations in Migration Rates: The Ovambo Case." *Journal of Southern African Affairs* 3(3):261–294.

_____. 1984a. "The !Kung in the Kalahari Exchange." In Schrire. *Past and Present in Hunter Gatherer Studies*.

_____. 1984b. *What Future for the Ju-/wasi of Nyae Nyae?* Boston: Cultural Survival. Occasional Paper No. 13.

_____. 1985. "Conserving the Bushmen to Extinction: The Metaphysics of Bushman Hating and Empire Building." *Survival International Review* 44:22–42.

_____. 1987a. "End Note: A Namibian Perspective on Lorna Marshall's Ethnography." In M. Biesele et al., eds. *The Past and Future of !Kung Ethnography*. Hamburg: Helmut Buske Verlag.

———. 1987b. "Once Again: How Many Bushmen Are There?" In M. Biesele et al., eds. *The Past and Future of !Kung Ethnography.* Hamburg: Helmut Buske Verlag.

———. 1988. "Apartheid's Anthropologists: On the Genealogy of Afrikaner Anthropology." *American Ethnologist* 15(3):535–553.

———. 1989. "Can the Namibian San Stop the Dispossession of Their Land?" In Wilmsen, *We Are Here.*

———. 1990a. "Making Bushmen." Paper presented at the American Anthropological Association meeting, New Orleans.

———. 1990b. "People of the Sandface: People of the Great White Lie?" *Commission on Visual Anthropology Review.*

Gotthardt, Bishop J. 1933. *Auf zum Okavango.* Hunfeld: OMI.

Gray, Stephen. 1979. *Southern African Literature.* Cape Town: D. Philip.

Green, Frederick. 1860. "Narrative of a Journey to Ovamboland." *Cape Monthly Magazine* 41(7) May: 302–307, 353–362.

Green, Lawrence. 1945. *Where Men Still Dream.* Cape Town: Howard Timmins.

———. 1952. *Lords of the Last Frontier.* Cape Town: Howard Timmins.

———. 1980. *Secret Africa.* Cape Town: Howard Timmins.

Grimm, Hans. 1928. *Dreizehn Briefe aus Deutsch-Südwestafrika.* Munich: Langen.

Grobbelaar, Ben J. 1967. "'n Ondersoek na die verandering van die !Kung op tegnologiese en ekonomiese gebiede." M.A. thesis. Pretoria University.

Guenther, Mathias G. 1976. "The San Trance Dance: Ritual and Revitalization Among the Farm Bushmen of the Ghanzi District, Republic of Botswana." *Journal of the South West Africa Scientific Society* 30:45–53.

———. 1979a. "Bushman Religion and the (Non)Sense of Anthropological Theory of Religion." *Sociologus* 29(2):102–132.

———. 1979b. *The Farm Bushmen of the Ghanzi District, Botswana.* Stuttgart: Hochshulverlag.

———. 1980. "From 'Brutal Savages' to 'Harmless People.'" *Paideuma* 26:123–140.

———. 1985. "From Foragers to Miners and Bands to Bandits. On the Flexibility and Adaptability of Bushman Band Societies." *Sprache und Geschichte in Afrika.* 7(1):133–159.

Gusinde, Martin. 1953. "Anthropological Investigation of the Bushmen of South Africa." *Anthropological Quarterly* 26(1):20–28.

———. 1957. "Primitive Races Now Dying Out." *International Social Science Bulletin* 9:291–298.

H.J.K. 1920–1921. "A Trip to the Okavanga." *Nongqai,* December 1920: 626–628; January 1921: 2–5; February 1921: 58–62; March 1921: 115–120; April 1921: 174–178.

Hahn, Carl Hugo. 1985 (1837–1860). *Diaries of a Missionary in Nama- and Damaraland.* 5 vols. Ed. B. Lau. Windhoek: State Archives.

Hahn, Theophilus. 1867. "Die Nama-Hottentotten." *Globus* 12:238–242.

———. 1870. "Die Buschmänner." *Globus* 16:65–68, 81–85, 102–105, 120–123, 140–143, 153–155.

———. 1878. "The Graves of Heitsi-eibeb, a Chapter on the Pre-historic Hottentot Race." *Cape Monthly Magazine* 16(97):257–265.

_____. 1881. *Tsumi-//goam: The Supreme Being of the Khoi-Khoi.* London: Trubner.

Hailey, Lord. n.d. "A Survey of Native Administration in the Mandate of South West Africa." Manuscript.

Halfstuiver-Vereeniging. 1935. *Het Evangelie en de Boschjesmannen.* Hoenderloo: Doorgangshuis.

Hallinan, C. M. 1977. "The Subjugation and Division of Ireland: Testing Ground for Colonial Policy." *Crime and Social Justice* 8 (Fall-Winter): 53–57.

Heintze, Beatrix. 1972. "Buschmänner unter Ambo-Aspekte ihrer gegenseitigen Beziehungen." *Journal of the South West Africa Scientific Society* 26:45–56.

Heinz, Hans-Joachim. 1975. "Acculturative Problems Arising in a Bushman Development Scheme." *South African Journal of Science* 71:78–85.

_____. 1979. *Namkwa: Life Among the Bushmen.* Boston: Houghton Mifflin.

Helbig, Helga and Ludwig. 1983. *Mythos Deutsch-Südwest.* Weinheim: Beltz.

Hermans, Jane. 1977. "Official Policy Towards the Bushman of Botswana. A Review, Part 1." *Botswana Notes and Records* 9:55–67.

Hester, H. 1973. "Erkundungsritt durch die Namib." *Afrikanischer Heimatkalender:* 65–69.

Hitchcock, Robert K. 1980. "Tradition, Social Justice and Land Reform in Central Botswana." *Journal of African Law* 24(1):1–34.

_____. 1982. "Patterns of Sedentism Among the Basarwa of Eastern Botswana." In Leacock and Lee. *Politics and History in Band Societies.*

_____. 1987a. "Hunters and Herding: Local Level Livestock Development Among the Kalahari San." *Cultural Survival Quarterly* 11(1):27–30.

_____. 1987b. "Socioeconomic Change Among the Basarwa in Botswana: An Ethnohistorical Analysis." *Ethnohistory* 34(3):219–255.

_____. 1988a. "Decentralization and Development Among the Ju/wasi, Namibia." *Cultural Survival Quarterly* 12(3):31–33.

_____. 1988b. *Monitoring, Research and Development in the Remote Areas of Botswana.* Gaberone: Ministry of Local Government and Lands and NORAD.

Hobsbawm, Eric. 1969. *Bandits.* New York: Dell.

_____. 1973. "Social Banditry." In Henry Landsberger, ed. *Rural Protest: Peasant Movements and Social Change.* New York: Anchor.

Hobsbawm, E., and T. Ranger, eds. 1983. *The Invention of Tradition.* New York: Cambridge University Press.

Holz, P. 1956. "The Bushmen Are Dying Out." *African World,* July: 11–12.

Hooton, Ernest. 1946. "The Fat-buttocked Bushmen." In David McCord, ed., *The Pocket Book of Humerous Verse.* New York: Pocket Books.

Howell, Nancy. 1986. "Images of Tasaday and the !Kung: Reassessing Isolated Hunter-Gatherers." manuscript.

Hyden, Goran. 1980. *Beyond Ujamaa in Tanzania.* Berkeley: University of California Press.

Iliffe, John. 1987. *The African Poor.* New York: Cambridge University Press.

Isaacman, Alan. 1977. "Social Banditry in Zimbabwe and Mozambique." *Journal of Southern African Studies* 4(1):1–30.

Jackson, Albert. 1958. *Trader on the Veld.* Cape Town: Balkema.

Jacobs, Wilbur R. 1971. "The Fatal Confrontation: Early Native-White Relations on the Frontiers of Australia, New Guinea, and America—A Comparative Study." *Pacific Historical Review* 40:283–309.

Jenkins, Trefor. 1979. "Southern Africa's Model People." *South African Journal of Science* 75:280–282.

———. 1988. *The Peoples of Southern Africa: Studies in Diversity and Disease.* Johannesburg: Witwatersrand University Press.

Jenkins, Trefor, et al. 1987. "Transition from a Hunter-Gatherer to a Settled Lifestyle Among the !Kung San (Bushmen): Effect on Glucose Tolerance and Insulin Secretion." *South African Journal of Science* 83(7):410–412.

Jenny, Hans. 1982. *Südwestafrika,* 2nd ed. Windhoek: South West Africa Scientific Society.

Jordan, Will Worthington. 1881. "Journal of the Trek Boers." *Cape Quarterly Review* 1(1) October: 145–175.

Katjavivi, Peter. 1988. *A History of Resistance in Namibia.* London: J. Currey.

Katz, Richard. 1982. *Boiling Energy: Community Healing Among the Kalahari !Kung.* Cambridge: Harvard University Press.

Kienetz, Alvin. 1974. "Nineteenth Century German South West Africa As a German Settlement Colony." Ph.D. dissertation, University of Minnesota.

———. 1977. "The Key Role of the Orlam Migrations in the Early Europeanization of South-West Africa (Namibia)." *International Journal of African Historical Studies* 10(4):553–572.

Kjekshus, Helge. 1977. *Ecology Control and Economic Development in East Africa.* Berkeley: University of California Press.

Kloppers, Johannes. 1970. *Gee My 'n Man.* Johannesburg: Afrikaanse Pers.

Köhler, Oswin. 1957. "Dokumente zur Entstehung des Buschmannproblems in Südwestafrika." *Afrikanischer Heimatkalender:* 52–64.

———. 1959a. *A Study of Gobabis District.* Pretoria: Government Printer.

———. 1959b. *A Study of Grootfontein District.* Pretoria: Government Printer.

Kolata, Gina. 1981. "!Kung Bushmen Join the South African Army." *Science* 211:562–564.

Krause, A. 1939. "Von den Buschmännern im Sandveld." *Katholische missionsarztliche Fürsorge Jahrbuch* 16:79–82.

Kritzinger, J. J. 1972. *Sending en Kerk in Suidwes-Afrika.* Pretoria: RGN.

Kruger, G. P. n.d. "Outjo, 1885–1960." Mimeo.

Ku'eep. 1857. "Sketches and Recollections of Great Namaqualand." *Cape Monthly Magazine* 1(6) June: 365–369.

Kulz, Wilfried. 1909. *Deutsch-Südafrika im 25 Jahre deutscher Schutzherrschaft.* Berlin: Susserott.

Kuper, Adam. 1970. *Kalahari Village Politics.* New York: Cambridge University Press.

Kuper, Leo. 1981. *Genocide.* Harmondsworth: Penguin.

Lamar, Howard, and Leonard Thompson, eds. 1979. *The Frontier in History.* New Haven: Yale University Press.

Lamb, Geoffrey. 1974. *Peasant Politics.* New York: St. Martins.

Lategan, Felix. 1971. "Firearms." *Standard Encyclopaedia of Southern Africa,* vol. 4. Cape Town: Nasionale Boekhandel.

_____. 1974. *Die Boer se Roer.* Kaapstad: Tafelberg.

Lau, Brigitte. 1981. "'Thank God the Germans Came.' Vedder and Namibian Historiography." In K. Gottschalk and C. Saunders, eds. *Africa Seminar. Collected Papers 2.* Cape Town: University of Cape Town Center for African Studies.

_____. 1987. *Namibia in Jonker Afrikaner's Time.* Windhoek: State Archives.

Leach, Edmund R. 1976. *Culture and Communication.* New York: Cambridge University Press.

_____. 1977. *Custom, Law and Terroristic Violence.* Edinburgh: University Press.

Leacock, Eleanor, and Richard Lee, eds. 1982. *Politics and History in Band Society.* New York: Cambridge University Press.

League of Nations, Permanent Mandates Commission. 1928–1938. *Minutes of Proceedings. . . .* Geneva.

Lebzelter, Viktor. 1928. "Bei den !Kun-Buschleuten am oberen Omuramba u Ovambo." *Mitteilungen der Anthropologischen Gesellschaft Wien:* 12–16.

_____. 1934a. "Die Buschmänner Südwestafrikas." *Africa* 7:70–81.

_____. 1934b. *Eingeborenenkulturen in Süd- und Südwestafrika.* 2 vols. Leipzig: Hiersemann.

Lee, Richard B. 1979. *The Kung San.* New York: Cambridge University Press.

_____. 1983. *The Dobe !Kung.* New York: Holt, Rinehart & Winston.

Lee, Richard B., and Susan Hurlich. 1982. "From Foragers to Fighters: South Africa's Militarization of the Namibian San." In Leacock and Lee. *Politics and History in Band Society:* 327–345.

Lefebvre, Henri. 1971. *Everyday Life in the Modern World.* New York: Harper & Row.

Legendre, Sidney. 1939. *Okavango, Desert River.* New York: Messner.

Lehmann, F. Rudolf. 1956. "Die verhouding van die Duitse beskermingsadministrasie in Suidwes-Afrika tot die Ambovolke." *Journal of the South West Africa Scientific Society* 11:5–32.

Lemmer, C.J.C. n.d. *A History of South West Africa.* Cape Town: Maskew Miller.

Leser, Helmut. 1975. "Weidewirtschaft und Regenfeldbau im Sandfeld: Westliche Kalahari um Schwarzen Nossob und Epukiro, östliches SWA." *Geographische Rundschau* 27:108–122.

_____. 1982. *Namibia.* Stuttgart: Ernst Klett.

Leutwein, Theodor. 1906. *Elf Jahre Gouverneur in Deutsch-Südwestafrika.* Berlin: Mittler und Sohn.

Lewis-Williams, David. 1981. *Believing and Seeing: Symbolic Meaning in Southern San Rock Art.* London: Academic Press.

Lindfors, Bernd. 1983. "Clicks and Clucks: Victorian Reactions to San Speech." *Africana Journal* 14(1):10–17.

Lips, Julius. 1937. *The Savage Hits Back.* New Haven: Yale University Press.

Loeb, Edwin M. 1962. *In Feudal Africa.* Bloomington: Indiana University Press.

Lubbock, Sir John. 1913. *Prehistoric Times As Illustrated by Ancient Remains.* New York: H. Holt.

Luttig, H. G. n.d. *The Religious System and Social Organization of the Herero.* Utrecht: Kemink.

McClintock, Anne. 1988. "Maidens, Maps, and Mines. The Reinvention of Patriarchy in Colonial South Africa." *South Atlantic Quarterly* 87(1):147–192.

McKiernan, Gerald. 1954. *The Narrative and Journal of Gerald McKiernan in South West Africa, 1874–79.* Ed. G. Serton. Cape Town: van Riebeeck Society.

Maingard, L. 1937. "Some Notes on Health and Disease Among the Bushmen of the Southern Kalahari." *Bantu Studies* 11(3):285–294.

Makin, W. J. 1929. *Across the Kalahari Desert.* London: Arrowsmith.

Malan, J. S. 1980. *Peoples of South West Africa / Namibia.* Pretoria: Haum.

Malan, P. S., and C. F. Malan. 1982. *Geskiedenis van Suidwes-Afrika.* Kaapstad: Nasou.

Malinowski, Bronislaw. 1937. "Foreword." In Lips. *The Savage Hits Back.*

Mandel, Ernest. 1976. *Late Capitalism.* London: New Left Books.

Marais, François, and partners. 1984. *Ondersoek na die Boesmanbevolkingsgroep in Suidwes-Afrika.* Windhoek: Direktoraat, ontwikkelingskoordinering.

Marks, Shula. 1972. "Khoisan Resistance to the Dutch in the 17th and 18th Centuries." *Journal of African History* 13(1):55–80.

————. 1981. "Old, Thievish, and Not to Be Trusted." *History Today,* August: 15–21.

Marks, Shula, and Anthony Atmore, eds. 1980. *Economy and Society in Preindustrial South Africa.* London: Longman.

Marquard, Leo, and T. G. Standing. 1939. *The Southern Bantu.* London: Oxford University Press.

Marshall, John. 1989. "The Constitution and Communal Lands in Namibia. Land Rights and Local Governments. Helping 33,000 People Classified as 'Bushmen.'" Mimeo.

————. Forthcoming. "Filming and Learning." *Visual Anthropology.*

Marshall, John, and Claire Ritchie. 1984. *Where Are the Ju-/wasi of Nyae Nyae?* Cape Town: University of Cape Town African Studies Program.

Marshall, Lorna. 1976. *The !Kung of Nyae-Nyae.* Cambridge: Harvard University Press.

Mattenklodt, W. 1931. *Fugitive in the Jungle.* Boston: Little, Brown.

Maughan Brown, David. 1983. "The Noble Savage in Anglo-Saxon Colonial Ideology, 1950–1980." *English in Africa* 10(2):55–77.

Mbuende, Kaire. 1986. *Namibia, the Broken Shield: Anatomy of Imperialism and Revolution.* Malmo: Liber.

Memmi, Albert. 1967. *The Colonizer and the Colonized.* Boston: Beacon.

Metz, J., D. Hart and H. Harpending. 1971. "Iron, Folate and Vitamin B12 Nutrition in a Hunter-Gatherer People. Study of the !Kung Bushmen." *American Journal of Clinical Nutrition* 24:229–242.

Metzger, Fritz. 1950. *Narro and His Clan.* Windhoek: John Meinert.

Mill, D. 1987. "SADF's Bushmen: Desert Nomads on SWAPO's Track." *Soldier of Fortune,* January: 32–37.

Moller, P. 1974. *Journey Through Angola, Ovamboland and Damaraland, 1895–1896.* Cape Town: Struik.

Moorsom, Richard. 1977. "Underdevelopment, Contract Labour and Worker Consciousness in Namibia, 1915–1972." *Journal of Southern African Studies* 4(1).

———. 1982. *Transforming a Wasted Land*. London: Catholic Institute of International Relations.

Moritz, Walter. 1980. *Erkundungsreise ins Ovamboland, 1857. Tagebuch Carl Hugo Hahn*. Schwäbisch Gmünd: Lempp.

Morphy, Howard, and Frances Morphy. 1984. "The 'myths' of Ngalakan History: Ideology and Images of the Past in Northern Australia." *Man* 19(3):459–478.

Morton Seagars, E. T., with L. O. Honeyborne. 1941. "At War with the Bushmen." *Nongqai* 32(5):547–550, 588.

Mosse, George. 1985. *Nationalism and Sexuality*. Madison: University of Wisconsin Press.

Mueller, Hauptmann. 1912. "Die Buschleute im Kaukauveld." *Deutsch-Südwestafrikansche Zeitung* 65:66.

Muller, Fritz F. 1962. *Kolonien unter der Peitsche*. Berlin: Rutten & Loening.

Muller-Hill, Benno. 1989. *Murderous Science*. New York: Oxford University Press.

Newton, L. M. n.d. *Faraway Sandy Trails*. Johannesburg: Central News Agency.

Nienaber, G. S. 1950. "Die Woord 'Boesman.'" *Theoria* (Pietermarizburg): 36–40.

———. 1989. *Khoekhoense Stamname*. Kaapstad: Academica.

Nolte, K. 1886. "Die westliche Kalahari Wüste und die angrenzenden Distrikte." *Deutsche Kolonial Zeitung:* 341–344.

Norval, M. 1984. "SADF'S Bushman Battalion: Primitive Trackers Fight 20th Century War." *Soldier of Fortune*, March: 71–75.

O'Keefe, Stephen, and Robyn Lavender. 1989. "The Plight of Modern Bushmen." *Lancet*, 29 July: 255–258.

O'Malley, Patrick. 1981. "The Class Production of Crime: Banditry and Class Strategies in England and Australia." In R. Simon and S. Spitzer, eds. *Research in Law and Sociology*. Greenwich: JAI Press.

Oelhafen von Schoellenbach, Hans. 1926. *Die Besiedlung Deutsch-südwestafrikas bis zum Weltkriege*. Berlin: Reimer.

Offe, Hans. 1937. "Die Reservatfrage bei den Buschmännern." *Koloniale Rundschau* 28(2):136–139.

Oldevig, Margarita. 1944. *The Sunny Land*. Cape Town: Howard Timmins.

Olivier, Martinus J. 1961. "Inboorlingbeleid en -Administrasie in die Mandaatgebied van Suidwes-Afrika." Ph.D. dissertation, Stellenbosch University.

Palgrave, William Coates. 1877. *Report of W. Coates Palgrave, esq. Special Commissioner to the Tribes North of the Orange River, of His Mission to Damaraland and Great Namaqualand in 1876*. Cape Town: Government Printer, G.50/1877.

Paratus. 1978. "Hier is die SAW die Alfa en die Omega." May: 24–26.

Parkington, John. 1984. "Soaqua and Bushmen: Hunters and Robbers." In Schrire. *Past and Present in Hunter Gatherer Studies*.

Passarge, Siegfried. 1907. *Die Buschmänner der Kalahari*. Berlin: Dieter Reimer.

Pearson, Patrick. 1981. "The Rehoboth Rebellion." In Phillip Bonner, ed. *Working Papers in Southern African Studies*. Johannesburg: Ravan.

Peringuey, Louis. 1911. "The Stone Ages of South Africa." *Annals of the South African Museum* (Cape Town) 8.

Permanent Mandates Commission of the League of Nations. 1930. *Minutes of Meetings.* Geneva: League of Nations.

Peterson, Jean T. 1984. "Cash, Consumerism, and Savings: Economic Change Among the Agta Foragers of Luzon, Philippines." In Barry Isaac, ed. *Research in Economic Anthropology,* vol. 6. Greenwich: JAI Press.

Poewe, Karla. 1986. *The Namibian Herero.* New York: Mellen.

Pool, Gerhard. 1979. *Die Herero-Opstand, 1904–07.* Cape Town: HAUM.

Potgieter, D. J. 1937. "Geneesheer veel nodiger as reservaat." *Brandwag* 20 February: 9, 11.

Potgieter, Ewart F. 1955. *The Disappearing Bushmen of Lake Chrissie.* Pretoria: University of South Africa.

Pratt, Marie Louise. 1986. "Fieldwork in Common Places." In J. Clifford and G. Marcus, eds. *Writing Culture.* Berkeley: University of California Press.

Prichard, J. C. 1851. *Researches into the Physical History of Mankind.* 5 vols. London: Sherwood, Gilbert & Piper.

Prinsloo, J. G., and J. G. Gauche. 1933. *In die Woeste Weste.* Pretoria: de Bussy.

Proctor, Robert. 1988. *Racial Hygiene.* Cambridge: Harvard University Press.

Pyper, Cornelius R. 1950. "Jottings on the Epukiro Bushmen." *Student* 3:51.

Rädel, Fritz E. 1947. "Die Wirtschaft und die Arbeiterfrage Südwestafrikas." D. Comm. dissertation, Stellenbosch University.

Rafalski, Hans. 1930. *vom Niemandsland zum Ordnungsstaat.* Berlin: E. Werseitz.

Raif, Karl. 1935. *Kampfe im Busch.* Berlin: Allstein.

Rao, Aparna, ed. 1987. *The Other Nomads.* Cologne: Bohlau Verlag.

Ratzel, Friedrich. 1897. *The History of Mankind,* vol. 2. London: Macmillan.

Rheinhallt-Jones, David, and Clement Doke. 1937. *The Bushmen of the Southern Kalahari.* Johannesburg: Witwatersrand University Press.

Richards, Paul. 1983. "Ecological Change and the Politics of African Land Use." *African Studies Review* 26(2):1–72.

Robertson, A. F. 1984. *People and the State.* New York: Cambridge University Press.

Rohrbach, Paul. 1907. *Deutsche Kolonialwirtschaft,* Band 1. *Südwestafrika.* Berlin: Schönberg.

Romanyshyn, J. M. 1971. *Social Welfare: Charity to Justice.* New York: Random House.

Rosaldo, Renato. 1982. "Utter Savages of Scientific Value." In Leacock and Lee. *Politics and History in Band Societies.*

Russell, Margo. 1976. "Slaves or Workers? Relations Between Bushmen, Tswana and Boers in the Kalahari." *Journal of Southern African Studies* 2(2):178–197.

Russett, Cynthia. 1989. *Sexual Science: The Victorian Construction of Womanhood.* Cambridge: Harvard University Press.

Sachs, Albie. 1973. *Justice in South Africa.* Berkeley: University of California Press.

Sangiro. 1954. *En die Oranje Vloei Verby.* Johannesburg: Afrikaanse Pers.

Saunders, Christopher. 1988. *The Making of the South African Past.* Cape Town: D. Philip.

Schapera, Isaac. 1930. *The Khoisan Peoples of South Africa.* London: Routledge & Kegan Paul.

———. 1938, 1939. "Memorandum to the Standing Committee in Connection with the Proposed Bushman Enquiry." Mimeo available at State Archives, Windhoek: Also published as "A survey of the Bushman question," *Race Relations* (1939) 6(2):68–82.

Schenk, G. T. 1974. "German South West Africa." Ph.D. dissertation, New York University.

Schinz, Hans. 1891. *Deutsch-Südwest-Afrika.* Leipzig: Schulzesche Hofbuchhandlung.

Schmokel, Wolfe. 1985. "The Myth of the White Farmer: Commercial Agriculture in Namibia, 1900–1983." *International Journal of African Historical Studies* 18(1):93–108.

Schoeman, Amy. 1982. "Wilderness and Its Preservation in South West Africa." *South West Africa Annual, 1982:* 69–80.

Schoeman, Pieter J. n.d.(a). "Voorlopige verslag van die Kommissie vir die behoud van die Boesmanbevolking in Suidwes-Afrika, 1950" (interim report). Mimeo.

———. n.d.(b) (circa 1952). "Report of the Commission for the Preservation of Bushmen in South West Africa" (final report). Mimeo.

Schoeman, P. J. n.d.(c). "Memorandum on the Study of the Bushmen." Mimeo, lent by Mrs. MacIntyre.

———. 1952. "Seventien Boesmans kom na Grootfees." *Die Huisgenoot* 36 (21 March): 16–17, 34–35.

———. 1957. *Hunters of the Desert Land.* Cape Town: Howard Timmins.

———. 1971. "Weeskinders van Afrika." *Landbouweekblad,* 12 October: 10–15.

Schoeman, S. J. 1975. "Suidwes-Afrika onder militere bestuur." M.A. thesis, University of South Africa.

Schott, Rudiger. 1955. "Die Buschmänner in Südafrika. Eine Studie über die Schwierigkeit der Akkulturation." *Sociologus* N.S. 5:132–149.

Schrire, Carmel. 1980. "An Inquiry into the Evolutionary Status and Apparent Identity of San Hunter-gatherers." *Human Ecology* 6(1):9–31.

———, ed. 1984. *Past and Present in Hunter Gatherer Studies.* New York: Academic Press.

Schulte, Pater J. 1912. "Die ersten Missionierungs-Versuche unter den Buschleuten im Bezirk Grootfontein." *Maria Immaculata* 20:19–22.

Schultze, Leonard. 1907. *Aus Namaland und Kalahari.* Jena: Fischer.

———. 1914. "Südwestafrika." In Hans Meyer, ed. *Das Deutsche Kolonialreich,* vol. 2, pt. 2. Leipzig: Verlag des Bibliographischen Instituts.

Seiner, Franz. 1912. "Die Buschmannsgefahr in Deutsch-Südwestafrika." *Deutsche Kolonial Zeitung:* 311–312.

———. 1913a. "Beobachtungen an den Bastard-Buschleuten der Nord-Kalahari." *Mitteilungen der Anthropologische Gesellschaft in Wien* 43:311–324.

———. 1913b. "Die Buschmannfrage im nördlichen Deutsch-Südwestafrika." *Deutsche Kolonial Zeitung:* 745–746.

Shineberg, Dorothy. 1971. "Guns and Men in Melanesia." *Journal of Pacific History* 6:61–82.

Shostak, Marjorie. 1983. *Nisa, the Life and Words of a !Kung Woman.* New York: Vintage.

Silberbauer, George, and Adam Kuper. 1966. "Kgalagari Masters and Bushman Serfs." *African Studies* 25(4):171–179.

Snow, A. H. 1921. *The Question of Aborigines.* New York: Putnam.

Sohnge, Walter. 1967. *Tsumeb: A Historical Sketch.* Windhoek: South West African Scientific Society.

Solway, Jacqueline, and Richard Lee. 1990. "Foragers, Genuine or Spurious? Situating the Kalahari San in History." *Current Anthropology* 31(2):109–146.

South Africa. 1918. *Report on the Natives of South West Africa and Their Treatment by Germany.* London: HMSO, cd.9146.

―――. 1923. *Annual Report on South West Africa Submitted to the League of Nations.* Pretoria: Government Printer.

―――. 1925. *Annual Report on South West Africa Submitted to the League of Nations.* Pretoria: Government Printer.

―――. 1927. *Annual Report on South West Africa Submitted to the League of Nations.* Pretoria: Government Printer.

―――. 1931. *Annual Report on South West Africa Submitted to the League of Nations.* Pretoria: Government Printer.

―――. 1934. *Annual Report on South West Africa Submitted to the League of Nations.* Pretoria: Government Printer.

―――. 1936. *Report of the South West Africa Commission.* Pretoria: Government Printer, UG 26/1936.

―――. 1939. *Annual Report on South West Africa Submitted to the League of Nations.* Pretoria: Government Printer.

―――. 1951. Verbatim Record of Proceedings. June 7th. *South African Senate Hansard.*

―――. 1964. *Report of the Commission of Inquiry into South West African Affairs.* Pretoria: Government Printer.

South Africa, Department of Welfare. 1962. "Die Boesmans in die Noordoostelke dele van Suidwes-Afrika." Mimeo.

South African Farm Consultants. 1983. "Report on Agriculture to the Administration for Whites." Windhoek. Mimeo.

South West Africa (South Africa). 1922. *South West African Native Reserves Commission.* Pretoria: Government Printer, UG 32/1922.

―――. 1925. *SWA: Land of Opportunity.* Windhoek: Administration.

―――. 1936. *Report of the Constitutional Commission (van Zyl).* Windhoek: Government Printer.

―――. 1949. "Report of the Game Preservation Commission." Windhoek. Mimeo.

―――. 1950a. *Report of the Long Term Agricultural Policy Commission.* Windhoek: Govenment Printer.

―――. 1950b. "Report of the Native Labour Commission, 1945–8." Windhoek. Mimeo.

―――. 1957. *Minutes of the Legislative Assembly.* Windhoek: Legislative Assembly.

―――. 1958. "Report of the Commission of Enquiry into Non-European Education." Windhoek. Mimeo.

Spies, J. J. 1948. "Soektog na ontvoerde meisie." *Die Huisgenoot,* 19 November: 74–76.

Stals, Ernst L.P. 1962. "Die Geskiedenis van die Beesteelt in Suidwes-Afrika tydens die Duitse tydperk (1884–1915)." *Archives Yearbook for South African History,* 25.

_____. 1968. "Die aanraking tussen blankes en Ovambos in SWA 1850–1915." *Archives Yearbook for South African History* 31(2).

_____. 1984. "Duits Suidwes-Afrika na die Groot Opstande." *Archives Yearbook for South African History* 46(2).

Steyn, H. P. 1985. *The Bushmen of the Kalahari.* Hove: Wayland.

Stockenstrom, Wilma. 1983. *The Expedition to the Baobab Tree.* Boston: Faber & Faber.

Stocking, George. 1987. *Victorian Anthropology.* New York: Free Press.

Strydom, S. Scheepers. 1929. "Boesmans en Korannas: Hoe die Noordweste van hulle gesuiwer is." *Die Huisgenoot,* 29 November, 13 December, 20 December.

Swanepoel, J. M. 1978. "Onderwysvoorsiening-Haikom." Mimeo.

Swanepoel, P. G. n.d. *Polisie-avonture in Suidwes-Afrika.* Johannesburg: Perskor.

Szalay, Milos. 1983. *Ethnologie und Geschichte.* Berlin: Dietrich Reimer.

Tabel, W. 1975. "Erlebnisschilderungen von Soldaten und Siedlern aus der Kolonial -und Mandatzeit Südwestafrikas." *Afrikanischer Heimatkalender:* 81–122.

Tabler, Eric G. 1973. *Pioneers of South West Africa and Ngamiland, 1738–1880.* Cape Town: Balkema.

Taussig, Michael. 1984. "Culture of Terror—Space of Death. Roger Casement's Putumayo Report and the Explanation of Torture." *Comparative Studies in Society and History* 26(2):467–497.

Thomson, A. A., and Dorothy Middleton. 1959. *Lugard in Africa.* London: Robert Hale.

Tindall, Joseph. 1856. *Two Lectures on Great Namaqualand.* Cape Town: Mechanics Institute.

Tlou, Thomas. 1985. *A History of Ngamiland—1750 to 1906.* Gaberone: Macmillan.

Tobias, Philip V., ed. 1978. *The Bushmen: San Hunters and Herders of South Africa.* Cape Town: Human & Rousseau.

Todorov, Tzvetan. 1985. *The Conquest of America.* New York: Harper Colophon.

Tomaselli, Keyan, et al. 1986. *Myth, Race and Power: South Africans Imaged on Film and TV.* Bellville, SA: Anthropos.

Trumpelmann, G.P.J. 1948. "Die Boer in Suidwes-Afrika." *Archives Yearbook for South African History* 11(2).

Turner, Victor. 1974. *Dramas, Fields and Metaphors.* Ithaca: Cornell University Press.

Unterkötter, Rev. A. 1935. "Gilt das Evangelium auch den Buschleuten?" *Berichte der Rheinischen Mission* 92(1):21–28.

_____. 1938. "Ich will die Zauberei bei Dir ausrotten." *Berichte der Rheinischen Mission* 95:275–83, 308–315.

_____. 1955. *Schatten über dem Windschirm.* Wuppertal-Barmen: RMG.

van der Post, Laurens. 1988. *Lost World of the Kalahari, with a New Epilogue.* New York: Morrow.

van der Walt, A. J. 1926. *Noordwaarts!* Cape Town: Nasionale Pers.

van der Westhuizen, J., et al. 1987. "Thiamin and Biochemical Indices of Malnutrition and Alcholism in Settled Communities of !Kung San." *Journal of Tropical Medicine and Hygiene* 90:283–289.

van Oordt, Gregorius August. 1980. *Striving and Hoping to the Bitter End.* Cape Town: Nasionale Boekwinkel.

van Reenen, Reenen J. 1920. *Iets oor die Boesmankultuur.* Bloemfontein: Nasionale Pers.

van Zwanenberg, Roger M. 1976. "Dorobo Hunting and Gathering: A Way of Life or a Mode of Production?" *African Economic History* 2:12–21.

Vedder, Heinrich. 1913. "Die Buschmänner." *Deutsche-Südafrikanische Zeitung:* 102, 103, 104, 105.

————. 1928. "The Herero." In C. Hahn, H. Vedder, and L. Fourie. *The Native Tribes of South West Africa.* Cape Town: Cape Times.

————. 1937. "Die Buschmänner Südwestafrikas und ihre Weltanschauung." *South African Journal of Science* 24:416–436.

————. 1938. *South West Africa in Early Times.* London: Oxford University Press.

————. 1981 (1934). *Das alte Südwestafrika.* Windhoek: SWA Scientific Society.

Voeltz, R. A. 1988. *German Colonialism and the South West Africa Company, 1894–1914.* Athens: Ohio University Press.

Voigt, B. 1943. *Diri: Ein Buschmannleben.* Potsdam: Voggenreiter.

Volkman, Toby A. 1986. "The Hunter-Gatherer Myth in Southern Africa: Preserving Nature or Culture?" *Cultural Survival Quarterly* 10(2):25–31.

Volkmann, Hauptmann. 1901. "Reise von Grootfontein nach dem Okavango." *Deutsches Kolonialblatt* 12:866–868, 908–009.

von Luschan, Felix. 1906. "Bericht über eine Reise in Süd-Afrika." *Zeitschrift für Ethnologie* 38(6):863–895.

————. 1908. "Die Frage der Buschmänner." *Deutsche Kolonial Zeitung:* 99.

von Moltke, Johannes. n.d.(a). *Veldsmanne.* Johannesburg: Afrikaanse-Pers.

————. n.d.(b). von Moltke collection, A100. State Archives, Windhoek.

von Weber, Otto. 1983. *Geschichte des Schutzgebietes Deutsch-Südwest-Afrika.* Windhoek: South West Africa Scientific Society.

von Zastrow, Beringar. 1914. "Über die Buschleute. . . ." *Zeitschrift für Ethnologie* 46:1–7.

von Zastrow, Beringar, and Heinrich Vedder. 1930. "Über die Buschmänner." In H. Schultze-Ewerth and L. Adam, eds. *Das Eingeborenenrecht,* vol. 2. Stuttgart: Strecker & Schroder.

Wadley, Lynn. 1979. "Big Elephant Shelter and Its Role in the Holocene Prehistory of Central South West Africa." *Cimbebasia* Ser. B. 3(1):1–76.

Wagner, Gunther. 1952. "Aspects of Conservation and Adoption in the Economic Life of Hereros." *Sociologus* 2:1–25.

Walbaum, Gunther. n.d. "Kriegstagebuch von Guenther Walbaum, 1914–1915." Unpublished manuscript on file in State Archives. A.214.

Wallis, J.P.R. 1936. *Fortune My Foe.* London: J. Cape.

Wannenburgh, Alf. n.d. *Forgotten Frontiersmen.* Cape Town: Howard Timmins.

Watts, Ainsley. 1926. "The Early Hunters and Explorers in SWA, 1760–1886." M.A. thesis, University of South Africa.

Weich, Ferdinand. 1964. (Article on Bushmen) in *Die Huisgenoot,* 5 June.

Weineke, Rev. W. A. 1956. "Buschmann-Mission in der Kalahari." *Berichte der Rheinischen Mission* 2(10):28–35.

Wellington, John. 1967. *South West Africa and Its Human Issues.* Cape Town: Oxford University Press.

Wendt, W. E. 1981. "Die letzten Sammler und Jäger aus der südlichen Namib." *Afrikanische Heimatkalender:* 45–62.

Werner, Wolfgang. 1982. "Production and Land Policies in the Herero Reserves, 1915–circa 1950." Mimeo.

Western, David. 1981. "A Challenge for Conservation." *L.S.B. Leakey Foundation News,* 21 (Winter): 1, 14–15.

———. 1982. "The Environment and Ecology of Pastoralists in Arid Savannas." *Development and Change* 13:183–211.

Westphal, E. Otto. 1971. "The Click Languages of Southern and Eastern Africa." In J. Berry and J. Greenberg, eds. *Linguistics in Sub-Saharan Africa: Current Trends in Linguistics,* vol. 7. The Hague: Mouton.

Wiessner, Polly. 1982. "Risk, Reciprocity and Social Influences on !Kung San Economics." In Leacock and Lee. *Politics and History in Band Societies.*

Wilhelm, J. H. 1954. "Die !Kung-Buschleute." *Jahrbuch des Museums für Völkerkunde zu Leipzig* 12:91–188.

Wilkins, Ivor, and Hans Strydom. 1978. *The Super-Afrikaners.* Johannesburg: J. Ball.

Wilkinson, Paul. 1978. "The Global Distribution of National Parks and Equivalent Reserves." In J. G. Nelson, R. D. Needham and D. L. Mann, eds. *International Experience with National Parks and Related Reserves.* Waterloo: University of Waterloo Press.

Wilmot, A. 1895. *The Story of the Expansion of South Africa.* London: Fisher Unwin.

Wilmsen, Edwin. 1983. "The Ecology of Illusion: Anthropological Foraging in the Kalahari." *Reviews in Anthropology* 10(1):9–20.

———. 1989a. *Land Filled with Flies.* Chicago: University of Chicago Press.

———, ed. 1989b. *We Are Here: Politics of Aboriginal Land Tenure.* Berkeley: University of California Press.

Wilmsen, Edwin, and James Denbow. 1990. "Almost Free as Birds. Pre-Harvard History of San-speaking Peoples and 'Post-Modern' Attempts at Reconstruction." *Current Anthropology* 31(5).

Wolf, Eric. 1982. *Europe and the People Without History.* Berkeley: University of California Press.

Worsley, Peter. 1984. *The Three Worlds.* Chicago: University of Chicago Press.

Wright, John B. 1977. "San History and non-San Historians." In University of London, Institute of Commonwealth Studies. *The Societies of Southern Africa in the 19th and 20th centuries,* vol. 8, pp. 1–10.

Wulfhorst, Rev. A. 1937. "Buschleute im Norden von SWA." *Berichte der Rheinischen Mission* 94(2):36–40.

Wust, Pater. 1938. "Ein sterbendes Volk." *Monatsblatt des Oblaten* 45: 254–259, 292–297, 325–329.

Newspapers and Journals

Allgemeine Zeitung, 10 October 1980.
Die Burger, 13 August 1960; 8 February 1980; 12 July 1981; 6 January 1982.
Cape Argus, 3 September 1935; 26 February 1937; 12 July 1958; 29 July 1959; 7 June 1960; 3 October 1960; 10 July 1961; 15 April 1963; 14 June 1963.
Cape Times, 1 January 1926.
Christian Science Monitor, 19 March 1981; 19 May 1981.
Daily News, 24 February 1981.
Deutsche Kolonial Zeitung, 1908:91; 1909:452; 1911:17, 73; 1912:463–464; 1913:88; 6 December 1913; 1913:672–673.
Deutsche Südwest-Afrika Zeitung, 24 December 1913.
Eastern Province Herald, 2 February 1980; 8 February 1980; 21 August 1980.
Frankfurter Allgemeine Zeitung, 23 April 1979.
Die Huisgenoot, 5 June 1964; 14 April 1978.
Namibian, 16 October 1987.
New York Times, 24 February 1981.
Paratus, May 1978; August 1979; February 1983.
Pretoria News, 26 February 1981; 16 May 1985.
Die Republikein, 4 July 1978; 3 December 1980; 21 January 1983.
St. Helena Gazette, 31 January 1852.
Star, 9 September 1981; 9 October 1981; 24 November 1982.
Südwest Zeitung, 1907:15, 17, 40; 25 November 1908; 17 October 1911; 1912:13; 24 July 1912; 19 November 1912; 1913:104.
Die Suidwester, 3 May 1969; 29 January 1973; 15 May 1973; 12 September 1973; 23 September 1973.
Sunday Times, 27 July 1980.
Sunday Tribune, 1 March 1980.
Time, 2 March 1981.
To the Point, 12 September 1980; 17 October 1980.
Valley News, 15 December 1987.
Die Volksblad, 6 September 1980; 3 July 1981; 15 July 1981.
Vrye Weekblad, 30 March 1990.
Windhoek Advertiser, 31 March 1951; 24 October 1973.

Files*

GERMAN ERA

BSW. G35. Gefängene Buschleute, 1911–1914.
ZBU. 1008–1010 Geographische und Ethnographische Forschungen, 1885–1913.

---

* This list includes files consulted but not directly cited in the text.

_____ . 1009–1010. Geographische und Ethnographische Forschungen, 1902–1913.

_____ . 2043. W11. 1–5. Buschleute, 1895–1915.

_____ . 694. Gefängniswesen, 1898–1915.

ADM (MILITARY ADMINISTRATION, 1915–1920)

13/26. Bushman Raiders, Grootfontein.

13/35. Grootfontein, Lawlessness of Bushmen, 1915.

29/25. Grootfontein Patrol Report.

112. Annual Report, 1916.

116-3823/8. Ovambo Labour, Murder of Ovambos by Bushmen, 1918–1920.

148. Confidential Staff Files, G. F. Swemmer.

273. Stockthefts, Otjituo, 1916.

1080. Shooting of Bushmen, 1916.

2279. Native Deserters (Excluding Ovambo), 1916–1924.

3360. Bushmen, Treatment of Vagrants, 1916–1923.

3768/7. Bushmen, Shooting of, 1917.

3823/8. Ovambo Labour. Murder of Ovambo by Bushmen, 1918–1923.

3979. Otjiwarongo Native Affairs, General, 1917.

4185/2. Tsintsabis Police, 1919–1921.

4508. Tsumeb Police.

5503/1. Etosha Game Reserve Reports, 1920–1925.

NAR (NATIVE AFFAIRS RUNDU)

11/7. Native Labour Recruits, Escorts, 1929–1942.

NAT (NATIVE AFFAIRS TSUMQEB [TSUMEB])

28/1. Otavi Mines and Engineering Native Labour, 1937–1947.

29. Bushmen, General, 1937–1941.

29/1. Removal of Diniab Bushmen, 1938–1940.

34/1. SWACO Native Labour, 1938–1940.

NAO (NATIVE AFFAIRS OVAMBOLAND)

17/6. Trading in Game Reserve, 1947–1948.

24/6. Game Reserves, General, 1947–1955.

24/8. Bushmen Living in Game Reserves, 1947.

33/1. Namutoni Game Reserve, 1928–1932; 1932–1936; 1936–1940.

LGR (MAGISTRATE GROOTFONTEIN)

1/1/1–16. Records of Proceedings, Criminal Cases.

1/2/1–6. Records of Proceedings, Preparatory Examinations.

1/3/1–54. Criminal Record Book.

3/1/7. Treatment of Wild Bushmen; Native Affairs Annual Reports, 1935–1937; 1945–1947.

3/1/8. Game; Scientific Research.

3/1/16. Criminal Matters, Bushman Thefts, 1931–1935; Annual Reports, 1924–1933.

3/1/17. Annual Reports, 1934ff.

3/1/26. Annual Report, Native Affairs, 1948; Native Labour.

3/2/1. Economic Position, Grootfontein.

LGO (MAGISTRATE GOBABIS)

1/1/1–16. Records of Proceedings, Criminal Cases, 1919–1969.

1/2/1–72. Criminal Record Book, 1932–1976.

1/3/1–2. Preparatory Examinations, 1932–1953.

3/1/4. Complaints; Distribution of Bushmen.

3/1/60. Annual Report, Native Affairs, 1944–1947.

N5/1–2. Inquests.

SWAA (SOUTH WEST AFRICA ADMINISTRATION)

A3/35. Police Crime Reports (pt. 5:1923; pt. 6:1947–1950).

A3/36/1. Kavango Patrol, 1924–1926.

A13/26.

A33/1.

A3/50. Police Offences, 1921–1955.

A3/111. Relations S.A. Police and Natives, 1947–1953.

A50/5. Bushman Relics, 1920–1948.

A50/6. Squatters, 1924–1937; Bechuanaland Border, 1937–1957.

A50/25. Bushman Depredations, Gobabis, 1927–1948.

A50/26. Bushman Depredations, Grootfontein, 1925–1946.

A50/27. Native Vagrants, 1915–1949.

A50/34. Passports for Natives.

A50/46. Ethnological Research, 1927–1952.

A50/57. Complaints re Etosha Bushmen.

A50/67. Native Affairs, Bushmen.

A50/67/1. Carrying of Bows and Arrows by Bushmen, 1935–1948.

A50/67/2. Removal of Dineib Bushmen to Okavango, 1926–1947.

A50/101. Bechuanaland Border.

A50/120. Hunting of Game by Bushmen, 1936–1953.

A50/188/1. Annual Report, 1936.

A50/188/2. Annual Report, 1937.

A50/188/4. Annual Report, 1938.

A50/188/5. Annual Report, 1940.

A50/188/10. Annual Report, 1944–1946.

A50/188/11. Native Affairs, Annual Report, 1946.

A82/19. Police Station, Nurugas, 1919–1954.

A82/21. Police Station, Tsintsabis, 1919–1952.

A82/26. Police Station, Gobabis, 1920–1951.

A82/27. Police Station, Grootfontein, 1920–1957.

A158/7/1–5. Native Reserves Epukiro, General, 1919–1950.

A158/64. Native Reserves Gobabis, General, 1913–1919.

A158/10/1–6. Native Reserves Otjituo, General, 1919–1951.

A158/23/1–6. Native Reserves Waterberg, General, 1922–1952.

A158/23/9. Native Reserves Waterberg, Crime, 1949.

A58/101. Natives on Eiseb Omuramba, 1933–1934.

A158/114. Native Reserves, Eastern, General, 1934–1955.

A158/178. Native Reserves, Famine Amongst Natives, 1946–1947.

A198/3. Museums, Anthropological Research, 1916–1949.

A198/6/15. Botanical and Zoological Research, J. H. Wilhelm.

A198/26. Ethnology of Bushmen, 1934–1947.

A205/12. Shooting in Native Reserves, 1926–1952.

A205/12/1. Poaching in Native Reserves, 1938–1939.

A287/7. Gaol. Gobabis Escapes, 1921–1948.

A288/6. Gaol. Grootfontein Transfer, 1916–1947.

A288/7/1–2. Gaol. Grootfontein Escapes, 1917–1952.

A396/2. Native Unrest, Grootfontein, 1915–1922.

A396/7. Native Unrest, Gobabis, 1916–1952.

A396/11. Native Unrest, Outjo, 1916–1923.

A403/1/1–2. Slavery, 1922–1937.

A511/1/1–4. Game Reserves, General, 1919–1952.

A511/11. Game Reserves, General, 1940–1949.

A521/3. Ill-treatment of Natives, 1916–1947.

A521/10/1. Complaints, Kavango Labour, 1928–1930.

A521/13/1–6. Farm Labour Desertions, 1923–1952.

A521/52. Native Labour, Deserters, 1926–1936.

A521/92. Rural Labour Inspection, 1944–1948.

A659. Bushmen. General, 1955.

SW51/47.

Court Cases

Rex v. Kremer 1915 Special Criminal Court (hereafter, SCC).

Rex v. Venuleth 1916 SCC.

Rex v. Becker 1916 SCC.

Rex v. Orthey 1917 SCC.

Rex v. Thomas 1917 SCC.

Rex v. Tinschmann 1917 SCC.

Rex v. Halberstadt 1917 SCC.

Rex v. Anton and three others, 1917 SCC.

Rex v. Smith 1917 Outjo Magistrate's Court.

Rex v. Voswinkel 1918 SCC.

Rex v. Feuerstein 1918 SCC.

Rex v. Johannes Fritz 1918 SCC.

Rex v. Massinab 1918 SCC.
Rex v. Nauhas and Jakubowski 1919 SCC.
Rex v. Qouigan and Habuson 1919 SCC.
Rex v. Schilg 1919 SCC.
Rex v. Link 1919 Gobabis Magistrate Court.
Rex v. Quben Qubu 1920 SCC.
Rex v. Thuantha et al. 1920 SCC.
Rex v. Hans and Josef 1922 Supreme Court Windhoek (hereafter, SCW).
Rex v. Kahoekaboud et al. 1923 SCW.
Rex v. Xaie et al. 1927 SCW.
Rex v. Namseb and Toetab 1927 SCW.
Rex v. Brand and two others 1929 SCW.
Rex v. Wetondowando and Kanomotwa 1932 SCW.
Rex v. Zh. Boesman 1934 SCW.
Rex v. Tjamp and Kutha 1936 SCW.
Rex v. Duma 1938 SCW.
Rex v. Smith, Odendaal and Abraham 1940 Grootfontein Mag. Court.
Rex v. Majarero and twenty-three others 1947 SCW.
Rex v. Kgau 1958 SCW.
State v. Britz and Gougorob 1962 Grootfontein Mag. Court.

Legislation

Masters and Servants Proclamation (1920).
Stock-theft Proclamation (Proc. 5/1920).
Vagrancy Proclamation (Proc. 25/1920).
Proclamation 11/1927.
Proclamation 31/1927.

Miscellaneous

Charles Templeman Loram Papers, 10 II No. 54, Sterling Library, Yale University.
Elok (Evangelical Lutheran Church) Archives, Windhoek, unsorted material.
DRC Bushman Mission, *Die Regte Mense.* Newsletter: copies on file at DRC Mission secretariat in Windhoek.
———. Tsumkwe mission. Annual report (mimeo): available at the DRC Mission secretariat in Windhoek.
SWA Constitutional Commission. 1936, Minutes of Evidence, p. 1234, on file in State Archives.

About the Book and Author

Images of the Bushman—from the innocent hero of the hit movie, *The Gods Must Be Crazy*, to "vermin" eradicated by the colonists, to the superhuman trackers conscripted by the South African Defense Forces, to the living embodiment of prehistory for the academic—shape our perceptions of the Bushman. Looking at this interplay between imagery, history, and policy, Robert Gordon focuses not on the Bushmen but on the colonizers' image of them and the consequences of that image for the people assumed to be Bushmen.

To understand the image of the Bushmen, we must place them into the context from which they were abstracted. *The Bushman Myth* then explores not only history but also the sociology of knowledge and the relationship between perceived role and economic class. Lavishly illustrated with archival and recent photographs, the book attempts to convey the extent to which Westerners have participated in the creation of the "Bushmen" identity. With its poignant example of the Bushmen, this work brings us face to face with the complexities and deceptions of our constructions of the "Other."

Robert J. Gordon is associate professor of anthropology at the University of Vermont, currently on leave of absence as Head of Research at the Institute of Southern African Studies, National University of Lesotho. He is author of *Mines, Migrants and Masters* (1977) and *Law and Order in the New Guinea Highlands* (with Mervyn Meggitt, 1985).

Index